CANADA
Celebrating Our Faith

JOHN PAUL II

Compiled and Indexed
by the Daughters of St. Paul

ST. PAUL EDITIONS

Translations provided by *L'Osservatore Romano*, English edition, reprinted with permission and cited after each. Translations provided directly by the Vatican are acknowledged after each message.

Cover and inside photos: *Famiglia Cristiana*—Giuliani
Second insert of photos: Arturo Mari

ISBN 0-8198-1440-7 c
      0-8198-1441-5 p

Printed in the U.S.A. by the Daughters of St. Paul
50 St. Paul's Ave., Boston, MA 02130

The Daughters of St. Paul are an international congregation of women religious serving the Church with the communications media.

CONTENTS

SEPTEMBER 10

To Canada
in a Sign of Unity,
Justice and Peace

Before beginning his apostolic journey to Canada on September 9, 1984, the Holy Father sent the following TV message which was transmitted on September 7 at 10:00 Montreal time.

Dear Canadian friends,

You have been told that my visit among you is that of a Shepherd. The Shepherd is one who gathers together. The bishops, the religious leaders do this in their own areas. We gather together to celebrate our faith.

I know that I will be able to see for myself your human energy and your Christian vitality, both inherited from a noble past. For my part, I hope to make you share the faith and feelings which inspire me as Successor of Peter, in the light of the faith and hope of the whole Church.

We will gather together as brothers and sisters in humanity; we will intensify our feelings of brotherhood, our desire for justice and peace.

We will gather together as believers in God; we will discover that we are sons and daughters of the same Father, and we will learn what is the basis of true happiness.

We will gather together as believers in the Lord Jesus; we will discover a lasting hope which leads to new life in Christ and, in Him, commits us to better serve the men and women of our day.

As for us Catholics, we will unite to celebrate this faith in our Eucharistic gatherings, thus proclaiming the death and resurrection of our Lord Jesus Christ from whom the Apostolic Church holds life and who is eternally blessed.

The Canadian Conference of Catholic Bishops invited me many years ago. The civil authorities assured me of a warm welcome on the part of the Canadian people. Some of you have written to tell me of your joy and your hopes. Many have helped to prepare this visit. My wholehearted thanks to all of you.

May God bless you and may He cause this journey to lead to greater faith, brotherhood and peace for all!

From the English edition of L'Osservatore Romano

May Canada Continue
To Grow in the Light
of the Cross

The beginning of the evangelization of Canada was recalled by the Holy Father in a radio message that was transmitted throughout Canada as his plane flew over the area of Gaspé, where in 1534 the explorer Jacques Cartier erected the first cross on Canadian soil. Following is the text of the Pope's message.

Hail, Cross of Jesus, Symbol of our hope!

Hail, Cross of Gaspé!

Here, 450 years ago, Jacques Cartier planted the cross.

In the presence of the first inhabitants of this land, he knelt down with his men to venerate the sign of our salvation.

Here Jacques Cartier opened a new page in the history of the world and of the Church.

Cross of Gaspé, guide our steps towards the Lord!

Today I pay heartfelt homage to the dauntless faith of the men and women who accepted, in the footsteps of Jacques Cartier, to cross the ocean and to implant the faith and the Church in Canada.

3

My greetings to all the Canadians, and more particularly to you, the people of Gaspé, whose life is so closely linked to the land, the forest and the sea.

My greetings to the Amerindians and Innuit who have lived here from time immemorial. May you live always with the full recognition of your dignity and of your rights!

I call to mind all the great pioneers who contributed to the building of this wide, prosperous and peaceful country. Let us pray God that it will keep on growing in the light of the Cross, which is still for its inhabitants a "tree of life" (Rv. 2:7). To all, I offer my blessing.

From the English edition of L'Osservatore Romano

I Come in God's Name
To Seek with You
the Way To Grow Together

The Holy Father's first meeting with the Canadian people took place at the international airport in Quebec on September 9, 1984. Welcomed by the Governor General and by numerous civil and religious authorities, Pope John Paul II delivered the following address, partly in French and partly in English.

Madame Governor-General of Canada;

Your Eminences;

Your Excellency the President of the Canadian Conference of Catholic Bishops;

Your Grace the Archbishop of Quebec; and all of you, dear brothers in the episcopate;

Mr. Lieutenant Governor of Quebec;

Mr. Prime Minister of Canada;

Mr. Prime Minister of Quebec;

Mr. President of the Urban Community of Quebec;

Mr. Mayor of Quebec City;

Mr. Mayor of Sainte-Foy;

To all of you, dignitaries and authorities of civil society and of religious groups in this country,

"Grace and peace from God our Father and the Lord Jesus Christ" (1 Cor. 1:3).

Before giving my message to all those whom you represent, I want to express my heartfelt thanks to Her Excellency the Right Honorable Jeanne Sauvé. Madam, I cannot take up here all the various points of your address. We will have another meeting in Ottawa. But I want to tell you even now that I am deeply touched by your words. The tact and dignity of your speech, the true perception you have expressed of the meaning of my apostolic mission in the world, the deep insight of my pastoral visit to Canada, such a touching reference to the Canadian people, your warm yet demanding words concerning the destiny of this dear country, the personal witness which you give in the exercise of your high office—all this is for me the best expression of welcome and a powerful encouragement to approach with confidence the various stages of my pilgrimage in your country. I am deeply grateful to you.

1. Greetings to you, people of Canada, in the diversity of your history, of your cultures, of your provinces, of your regions.

2. In this immense country which is Canada, it is in Quebec that I begin my pilgrimage, and this makes me very happy. Greetings to you, Quebec, first Church in North America, first witness to the Faith, you who planted the cross at the intersections of your highways and caused the Gospel to spread over this blessed land!

Greetings to you, the people of Quebec, whose traditions, language and culture give your society such a unique character in North America.

Greetings to you, the people of this country, Amerindians, people of French and English extraction, immigrants who have come from everywhere and who live together so as to advance together, with each other's help, on the path of history, so arduous and so fascinating.

3. Greetings to you, believers in Jesus Christ and members of the Catholic Church. Let us seek together the firmness of the Faith, which expresses itself in the perfection of love.

Greetings to you, believers in Jesus Christ and members of other Christian confessions. Let us seek together the same Christ and Lord.

Greetings to you, believers in God and heirs of the people of Israel. Let us seek together the Word of Life.

Greetings to you, believers and members of other spiritual families. Let us seek together the face of God.

4. Greetings to you, men and women who are looking for a meaning to your life and do not find a satisfactory answer to your deepest aspirations. You are trying to live your life with dignity and in a responsible way. Let us seek together the best way to live.

To all of you, I bring the greetings of the Church of Rome and of the entire Church of God which lives in communion with her, spread throughout the world. I bring you the love, joy, sufferings and hope of your brothers and sisters in all parts of the world. In return, I hope I can bring to the world something of yours, an idea of your human energy and of your religious vitality.

5. For a long time you have waited for me. And I, for my part, have greatly longed to be with you.

It is not as a Head of State that I come to visit you. The Vatican is indeed recognized as a "State" on the international plane in order better to ensure the freedom of the Holy See, in the service of the spiritual mission of the Successor of Peter. The Holy See is entitled to have its diplomatic representatives, and I am pleased that Canada has appointed to it an ambassador. In this way the Holy See is able to give its witness on the international scene and to take part in important discussions which affect the destiny of the world community.

6. But it is above all as a shepherd and a brother that I come to you. I am the shepherd who follows in the footsteps of the first Shepherd, the Apostle Peter. I am a father, which is what the word "Pope" means. But I am also your brother, your human brother and your brother in obedience to the Good Shepherd of the Church, Jesus Christ.

I am among you to share the bread and the word, to share your hopes, to transmit to you the Word of God and the Eucharistic Bread.

7. In the next eleven days I shall cross your country from one ocean to the other, *a mari usque ad mare.* I have some questions to ask you, and I would like also to hear yours. I would like to speak to you about the issues of our times, concerning culture, the community, technology, the family, sharing and justice. This is because nothing is irrelevant to the charity of the believer, to his or her love for humanity. I wish, above all, to speak to you about the fundamental problems: about the faith, about the experience of God, about hope. My word does not claim to furnish an answer to all your questions, or to

replace your searching. But it will offer you the light and the strength of faith in Jesus Christ as proclaimed by Peter himself in Galilee: "You are the Christ, the Son of the living God!"

8. I would hope that my word will be a sharing. Sharing with a brother in the faith. Sharing with a pilgrim who is witness to how the men and women of today live. Sharing with a man who is aware of the spiritual crisis of our day, who is preoccupied about justice; a man who is equally confident in the possibilities of the human heart when it is transformed by God's love. "But be brave," Jesus said, "I have conquered the world" (Jn. 16:33).

9. As your bishops have said so well: Let us celebrate our faith in Jesus Christ. My visit is intended to be essentially pastoral. I would like to recount to all believers the joy of believing in Jesus Christ. For, of all the blessings in life, faith is the most precious, the most beautiful. May my pilgrimage here be the symbol of your journey in the faith. For this very reason, I would like to come among you as a witness of hope. I would like to assure the bishops of my fraternal interest. I would like to offer a special word of support to the priests, to the men and women religious, and to the laity in charge of many sectors of the apostolate.

Brothers and sisters, friends already, let us walk together, let us look to the One who unites us. O Lord, our God, "how great your name throughout the earth!" (Ps. 8)

May the name of God echo in your hearts and may this visit bring to us, both to you and to me, comfort and fresh joy.

From the English edition of L'Osservatore Romano

May Mary Sustain the People of Quebec

Before reciting the angelus in the Quebec cathedral on Sunday, September 9, the Holy Father gave the following brief address.

Dear brothers and sisters,

I thank you for receiving me in your cathedral immediately after my arrival in Quebec. And I am happy to meet again here the Archbishop of Quebec, His Excellency Luis-Albert Vachon, with his auxiliary bishops, and surrounded by the cathedral chapter, their collaborators and the representatives of the communities which make up the living Church in the historic center of your province. I greet you all most cordially.

I also greet the Mayor of Quebec and the civil dignitaries here present. To them I express my gratitude for their courteous welcome and for all the care they have taken in organizing in their city, in association with the bishops, this first stage of my pastoral visit in Canada.

Shortly, I will be going to the tomb of your first bishop, Blessed François de Laval. But how can I not recall here the memory of this founder? He came to Quebec as a zealous witness of the spiritual renewal in which he had participated in France, as a missionary, as a pastor. As vicar apostolic, he took care to link solidly to the Apostolic See of Rome the young Christian community whose influence was to spread over most of North America. He knew the joy of founding a diocese in its own right, thus strengthening even more those links with the Pope. My coming among you shows their continuity.

Just as I am about to meet the community of this diocese, it is good that I have been able to come directly to this cathedral basilica. First seat of episcopal authority, center from which the presbyterate reaches out to the parishes and other institutions, center of prayer, the mother church recalls to all the unity of Christ's body whose members are different but all sharing in the same life. With you, even now, I want to give thanks for the Word and the Bread of Life given in this place and passed on from here. With you I ask God to give you the strength to carry out your missions in hope and joy.

We entrust our prayer to Our Lady of Quebec to whom this basilica is dedicated. May the Mother of the Lord keep the sons and daughters of Quebec in the faith and unselfish generosity of which she is the perfect example! And let us now invoke her in simplicity with the angelic salutation.

(Recitation of the angelus)

With all my heart I bless you in the name of the Father, and of the Son, and of the Holy Spirit.
Amen.

Gift of Oneself to Consecrated Celibacy, Life of Prayer and Active Charity

The person and work of Blessed François de Laval were recalled by the Holy Father in a brief address delivered to religious in the chapel of the minor seminary of Quebec on Sunday, September 9. Blessed François de Laval was appointed Vicar Apostolic of New France in 1674 and is considered the founder of the Canadian Church. His remains are preserved in the chapel of the minor seminary.

Following is our translation of the Pope's address, which was delivered in French.

Dear brothers and sisters,

On this first day of my pilgrimage, I am happy to have been able to venerate the tomb of Blessed François de Laval, the first Bishop of Quebec and of all of North America, whom I had the joy of beatifying in 1980 at the same time as Marie de l'Incarnation and Kateri Tekakwitha.

In 1639, François de Laval found here a young Church, the result of the courageous activity of priests and religious men and women who brought the Gospel to this land. As Vicar Apostolic, he worked without sparing to bring the first native converts and the Christian colonists together in the unity of what was soon to be a diocese, while taking part himself in the missionary effort and experiencing his share of the trials of the pioneers.

In France, he had seen the vitality of a Christianity undergoing renewal under the influence of numerous founders and remarkable mystics whose sense of God and of charity he shared. He wanted to establish the Church in this new land firmly in communion with the Bishop of Rome. And one of his most important acts was the foundation of the major seminary and of the minor seminary where we are now, so as to make possible the rapid development of the clergy of Quebec.

With you, I want to give thanks for the gift of God which was manifested in this land especially by the holiness of this first bishop as well as by that of all the founders.

In particular, I want to recall the religious communities whose missionary zeal produced so many fruits of holiness. The Jesuits, the Récollets, the Ursulines, the Augustinian Hospital Sisters of the Mercy of Jesus were among the first to come from France to North America. The Sulpicians soon followed, along with many others. Then there arose many institutions, proof of the flowering of a generous ecclesial community.

Dear religious men and women gathered in this chapel, let us praise the Lord for all that He allowed your predecessors to accomplish.

And now I want to tell you, and I will do so again in the course of my journey, that the Church relies solidly on your action and your witness. No doubt your role has been changing for some years, but the essentials of your particular vocation remain: the gift of self in consecrated celibacy, the life of prayer and of active charity are signs for all. The specific services which you provide are irreplaceable, whether it be in pastoral work, in the different types of formation for young people and for adults, and especially in help provided to the least capable. I ask God to call a sufficient number of generous young people to work with you so that your missions may continue and be ever renewed.

Allow me to address an especially warm greeting to the priests who work in the seminaries of Quebec and to give them my confidence and good wishes for the most important task which they must carry out.

And most cordially I give all of you my apostolic blessing.

From the English edition of L'Osservatore Romano

In a Changing Society the Faith Must Learn To Speak Out and Be Lived

The Pope's first Mass in Canada was celebrated on Sunday, September 9, on the campus of Laval University. The following is the text of the Holy Father's homily.

1. "You are the Christ, the Son of the living God!" (Mt. 16:16)

These words were spoken for the first time in the neighborhood of Caesarea Philippi in reply to Jesus' question: "Who do people say the Son of Man is?" (Mt. 16:13)

These words—it is Simon Peter who spoke them in Galilee. He spoke them again later in many other places. He spoke them in Jerusalem, especially on the day of Pentecost. He spoke them in Antioch after he left Jerusalem. He spoke them finally in Rome until the day he was made to suffer death on a cross to give witness to the truth of these words.

These words proclaiming the divine sonship of Jesus Christ, Simon Peter handed over as a heritage to the Church. He handed them down in a special way to all his successors in the episcopal See of Rome.

SON OF THE LIVING GOD

2. As Bishop of Rome and Successor of Peter, I want to repeat these same words here today on Canadian soil.

"You are the Christ, the Son of the living God!" (Mt. 16:16)

The Bishop of Rome treads this soil for the first time, in the city of Quebec. Here began the evangelization of Canada. Here the Church was founded. Here was established the first diocese in all of North America. Here, from the seed planted in earth, began an immense growth.

This is why I desire that, right at the start of this pilgrimage, we should meet and unite ourselves in this profession of faith on which is built the Church of Christ on earth:

Christ, the Son of man, the Son of the living God;

the Son, of the same nature as the Father: God from God, Light from Light; begotten, not made, Eternal Word through whom all things were made;

and at the same time: Christ, true man.

"For us men and for our salvation, He came down from heaven; by the power of the Holy Spirit He became incarnate from the Virgin Mary, and was made man."

Christ: true God and true man. Such is the faith of the Church.

Christ: crucified under Pontius Pilate, He suffered death and was buried....

Christ: the third day He rose from the dead; He ascended into heaven and is seated at the right hand of the Father, whence He will come again to judge the living and the dead.

3. Such is the faith of the Apostles. Such is the faith of Peter. This faith is the foundation on which the Church of God on earth is built.

Simon Peter, who was the first to profess this faith, in the neighborhood of Caesarea Philippi, was also the first to receive Christ's reply: "You are Peter and on this rock I will build my Church..." (Mt. 16:18).

How wonderful it is to hear the same Apostle Simon Peter, in his first letter which is being read in today's liturgy, give witness to Christ by calling Him the foundation stone!

Christ is "the living stone" (1 Pt. 2:4).

This stone, however, was discarded, utterly "rejected by men" (1 Pt. 2:4) who went so far as to condemn Jesus to death on the cross and to carry out this sentence a few hours before celebrating the Passover of the Old Law.

It is precisely in this rejection that He is recognized for what He is: Jesus, the Christ, "chosen by God and precious to him" (1 Pt. 2:4).

It is through Him, the living stone, the foundation stone, that we are all made part of the construction of "a spiritual house" (1 Pt. 2:5).

Yes, all of us: "as living stones," we form part of the construction which has Christ as foundation, so as to create "a holy priesthood that offers the spiritual sacrifices which Jesus Christ has made acceptable to God" (1 Pt. 2:5).

Thus are we "a chosen race, a royal priesthood, a consecrated nation, a people set apart" for God (1 Pt. 2:9), and this because of Jesus Christ who is the Son of the living God, who is true God and true man, crucified and risen. Yes, because of Jesus Christ: He is the foundation stone of the divine edifice, made up of the sons and daughters of the whole earth, which will stand for all eternity in the indescribable glory of the most Holy Trinity!

From Jesus Christ, the living stone, rises the ultimate future of our construction.... Such is man's future on earth. A future of divine destiny.

FAITH IN JESUS CHRIST

4. This then is the faith in Jesus Christ proclaimed by Simon Peter!

This is the faith concerning the Church proclaimed by Simon Peter!

What surprising unity! And what strength in this faith!

Today the Bishop of Rome, on Canadian soil, wants to profess this faith with all his heart. He wants to make it the basis of his mission among you, beloved brothers and sisters, in this city of Quebec and throughout Canada which I will then visit in each of its regions.

IMPLANTING THE FAITH

5. For we are here at the first center of Christ's Church in North America. Coming from France, people like Jacques Cartier, Champlain and so many

others, while bringing to this continent their culture and language, contributed to implanting the faith in Christ the Savior.

Many servants of God, both men and women, came right at the beginning of colonization to help build up the Church in your land. The Recollect Fathers, the Jesuits, the Sulpicians, the Ursulines with Marie de l'Incarnation radiating her incomparable spiritual experience, the Hospital Sisters of Dieppe influenced by the inexhaustible charity of Catherine de Saint-Augustine: these religious men and women were among the first to witness to the faith and the love of Christ among the colonists and the Indians. Bearers of the Word, educators of youth, good samaritans to the sick, they shaped the form of the Church in this new country. There was reference to a real "mystical epic" as early as the first half of the seventeenth century. Some of these pioneers gave their life in martyrdom. Many others came later, bringing their living stone to the construction, often in poverty, but strengthened by God's Spirit.

Here we recall especially François de Montmorency Laval, Vicar Apostolic and later first Bishop of Quebec. I cannot forget that the seminary which bears his name was the cradle of the university where we are now, in this beautiful location.

Your ancestors forged a culture here by drawing from the sources in their native land. Over the centuries, this heritage has taken root and become diversified; it has been influenced by the Amerindians and has gained much from the presence of the English on this continent. It has been further enriched by successive waves of immigrants from everywhere. Your people was able to keep its identity while remaining open to other cultures.

The Church has recognized or is about to recognize the holiness of some of these pioneers. They are striking witnesses among so many men and women, simple believers going about their everyday lives; they little by little fashioned this land in their image, according to their faith.

The energy and zeal of your predecessors also led them to carry the Good News farther afield: I acknowledge here a Church which early on sought to spread to the Canadian West, the Great North and many areas of America. What is more, she has contributed generously to the missionary effort of the universal Church throughout the world.

Your motto is *"Je me souviens"* ("I remember"). What treasures there are both in the memory of the Church and in the memory of a people!

But, in each generation, living memory allows us to recognize the presence of Christ who asks us, as He did in the neighborhood of Caesarea: "And you, who do you say that I am?"

A CHANGING SOCIETY

6. The answer to this question is crucial for the future of the Church in Canada, and also for the future of your culture.

You are aware that traditional culture, characterized by a certain "Christianity," has been shattered: it is open to a multitude of trends of thought and must find answers to many new questions;

science, technology and the arts take on ever more importance; material values are everywhere; but there is also greater sensitivity for the promotion of human rights, peace, justice, equality, sharing, freedom....

In this changing society, your faith, dear brothers and sisters, must learn to speak out and to be lived. I said it to your bishops last October: "This time is always God's time, and He never fails to raise up what His Church needs when she remains docile, courageous and prayerful." You must remember your past, the boldness and loyalty of your predecessors, so as to bring the Gospel message in your turn to new situations. You must promote a new culture, integrate the modernity of America without denying its deep humanity coming no doubt from the fact that your culture has been inspired by Christianity. Do not accept the divorce between faith and culture. You are being called today to a new missionary effort.

SAME FAITH AS PETER'S

7. Culture, and so also education which is its primary and essential duty, is basically the search for beauty, truth, good, that which best defines man "in light of his transcendency" (cf. my discourse at UNESCO, June 2, 1980; no. 10), that which helps him to become what he should *be* and not only to take advantage of what he *has* or of what he *owns*. Your culture is not only the reflection of what you are, but the key to what you will be. Accordingly, develop your culture in a lively and dynamic way in hope, without fear of difficult questions or new challenges;

without for all that allowing yourself to be blinded by the glare of novelty, and without allowing a vacuum, a break to come between the past and the future; in other words, with prudence and discernment, and with the courage of critical freedom in the face of what could be called the *culture industry*, and especially with the greatest concern for truth.

FAITH ILLUMINES CULTURE

But in addressing myself here to believers, I again repeat what I expressed at UNESCO: "I am thinking above all of the fundamental link between the Gospel, that is, the message of Christ and the Church, and man and his very humanity" (no. 10). Yes, dear brothers and sisters, in the culture that you are now developing, which is in line with what you already are by reason of a rich past, in this culture which is always the soul of a nation (cf. *ibid.*, no. 14), faith plays a great part. Faith will illuminate culture, it will give it savor, it will enhance it, as the Gospel says in regard to that *light, salt* and *leaven* which the disciples of Jesus are called to be. Faith will ask culture what values it promotes, what destiny it offers to life, what place it makes for the poor and the disinherited with whom the Son of man is identified, how it conceives of sharing, forgiveness and love. If it is this way, the Church will continue to accomplish her mission through you. And you will render service to all society, even to men and women who do not share the same spiritual experience as yourselves. For such a witness respects freedom of consciences, without thus abandoning them to certain "imperatives" of modern civilization which claim to serve human advancement but which in fact detract from respect for life, from the dignity of a love that involves persons, and from the search for the true values of humanity (cf. Discourse to UNESCO, no. 13).

But again, your faith must remain active and strong; it must become always more personal, more and more rooted in prayer and in the experience of the sacraments; it must reach the living God, in His Son Jesus Christ the Savior, through the help of the Holy Spirit, in the Church. This is the faith that you ought to deepen with joy, in order to live it and to bear witness to it in daily life and in the new realms of culture. This is indeed the grace which we must request for the future of Quebec, for the future of all Canada. And here we are back to the fundamental question of Jesus Christ: "And you, who do you say that I am?"

SEARCH FOR BEAUTY AND TRUTH

8. In the faith which Simon Peter professed in the neighborhood of Caesarea Philippi, in the faith which he expressed so beautifully in his first letter, in that same faith, I, John Paul II, Bishop of Rome, want to greet you with all my heart at the beginning of my pilgrimage in your country.

I want to greet you all, you who are a chosen race, a royal priesthood, a consecrated nation, a people set apart for God, you who have been called by Jesus Christ "to sing the praises of God who called you out of the darkness into his wonderful light" (1 Pt. 2:9).

Today we begin a celebration that will have great repercussions in your hearts.

The Church puts an appropriate song on our lips:

"Sing to Yahweh, bless his name.
Proclaim his salvation day after day,
tell of his glory among the nations,
tell his marvels to every people" (Ps. 96:2-3).

Let the Canadian nation sing to the Lord from the shores of the Atlantic to those of the Pacific, from the South to the frozen wastes of the North....

Behold that Christ, the Son of the living God, has become the foundation stone for you!

Behold that Christ, the Son of the living God, has become a living stone for all generations!

Gloria Tibi, Trinitas!
Glory to You, Holy Trinity!
Amen.

After the homily the Holy Father greeted those present as follows:

Dear brothers and sisters,

I thank you for this warm welcome.

I greet first of all His Excellency Louis-Albert Vachon, Archbishop of Quebec, and each of my other brothers in the episcopate who exercise their ministry in Canada.

I greet the representatives of the other churches who have come to join us here from America and other continents, especially from Europe with which Canada has such strong links.

I greet the Canadian missionaries and the representatives of the young churches where they exercise their ministry.

I greet the Rector of Laval University, the professors and students, and all those who are striving to renew and strengthen culture to make it always more human, in a trusting dialogue with faith.

I greet the priests, deacons, seminarians, religious, and the lay people from the different parishes of this archdiocese and of neighboring dioceses who have been able to come here thanks to the twinning of parishes.

I greet those for whom Jesus had particular affection: children, young people, elderly people, the sick, prisoners, all those who suffer because they are not loved, or are without work and on the fringes of society, or are sorely tried.

Together, following the example of the Apostle Peter, let us turn towards the Lord Jesus. May He strengthen our faith!

The Life of the Disabled Person Must Be Respected from the Moment of Conception

On September 10, the Pope's first address was to the handicapped persons in the François-Charon Center at Quebec. The Holy Father spoke in French.

Dear brothers and sisters,

1. I have very much wanted to meet personally with you, you who suffer in your bodies from illness or accident. I would like to greet each and every one of you as well as all those who surround you with affection and assistance and who help you to love life and to make it blossom in you like a gift from God. I mean, of course, your parents and your friends and all the people who work in this center. I would also like to extend my greetings to the other handicapped men and women in Quebec and throughout Canada. Like Jesus of Nazareth, I want to come near you and to explore with you the spiritual meaning of your suffering and your hope for a full life.

PRAISE FOR ORGANIZERS

2. First of all, I express spontaneously my admiration, my congratulations and my encouragement to those who organized this center and who see to its daily operation. The name François-Charon is, in itself, quite evocative. When this land was first being settled, he fell prey to illness and decided to abandon his lucrative fur business to devote his efforts and money to the underprivileged, children, orphans the crippled, the old and the infirm. To all, according to their needs he provided care, education and training. Was it not his house of charity that later became the Montreal General Hospital?

Today, five years after the merging of two institutions of somewhat similar nature, the François-Charon Center wants to be in the forefront of science, technology and pedagogy in order to offer physical and psycho-social rehabilitation services to an increasing number of physically handicapped adults in eastern Quebec.

Not only are tools and sophisticated rehabilitation methods made available to the handicapped, but also the means of acquiring as much independence as possible in their own milieu, as well as occupational training for reintegration into society. Teams of specialists from all disciplines work according to the philosophy that everyone has the right to equal opportunity and to equal human dignity. It is marvelous and I hope that scientists continue to invent every possible means of effectively relieving suffering.

But, dear members of the staff, despite all these tools and qualifications, the handicapped could not develop without the devotion, dedication, support and human warmth they also require and which I know you offer them here. I am struck by the young age of the employees who, inspired by an ideal of service, offer their abilities and their dynamism. I am not forgetting all the volunteers who by their visits here and in the home help to provide a climate of friendship and service.

A word of encouragement must also be given to the concern this center has for integrating the spiritual dimension into its work of human rehabilitation. This chapel in the heart of the center is a sign of this concern. It is a place where all those who want to gather before the Lord, partake of the Eucharist, meditate and sing with others and meet the priest and those who are involved with him in pastoral activities, can do so. The human person constitutes a whole—body and soul—and every personal event—trial, effort or healing—has a spiritual dimension.

Yes, my best wishes for the expert service offered in this center and in other institutions in Quebec.

BECOMING MORE AWARE

3. I see in all this a sign of the value that your people attach to the dignity of the disabled, in spite of the fascination the modern world feels for productivity, profit, efficiency, speed, and records of physical strength.

Our societies, thank God, appear to be becoming progressively more aware of the situation of the handicapped. They have rights which have often been neglected. On December 9, 1975, the United Nations Organization issued a statement on these rights which deserves our praise. In addition, the UN decreed 1981 the International Year of the Disabled. However, all these good intentions must take form in every region. For this to happen, there are psychological and material obstacles to overcome and progress to be made.

The Church has always taken a vivid interest in this question. Over the centuries the Church fostered many undertakings involving great generosity in order, like Christ, to come to the aid of the disabled. It did this because it was convinced of the unique value of every person. On March 4, 1981, the Holy See published a long document reasserting the basic principles and lines of action (*L'Osservatore Romano*, weekly French edition, March 24, 1981). I would like now to say once again clearly and forcefully: the handicapped person is a human subject in the full sense with all the innate, sacred and inviolable rights that that entails. This is true whether the person be handicapped by physical disability—whether due to birth defect, chronic disease or accident—or by mental or sensory deficiency. This is true too no matter how great the person's affliction might be. We must facilitate his or her participation in all facets of social life and at all possible levels: in the family, at school, at work, in the community, in politics and religion. In practice, this presupposes the absolute respect of the human life of the handicapped person from his or her conception through every stage of development.

We must attempt to overcome not only handicaps, but also their causes. Often, they are natural. A deformation of the organism or a disease; sometimes they are related to war or pollution, alcohol or drug abuse, or careless driving. There may be psychological and moral causes; a spiritual "ecology" is as important as an ecology of nature. We must help families who are in distress and deserve our help. To this end, we must build centers like this one where there is sensitivity to family bonds. We must provide training, suitable employment with a just wage, promotion opportunities and security to spare the handicapped traumatic experiences. All this requires imagination and boldness in order to develop various kinds of ideal initiatives. It also requires the aid of public authorities. I devoted a whole paragraph to this question in my encyclical on work (no. 22). It is important, finally, that the handicapped person not only be loved and helped but that he or she be as aware as possible of his or her dignity and resources, of his or her ability to will, to communicate, to cooperate, to love and give, while continuing daily the battle to maintain and develop his or her potential.

Unquestionably, the quality of a society or civilization is measured by the respect it has for its weakest members. A technically perfect society where only fully-productive members are accepted must be considered totally unworthy of human beings, perverted as it is by a type of discrimination that is no less reprehensible than racial discrimination. The handicapped person is one of us and shares in our humanity. To recognize and promote his or her dignity and rights is to recognize our own dignity and rights.

These are the convictions of the Church (cf. aforementioned document from the Holy See), and the Church is delighted to see that they are shared and practiced by many governments and societies.

BECOMING GOOD SAMARITANS
FOR ONE ANOTHER

4. But, dear friends, when it comes to working for the handicapped, Christians can find in their faith deeper motives and a very special source of strength.

The Gospel shows us Jesus going around doing good. He welcomed all those who were suffering whether physically or morally; He even sought them out. He proclaimed to them the Good News of the love of God and of their salvation by faith. And in this salvation He included both the body and the soul. By comforting the infirm—the crippled, the paralyzed, the blind and the deaf—He wanted to deliver them from their misery; their healing, in answer to their faith, was the sign of the fuller life that He proclaimed: "Arise and walk!"

He was not content simply to be near suffering and to relieve it, but He took it upon Himself. Voluntarily, He became the man of sorrows, acquainted with suffering including, in the end, the suffering of the tortured and of those condemned to death. Because He, the beloved Son of the Father, sacrificed His life, God raised Him from the dead, and Christ opened for us the gates of life. He guaranteed us that life would have the last word.

So the message He left us is that you, the handicapped, should seek with Him to fight against evil, to overcome the obstacle from which your body suffers, and to do this with the assistance of science and technology and with the courage of love.

This is how we become good samaritans for one another (cf. Letter *Salvifici Doloris*, nos. 28-30) not only by stopping beside a person suffering the wounds of life, but by bringing him or her efficacious help, by giving ourselves to this person with whom Christ identified Himself: "What you have done to one of my brothers or sisters, you have done to me."

THE INEVITABLE "WHY"
OF SUFFERING

5. Up to this point, dear brothers and sisters in Jesus Christ, I have spoken of the nobility of this tenacious fight against physical evil and of all the technical competency, courage, solidarity and hope that it involves. This is indeed the will of God.

But the mystery of your suffering is deeper still and I would like to descend into its depths with you as I did in my letter of February 11th this year on the occasion of the Feast of Our Lady of Lourdes: "At the heart of all human suffering appears the inevitable question: Why? It is a question about the cause, the reason; it is also a question about purpose and, finally meaning" (no. 9). "Almost every person enters suffering protesting, quite humanly: 'Why?...'" (no. 26). The person suffering addresses this question to God as Job did, and also to Christ. Even though one identifies the secondary cause of the handicap, even though one hopes to overcome it and manages to do so through will and rehabilitation, the subjective problem remains: Why this suffering? Why this restriction at this time in my life? This mystery accompanies us just as it accompanies all human trials, even human work. Christ gives an answer from His cross, from the depth of His own suffering. It is not an abstract answer, it is a call which requires time for us to hear.

Christ gave universal redemptive value to His own suffering which appeared to be imposed on Him from without. He accepted it out of obedience towards His Father and out of love for humanity in order to free it from its sin, the ultimate cause of suffering and death. And if we agree to do so, we also can participate in this redemption. This agreement is neither fatality nor resignation to suffering, which remains an evil against which we must continue to struggle. But God shows us how to draw good from evil by offering up our suffering with the cross of Christ. I'm sure that many of you are having or have had this experience in faith. The pain remains. But the heart is serene and peaceful. It overcomes the feeling of the uselessness of suffering (cf. *ibid.*, no. 27). It opens itself to love and helps those around to go out of themselves, to give themselves. Such a heart bears witness to faith and hope. It believes that in the mystery of the communion of saints it has something to offer for the salvation of its brothers and sisters throughout the world. It enters into the redemptive mission of Christ.

For this moving witness we thank the disabled and all those who discreetly accompany them on their spiritual journey. It is important that the handicapped persons and the sick help one another in associations, not only to make their living conditions more human and to have their rights recognized, but also to share better in this mystery. No one can impose his or her faith, but everyone can live it and bear witness to it and bring new inspiration and dynamism into these health institutions. Blessed are those who understand the language of the beatitudes! Human suffering becomes for them a force that can help to transform the world.

6. Yes, with Christ you must love life: "I have come so that they may have life and have it to the full" (Jn. 10:11). Natural life in your body, in your rehabilitated functions, in your senses; the life of the intellectual faculties and of your ability to love. But, also, the more mysterious, supernatural life which God gives believers at baptism, His divine life, a sharing in the life of the Trinity. This life is unaffected by physical handicaps; in fact, it is in contrast with the weaknesses of the body. This life is invisible to the eye, but it gives people their inner beauty and their hidden strength; it lasts and grows beyond this earthly life. The greatness of the sacraments, especially the Eucharist and Reconciliation, lies in introducing us into this life. This chapel is a chosen place for that to happen.

OUR RIGHT TO LIFE

7. That, dear friends, is the message the Bishop of Rome wants to leave with you today.

You seem to be well looked after here and encouraged to rediscover a taste for life. I cannot help but think—and this is an intention I entrust to your prayer—of all the other handicapped people in this country and in the world; of the mentally handicapped, of the gravely ill, of those who have injuries so serious that there is no human hope for improvement but who have the right to the same respect for life; of the handicapped who are defenseless, of children waiting to be born and of the elderly on whose behalf I would like to say: "We have the right to birth, we have the right to life!" I think of the countries who are too poor to have rehabilitation centers like this one.

We all share in the suffering of our brothers and sisters.

As I said at the outset of the International Year of the Disabled (January 1, 1981): "If we were to devote only a small part of the budget for the arms race to this task, we could make considerable progress and ease the fate of many suffering people."

AFFECTION AND ENCOURAGEMENT

8. Before we say goodbye—and I can assure you that the memory of this meeting will remain vivid with me—I would like to express again my affection and my encouragement to all the handicapped people here in this center. I express it also to their

families and to the deserving staff of this institution. Vatican II recognized that the vital center of the lay apostolate is found in works of charity like this (cf. *Apostolicam actuositatem*, no. 8). I think too of the religious men and women who have devoted their consecrated lives to serving the disabled and of all the priests who bring them the efficacious signs of Christ's love.

Peter the Apostle said to the lame man at the Beautiful Gate: "I have neither silver nor gold; but in the name of Jesus Christ, rise up and walk." This miraculous healing power belongs to Jesus Christ. Today, Peter's Successor thanks you for your welcome and your witness and he hopes that his presence among you will help to strengthen your faith, that faith which enlightens, expands and uplifts your life. I ask Mary, our Mother, to obtain for you this gift of the Holy Spirit. And I pray to God, Father, Son and Holy Spirit, to fill you with His blessings.

Open to Dialogue with Society, Be Architects of Your Own Future

On September 10, John Paul II met a group of Amerindians and Innuits (Eskimos) who represented 10 different national groups. The meeting took place at the Basilica of St. Anne de Beaupré, and the Holy Father spoke as follows:

Beloved brothers and sisters,

1. Thank you with all my heart for coming from so many regions, even from very far away, to give me this opportunity to meet you as I will meet your brothers and sisters in Huronia and in Fort Simpson. You represent the first inhabitants of this vast continent. For centuries you have made your mark in North America with your traditions and your civilization. Other waves of settlers came from Europe with their own culture and their Christian faith. They took their place beside you. The vastness of this continent allowed you to live together in a relationship that was not always easy, but that has also had its rewards. God gave the earth to all humankind. Today you have your own special place in this country.

Without losing any of your cultural identity, you have understood that God has sent the Christian message to you just as He did to others. Today, I come to greet you, the native peoples who bring us close to the origins of Canada. I come to celebrate with you our faith in Jesus Christ. I recall that beautiful day when Kateri Tekakwitha was beatified in Rome where several of you were present. I have not forgotten the heartfelt and insistent invitations you made then. But I could not visit all of your villages and territories, those of the different Amerindian nations, dispersed throughout the many regions of Canada, and those of the Innuit whose familiar horizons of snow and ice are near the North Pole. That is why I wanted to meet you here, in St. Anne de Beaupré, on the very spot where you pitch your tents every year. You come here as pilgrims, to pray to St. Anne whom you so lovingly call your grandmother. Your ancestors have often come here to pray since the Hurons made their first pilgrimage in 1671 and the Micmacs in 1680. They became part of a great popular movement which has made this one of the most visited sanctuaries in North America.

THANKS TO REDEMPTORISTS AND COLLABORATORS

2. On behalf of all pilgrims and in union with the Bishops of this country I would like to thank the Redemptorists and their collaborators. Thanks to them this shrine is still flourishing. Attentive to popular devotion, they have known how to leave place for gestures that express freely and forcefully

faith, prayer and the need for reconciliation. It is thanks to them that many Canadian families still pray to St. Anne, the mother of Mary.

But we should also give thanks for all those who, out of love for you, came to propose to your ancestors and yourselves that you become brothers in Jesus Christ so that you too could share the gift which they themselves had received. I am thinking of Jesuits like Fathers Vimont and Vieuxpont who from Fort Saint Anne to Cape Breton brought the word of the Gospel to the Micmacs and helped them to believe in Jesus as the Savior and to venerate His Mother Mary and the mother of Mary, St. Anne.

This brings to mind many other great religious men and women from the time of the founders to the present day. I would particularly like to mention the *Oblate Missionaries of Mary Immaculate*. They took charge of the vast region of the Canadian North. They devoted their lives to the evangelization and the support of many Amerindian groups by sharing their life, by becoming the pastors and the bishops of those who believed. They were the first Catholic missionaries to go among the Innuit and to stay with them to bear witness to Jesus Christ and to found the Church; the intercession of St. Theresa of the Child Jesus, patroness of missions, helped to enrich their difficult apostolate.

It must also be said that from the middle of the seventeenth century, the Amerindian peoples and, in their time, the Innuit, welcomed the news of Jesus Christ. Today, these Christians, full-fledged members of the Church, although not of society, are actively involved—often as couples—in the teaching of catechism to their brothers and sisters and their children, and in leading prayer. They are faithful to the celebration of the Eucharist and often take on responsibilities in pastoral councils. Yes, I am sorry that I cannot visit these places myself to encourage the courageous missionaries and the courageous Christians who have in them the blood and culture of the first inhabitants of this country.

GUARD YOUR WISDOM

3. Over the centuries, dear Amerindian and Innuit peoples, you have gradually discovered in your cultures special ways of living your relationship with God and with the world while remaining loyal to Jesus and to the Gospel. Continue to develop these moral and spiritual values: an acute sense of the presence of God, love of your family, respect for the aged, solidarity with your people, sharing, hospitality, respect for nature, the importance given to silence and prayer, faith in providence. Guard this wisdom preciously. To let it become impoverished would be to impoverish the people around you. To live these spiritual values in a new way requires on your part maturity, interiority, a deepening of the Christian message, a concern for the dignity of the human being and a pride in being Amerindian and Innuit. This demands the courage to eliminate every form of enslavement that might compromise your future.

Your encounter with the Gospel has not only enriched you; it has enriched the Church. We are well aware that this has not taken place without its difficulties and, occasionally, its blunders. However, and you are experiencing this today, the Gospel does not destroy what is best in you. On the contrary, it enriches as it were from within the spiritual qualities and gifts that are distinctive of your cultures (cf. *Gaudium et spes*, no. 58). In addition, your Amerindian and Innuit traditions permit the development of new ways of expressing the message of salvation and they help us to better understand to what point Jesus is the Savior and how universal His salvation is.

CHALLENGES YOU FACE

4. This recognition of your accomplishments cannot allow us to forget the great challenges your people face in the present North American context. Like all other citizens, but more acutely, you fear the impact of economic, social and cultural change on your traditional ways of life. You are concerned about the future of your Indian and Innuit identities and about the future of your children and grandchildren. For all that, you do not reject scientific and technological progress. You perceive the challenges it represents and you know how to make the most of it.

With reason, however, you want to control your future, to preserve your cultural traits, to establish an educational system where your languages are respected.

The Bishops' synod on "Justice in the World" (1971) stated that every people should, in mutual cooperation, fashion its own economic and social development and that each people should take part in realizing the universal common good as active and responsible members of human society (cf. Proposal no. 8). It is in this perspective that you must be the architects of your own future, freely, and responsibly. May the wisdom of your elders unite with the initiative and courage of your youth to meet this challenge!

Tenacity in safeguarding your personality is compatible with a spirit of dialogue and friendly acceptance among all those who have come to this country in successive waves and who are called to make up the very diverse group which must populate and settle this area as vast as a continent.

STRAIN OF PREJUDICE

5. I know that the relations between native people and white people are often strained and tainted with prejudice. Furthermore, in many places, the native people are among the poorest and most marginal members of society. They suffer from the fact that recognition of their identity and of their ability to participate in shaping their future is late in coming.

More and more, those who govern this country have your cultures and your rights at heart and want to rectify difficult situations. This is already evident in some pieces of legislation, open of course to further progress, and in the increased recognition of your own decision-making power. It is to be hoped that effective cooperation and dialogue based on good faith and the acceptance of the other in his or her difference will develop. The Church does not intervene directly in civil matters, but you know its concern for you and you know that it tries to inspire all those who want to live with the Christian spirit.

POWER OF HIS SPIRIT

6. As disciples of Jesus Christ, we know that the Gospel calls us to live as His brothers and sisters. We know that Jesus Christ makes possible reconciliation between peoples, with all its requirements of conversion, justice and social love. If we truly believe that God created us in His image, we shall be able to accept one another with our differences and despite our limitations and our sins.

In seeking a good understanding between the inhabitants of this country, faced with the difficulties of the modern world, it is necessary for you to have complete confidence in what you can do to help one another and to be renewed. Jesus Christ, in whom we believe, can break the chains of our personal and collective selfishness. He gives us the power of His Spirit so that we may triumph over difficulties and realize justice.

IT IS YOUR CHURCH

7. Assured of the love God has for you, put yourselves to the task; recall without ceasing that the Church of Jesus Christ is your Church. She is the place where the sun of the word enlightens you, where you find the nourishment and strength to continue on your way. She is like those "hiding places" that your ancestors constructed all along the route of their travels, so that no one might be caught

without provisions. Permit me to repeat this description of the Church in some of your own languages; this will be a way to come closer to you and to express to you my fraternal affection.

The Church is the ASADJIGAN of God for you (Algonquin).

The Church is the SHESHEPETAN of God for you (Montagnais).

The Church is the SHISHITITHEN of God for you (Cree).

The Church is the TESHITITAGAN of God for you (Atikamek).

The Church is the IA-IEN-TA-IEN-TA-KWA of God for you (Mohawk).

The Church is the APATAGAT of God for you (Micmac).

Now we must say goodbye. In the language of our Innuit brothers and sisters, I would like to assure you that you are my friends, all you who are loved by God! ILANNAARIVAPSI TAMAPSI NAGLIJAUVUSI JISUSINUT.

I will carry you in my heart and in my prayers. I will entrust you to Mary and to St. Anne so that you may grow in faith and bear witness, in your own way, to Jesus Christ in this country. In the name of Jesus Christ, I bless you with all my heart.

From the English edition of L'Osservatore Romano

Guide Pilgrims
to Conversion

On Monday, September 10th, the Holy Father visited the Sanctuary of Our Lady of the Cape in Trois Rivières, where he addressed in French the Oblates of Mary Immaculate and many others present.

Dear brothers and sisters:

As far back as we can trace the history of evangelization here, we find devotion to the Virgin Mary. How can the work of her Son be proclaimed and realized without looking towards His Mother, without admiring her availability and her faith, without imploring her intercession? This very ancient Sanctuary of Notre Dame du Cap de la Madeleine is the sign of this, and I am happy on my part to be a pilgrim here.

People come here from all over Quebec, from other provinces, and from all over Canada. These days of pilgrimage are powerful times in the Christian life, and they are great occasions of community and personal prayer, with a freedom and simplicity that is not always found at home; they are moments of refreshment through listening to the Word of God. We come to place our cares and petitions at the feet of Mary, with a trust that is pleasing to God; often we rediscover at the same time our own vocation, Christian, priestly, or religious. The contemplation of Mary Immaculate leads us to desire purification, the Sacrament of Penance, and the need for a new heart, animated by the Holy Spirit. And I am sure that many depart from here, after having prayed together with Mary as at Pentecost, with an increased apostolic zeal.

It is, therefore, very important that these pilgrimages be well received and guided; that the spirit of prayer and the best ecclesial sense be observed in them. I also congratulate and encourage the Missionary Oblates of Mary Immaculate, who for eighty-two years have been in charge of this sanctuary. I recalled this morning the very wonderful work of evangelization that your members, dear Oblate friends, have carried out and continue to accomplish in all of the Canadian Far North and in many other regions, especially in the service of the Amerindians. But in a sense, this ministry at Notre Dame du Cap de la Madeleine is also missionary. It must provide for a renewal of the People of God. And it is situated along the lines of your Marian spirituality which you have contributed to strengthen and spread in Canada.

In this place, I also greet the men and women religious who have come to unite themselves with the pilgrims, to serve them and to pray with them. I especially appreciate today the presence of the contemplative sisters who, like Mary, the sister of

Martha, remain before the Lord in adoration, to unite themselves to His praise of the Father and to His redemptive offering, to manifest their fervent love of Christ who has loved us so much and who dwells here in the Most Blessed Sacrament. Dear sisters, with Mary, the Mother of Jesus, you contemplate her Son: "Hail, true Body, born of the Virgin Mary!" This silent, spontaneous prayer is a very important testimony to all the pilgrims in this shrine, and it has a mysterious power for deepening their spiritual path.

Brothers and sisters, may the Most Holy Virgin obtain for you peace and joy in the service of the Lord. Through her intercession, may God bless the ministry which the Bishop of Rome accomplishes in this place! And may He receive the prayer which is going to ascend now, from this basilica, in our Eucharistic assembly!

From the English edition of L'Osservatore Romano

Mary, Primordial Model
of the Church,
Source of Our Faith
and Our Hope

*At four in the afternoon of Monday, September 10, Pope
John Paul II celebrated an outdoor Mass in French in honor of the
Blessed Virgin at the Sanctuary of Notre Dame du Cap de la
Madeleine, in Trois Rivières, Quebec, and delivered the following
homily in French.*

Dear brothers and sisters,

1. "Blessed is she who believed!" (Lk. 1:45)

These words were spoken to Mary of Nazareth
by her relative Elizabeth on the occasion of the
visitation.

They are contained in the second salutation that
Mary received. The first salutation was from the
angel at the annunciation: "Rejoice, so highly-
favored! The Lord is with you" (Lk. 1:28). These were
the words spoken by Gabriel, the herald who was
sent by God to a town in Galilee called Nazareth. At
the time of Mary's visit to the house of Zechariah, this
greeting of the angel finds in the mouth of Elizabeth

its human complement: "Of all women you are the most blessed, and blessed is the fruit of your womb" (Lk. 1:42).

This human greeting and that of the angel to Mary are blessed with the same light. Both are the Word of God in the mouths of the archangel and of Elizabeth.

Together they form a harmonious whole. Both have become our prayer to the Mother of God, the prayer of the Church. "Why should I be honored with a visit from the mother of my Lord?" (Lk. 1:43)

Elizabeth is the first to profess the faith of the Church: Mother of my Lord, Mother of God, Theotokos!

HANDMAID OF THE LORD

2. "Yes, blessed is she who believed that the promise made her by the Lord would be fulfilled!" (Lk. 1:45)

Today, Elizabeth's words to Mary at the visitation are repeated by the whole Church.

By these words, the entire Church blesses God Himself above all. "Blessed be God the Father of our Lord Jesus Christ" (1 Pt. 1:3).

Our Lord, Jesus Christ, is the Son. He is of the same nature as the Father. He was made man by the work of the Holy Spirit. He became incarnate at the annunciation in the womb of the Virgin of Nazareth and He was born from her as a true man. He is God made man.

Concretely, this took place in Mary at the time of the annunciation by the angel. And she was the first to believe in this mystery. She believed in God Himself on the word of the angel. She said *"Fiat,"* let what you have said be done to me! "I am the handmaid of the Lord."

And so it was.

When the Church blesses and gives thanks to God, the Father of Jesus Christ, with the words of the first letter of Peter, it also blesses the *"fiat"* of Mary, the handmaid of the Lord.

3. With these words of Peter the apostle, the Church is united with Mary in her faith.

"Blessed be God the Father of our Lord Jesus Christ, who in his great mercy has given us a new birth as his sons, by raising Jesus Christ from the dead, so that we have sure hope and the promise of an inheritance that can never be spoiled or soiled and never fade away, because it is being kept for you in the heavens. Through your faith, God's power will guard you until the salvation which has been prepared is revealed at the end of time" (1 Pt. 1:3-5).

This is the faith of the Church and the hope of the Church but, above all, it is the faith of Mary. She has her part, a most eminent part, in the faith and hope of the Church. She believed before all others and better than all others. She believed before the Apostles. Although His relatives did not believe in Jesus (Jn. 7:5), and although the crowds had more enthusiasm than faith, she was unshakable in her faith.

Mary is the primordial model for the Church as it makes its way along the path of faith, hope and charity. At the end of the Constitution on the

Church, Vatican II stated: "The Mother of God is the model of the Church in the order of faith, charity and perfect union with Christ.... It is in faith and in obedience that she brought the Son of the Father to earth...like a new Eve who believed, not in the serpent, but in the messenger of God with an unwavering faith. She gave birth to her Son, whom God made the firstborn among many brethren (Rom. 8:29), that is, the faithful, whose birth and upbringing benefit from her maternal love" (*Lumen gentium*, no. 63).

BLESSED BE ALL BELIEVERS

4. "Blessed is she who believed...."

These words, spoken by Elizabeth, which the whole Church has made its own, are being repeated by us today at the shrine Notre Dame du Cap on Canadian soil.

The Church on earth rejoices in professing here, in this place, its participation in Mary's faith.

With the whole universal Church, the Canadian Church thanks Mary for having helped it to build the faith of the People of God over many generations.

EVER DEVOTED TO MARY

5. Yes, once the witness of Catholic faith was brought to Canada and shared by the people, the Virgin Mary played an important part in their adhesion to Jesus, the Savior, the Word made flesh in her, and in the growth of this believing nation. The founders of this Church were people of great faith,

consecrated to our Lady. It could not have been otherwise. It is the same in every country. You know that my compatriots in Poland have experienced this very profoundly. We are talking about a devotion that is firmly anchored in the hearts of the Christian people, in their daily prayers, in their families and in their parishes. It becomes concrete by the building of important Marian shrines where the faithful come on pilgrimage and where the Virgin herself shows her tenderness and her powerful intercession in a special way.

Dear brothers and sisters, that happened here and I am sure you all know the story. I mention it because I myself was quite touched by it. In 1651, Abbé Jacques de la Ferté, the pastor of Sainte-Madeleine de Châteaudun in France, donated this part of the Cape to the Jesuit missionaries. Not long afterwards, on the Feast of the Presentation of Mary, they founded a village on this site. Marian devotion became so important in the parish, which they named Cap-de-la-Madeleine, that a Congregation of the Holy Rosary established itself here before the end of the 17th century. Thus in 1714 the shrine was built and it became the national Marian shrine and the oldest church in Canada. But tradition recounts some even more moving facts.

In 1879, the parishioners of Cap-de-la-Madeleine prayed to the Virgin Mary and worked with incredible courage all winter long transporting stones for the construction of the new Marian building. To do so they made use of a providential icebridge that had formed on the St. Lawrence known subsequently as

the Bridge of the Rosaries. This was a sign from the
Virgin that she approved this initiative. These facts,
dear brothers and sisters, attest admirably to the faith
of your forebears, to their clear understanding of the
role of Mary in the Church. Since that time, the same
Marian piety has brought thousands of pilgrims from
all over Canada to seek faith and courage from their
Mother! People of all ages and backgrounds; especially the humble and the poor; young families and
elderly couples; parents concerned about their children's upbringing; youth, people seeking the One
who is "the way, the truth and the life"; the sick in
search of strength and hope; missionaries who came
to consecrate their difficult apostolate to the Queen of
the Apostles; all those seeking new vigor to serve the
Lord, the Church and their brothers and sisters, just
as Mary visited Elizabeth.

These pilgrimages bring us "heavenly hours," as
some call them, in the joy of faith with Mary; far from
allowing us to escape our daily tasks, they give us
renewed strength to live the Gospel today while
assisting us to cross to the other shore of life where
Mary "already shines as a symbol of assured hope
and consolation before the People of God on pilgrimage" (Lumen gentium, no. 68).

Yes, this Marian pilgrimage remains as a great
gift to the Canadian people. May the stream of the
faithful who come to pray here never run dry. May
this basilica, which you have recently rebuilt and
extended, this church dedicated to Our Lady of the
Immaculate Conception, be often filled! It is with
satisfaction that I think of the twelve thousand

primary school students in Canada who came here to prepare for my visit. I have received their messages and I thank them. I congratulate them. I say to them: with Mary, build the Church of Canada.

I myself, so anxious to mark each one of my pastoral visits abroad by a pilgrimage to a great Marian sanctuary, am moved and touched to find myself a pilgrim of Mary in this place and to entrust my apostolic mission and the fidelity of all the Christian people in Canada to our Mother.

WITHOUT SEEING HIM, YOU BELIEVE

6. Today, we come to the shrine of Notre Dame du Cap as people of our own time.

We have come to pray with the Bishop of Trois Rivières, His Excellency Laurent Noël, with the members of his diocese and with those who have come from the whole region to this Marian shrine.

We have come to repeat the words of Elizabeth: "Blessed is she who believed that the promise made her by the Lord would be fulfilled!" (Lk. 1:45)

We have come to ratify the participation of past generations in the faith of the Mother of God. In the beautiful heritage which you received and which has made you what you are, faith was primordial. Devotion to Mary, to which your predecessors dedicated themselves, was essential for their loyalty to that faith.

We have come to transfer in some sense that faith into the hearts of our generation and of future generations.

The words spoken by God to Mary were fulfilled. That fulfillment is called Jesus Christ.

When the risen Christ appeared before the Apostles after the passion, one of them, Thomas, who had been absent at the time, did not want to believe. A week later, he saw Christ and proclaimed: "My Lord and my God!" (Jn. 20:28) And he heard the Master say to him: "You believe because you see. Happy are those who have not seen and yet believe" (Jn. 20:29).

And you, dear brothers and sisters, "you did not see him, yet you love him; and you believe in him still without seeing him..." (1 Pt. 1:8). Mary, the Mother of Christ, is there to help you in this faith. She was the first to believe! She will lead you to Him!

Let us pray now for our generation, so that future generations may share the faith of the Mother of God.

This faith will help you to bear the suffering and pain of life, it will help you to persevere with hope even in the midst of "all sorts of trials." Even more, these "trials will test your faith which is more precious than gold, which is corruptible even though it bears testing by fire" (1 Pt. 1:7).

Let us pray that our generation may have lucid and mature faith, unfailing faith! May this faith be a sharing in the faith of Mary who stood at the foot of her Son's cross on Calvary.

Was not Mary's great trial to see her Son rejected and condemned to death by the leaders of His people? She persevered to the end. She shared it all. She was united to Jesus who gave His life to save the world.... And we, when we feel God is far away, when we do not understand His ways, when the cross hurts our shoulders and our heart, when we suffer for our faith, let us learn from our Mother about steadfastness of faith in every trial, let us learn how to find strength and courage in our unconditional commitment to Jesus Christ.

THE PASCHAL MYSTERY

7. It was at the cross that Mary was able to repeat in a special way the words of the Magnificat: "He has looked upon his humble servant" (Lk. 1:48).

Mary's humility is joined in a saving union with the stripping of the garments of her crucified Son!

The whole Church, seeing Mary at the foot of the cross, rejoices: "blessed is she who has believed...." And in that faith of Mary's at the foot of the cross there appears as it were the first light of the Easter dawn.

The cross and the resurrection are joined in one mystery: the Paschal Mystery.

The Church lives this mystery from day to day.

The Church meditates on this mystery in prayer and, here, the prayer of the Rosary takes on its importance. It is with Mary, to the rhythm of the angelic salutation, that we enter the whole mystery of her Son, who was made flesh, died and rose from the dead for us. In a shrine like Notre Dame du Cap, but also in the life of each Christian, each family, this Marian prayer should be like daily breath.

The Church meditates, but it also celebrates, the ineffable Paschal Mystery in the Eucharist every day. Surely, this is the high point of our assembly this evening: with Mary, we approach the source, we are united with her Son's sacrifice, we are nourished by His life: "The mystery of faith!"

And day after day the Church expresses her overflowing joy before this mystery by drawing out its secret from the heart of the Mother of Christ at the moment in which she sings the Magnificat:

"My soul proclaims the greatness of the Lord ...for the Almighty has done great things for me. Holy is his name..." (Lk. 1:46-49).

We learn from Mary the secret of the joy which comes from faith, in order to enlighten with it our lives and the lives of others. The Gospel of the visitation is full of joy: the joy of being visited by God, the joy of opening the doors to the Redeemer. This joy is the fruit of the Holy Spirit, and no one can take it from us if we remain faithful to Him.

Holy Mother! Our Lady of the Cape!

May the Church on Canadian soil always take strength in the Paschal Mystery of Christ!

May it take strength from your Magnificat!

The Almighty has truly done great things for us.

Blessed is His name!

From the English edition of L'Osservatore Romano

Act of Consecration
of Canada to Mary

Before concluding the solemn Mass in the square in front of the Sanctuary of Notre Dame du Cap on Monday afternoon, September 10, the Holy Father, repeating an act that has become customary during his apostolic journeys, entrusted the present and the future of Canada to the Blessed Mother.

Following is the translation of the prayer the Pope offered in French.

1. Hail to you, full of grace, the Lord is with you!

Hail to you, humble servant of the Lord, blessed among all women!

Hail to you, holy Mother of God, blessed and glorious Virgin!

Hail, Mother of the Church, holy Mary: our Mother!

2. Our Lady of the Cape, you open your arms to welcome your children!

Great and small, you listen to and comfort everyone; you show them the source of all joy and all peace: Jesus, the fruit of your womb.

3. I present to your motherly love the men and women of this country.

I pray to you for the children and the young: may they go through life guided by faith and hope; may they open their hearts to the call of the Master of the harvest.

I pray to you for older people: may they enjoy peace and know that they are loved.

I pray to you for couples: may they discover the ever new beauty of a love that is generous and open to life.

I pray to you for families: may they enjoy the happiness of that unity, in which each gives to the other the best of himself or herself.

I pray to you for unmarried people: may they discover the happiness of serving and of knowing that they are useful to their brothers and sisters.

I pray to you for consecrated persons: may they bear witness, through their free commitment, to the call of Christ to build a new world.

4. I pray to you for those who have responsibility for the People of God: bishops, priests, deacons and all those who exercise an ecclesial ministry or an apostolate. Maintain them in the courage and the joy of the Gospel.

5. I pray to you for those who are ill, tired or discouraged. Grant them relief from their pain and the ability to offer it with Christ. May we be attentive to their sorrows and their needs.

6. I pray to you for those whom society isolates or rejects. Make us loving towards them. Help us to find in them the poor in whom your Son recognized Himself.

7. Guide political leaders in the path of justice for all. Help the human community to move in solidarity along the path of progress.

8. I pray to you for those who find themselves far from God. Lead them towards the love and the light of the Lord.

9. There are wars in many countries. Support the victims and convert those who spread misery.

10. So many of our brothers and sisters suffer the pangs of hunger. Make us capable of sharing more and of doing it freely.

11. Sustain the Church in Canada in the proclamation of the Gospel. Confirm within her the power of your Word.

Dispose her to be at the service of justice.

Strengthen within her the communion which your Son established among the members of His Body.

Help all the dispersed children of God find again the fullness of unity.

12. Mother of the faithful!

Pray for us all, poor sinners that we are.

Teach us to live in friendship with God

and in mutual fraternal help,

to walk along the ways of the Lord,

strong in faith

and fortified by the support of your presence.

13. I offer to you my brothers and sisters of this country. Receive them in your helpful goodness and motherly tenderness for they are loved by your Son Jesus. He confided them to you at the moment of giving up His life for the many. Amen.

From the English edition of L'Osservatore Romano

Let Us Ask
the Virgin Mary
for God's Light and Love

The last stop during the Pope's second day in Canada (September 10th) was a visit to Montreal's cathedral. Built from 1870 to 1894, the Cathedral-Basilica of Mary Queen of the World is a half-scale reproduction of St. Peter's Basilica in Rome.

After an introductory address by Archbishop Paul Gregoire and a prayer before the Blessed Sacrament, the Holy Father addressed in French those present.

Dear brothers and sisters,

I am touched to begin my pilgrimage in Montreal, in this Basilica-Cathedral, Mary Queen of the World. Its plan is very similar to that of St. Peter's Basilica in Rome. His Excellency Ignace Bourget, the second Bishop of Montreal, in the latter part of the last century, wanted to symbolize in this way the close ties between the Church in Canada and the Holy See. It is significant too that it was dedicated to Mary, under the title of Mary, Queen of the World.

Like all other cathedrals it is the center and symbol of the whole archdiocese. It is with much pleasure that I greet the Archbishop, His Grace Paul

Grégoire. I thank him most warmly for his welcome and for the words he spoke, words that show how close his Christian people are to his pastoral concern. I greet too his predecessor, my venerable brother Cardinal Paul-Emile Léger. Everyone knows the witness of love that he carried to Africa. I greet Archbishop Grégoire's auxiliary bishops and all other bishops of the ecclesiastical province of Montreal and of the region. I am equally happy to see here the cathedral chapter and the representatives of the presbyterium, of religious men and women and of the laity. I respectfully greet the Mayor of Montreal and all the civil authorities who have contributed to the organization of my stay with that sense of hospitality and efficiency for which they are so deservedly renowned.

After Quebec it was only natural that I should come to this great metropolis, remarkable for its size and for the high proportion and dynamic quality of its French-speaking population. This of course is characteristic of the province of Quebec. In Montreal, English-speaking groups too have their own place and more than twenty-five ethnic communities are recognized and heard. Because of its position and the spirit of initiative of its people and of its authorities it has enjoyed unmatched development and a well deserved international stature. In addition, over the last few decades, a number of large-scale cultural events have attracted the attention of the entire world to it.

Thinking of such a development it is all the more moving to remind oneself of its origins, both modest and extraordinary: the village of Hochelaga; the hill called Mont-Réal in the days of Jacques Cartier; the initiative of the pioneers who were to found Ville-Marie on the Island of Montreal with Paul de Chomédy, Soeur de Maisonneuve, Jeanne Mance; the apostolate of Marguerite Bourgeoys, the "Mother of the Colony"; and how many other devout Christian men and women, who gave this city its soul!

The city spread, was transformed, became modern. But God still has His place here. Rising in the heart of the city as it does, the cathedral bears witness to this. Yes, this land is holy because God dwells in it; His mystery remains as a light, as a call, as a force in the heart of every human person who remains open to His will as Sister Marie Léonie did, whom tomorrow we shall proclaim "blessed." A reflection of the presence of the Lord can be found in the heart of every activity that seeks to make the city more consonant with human dignity. God became man in Jesus Christ so that each and every human person might be imbued with the light and the love of God.

It is this grace that we ask through Mary, in this cathedral which honors her name. She gave us Christ and she continues to open His way for us. If she reigns with Him in heaven, sharing His resurrection, it is in order to continue to serve mankind in search for happiness, in search for true freedom and real progress, in search for love, truth and holiness.

Salve Regina!
Hail, our Queen!
(The Salve Regina was then sung.)

From the English edition of L'Osservatore Romano

Prayer at the Tomb of Blessed Brother André Bessette

Montreal's St. Joseph's Oratory was the first stop of the Holy Father's third day in Canada (September 11). The shrine is very dear to Canadians and contains the tomb of its founder, Frère André Bessette, a religious of the Congregation of the Holy Cross, whom Pope John Paul II beatified on May 23, 1982.

Following is a translation of the French text the Holy Father had prepared to deliver but instead signed and gave to the Superior of the Congregation.

Dear Religious of the Holy Cross,

Thank you for the warm welcome. I would have liked to have been able to talk to you longer, not only about Blessed Brother André, but also about the apostolate of the priests and brothers of the Holy Cross in Canada and in so many other countries where you offer a Christian education to children, to young people, to students, where you meet other spiritual needs in the area of Catholic action or of publications. For these human services and for this ecclesial witness, I would like to extend heartfelt wishes to your entire Congregation. From the very beginning, your founders sought the protection of the Holy Family and particularly of St. Joseph. And it was one of your most humble members, the porter of the college, André Bessette, who carried this confidence in St. Joseph's intercession to its highest degree. *"Pauper servus et humilis,"* Brother André is now among the blessed. In this high place in Montreal, in this great Oratory born of the fervent devotion of Brother André, rather than make a speech, I invite you to join me in my prayer to St. Joseph and to Blessed André.

St. Joseph, with you, for you, we bless the Lord.
He chose you among all men
to be the chaste spouse of Mary,
the one who would remain at the threshold of the mystery of her divine maternity, and who, after her, would accept it in faith as the work of the Holy Spirit.

You gave to Jesus legal paternity in the line of David.

You constantly watched over the Mother and the Child
with an affectionate concern,
in order to protect their lives
and to allow them to accomplish their destiny.

The Savior Jesus deigned to submit Himself to you, as to a father, throughout His childhood and adolescence
and to receive from you an apprenticeship in human life,
while you shared His life in the adoration of His mystery.

You remain at His side.
Continue to protect the whole Church,
the family born of the salvation of Jesus.
Protect especially the people of Canada
who have placed themselves under your patronage.
Help them to come closer to the mystery of Christ
in that attitude of faith, submission and love
that was your own.
See the spiritual and material needs of all those
who beg your intercession,
particularly families
and those who are poor, in every sense;
through you, they are certain to find Mary's
maternal face and the hand of Jesus to assist them.
And you, Blessed Brother André Bessette, porter
of the college and keeper of this Oratory,
give hope
to all those who continue to seek your help.
Teach them confidence in the virtue of prayer,
and, with it, the path of conversion and the
sacraments.
Through you and through St. Joseph, may God
continue to pour out His blessings
on the Congregation of the Holy Cross,
on all those who come to this Oratory,
on the city of Montreal,
on the people of Quebec,
on the Canadian people,
and on the whole Church.

From the English edition of L'Osservatore Romano

The Challenge of Secularism Demands an Increase of Faith Especially in Priests

On Tuesday, September 11, in the Basilica of St. Joseph's Oratory in Montreal, Pope John Paul II met with the priests, religious and seminarians of Montreal and neighboring dioceses. After a reading from the New Testament and some spiritual reflections offered by a number of the priests as personal testimonies, the Holy Father addressed the group as follows:

Dear brothers in the priesthood:

1. It is a great joy for me to meet you here, priests from Quebec and French-speaking priests from a number of other parts of Canada. The conversation with my brothers in the priesthood is always a high point in my travels. I undertake it in association with your bishops, whose principal collaborators you are. They transmitted to you the powers of Christ; each, in his own diocese, is the father of the presbyterium. Every year, on Holy Thursday, I write a letter to all the priests of the Catholic Church; I do it in

order to strengthen them in their sublime vocation and in their indispensable mission to the People of God.

It is indeed a demanding mission. But it is, above all, a gift, for which we must unceasingly give thanks to God. In spite of our unworthiness, Christ has called us to proclaim His Good News, to communicate His life! A difficult responsibility, perhaps, but one which I call on you to fulfill in hope. The words addressed by St. Paul to the Christians of Rome are even more relevant for you, you who share in the apostolic ministry. "May the God of hope bring you such joy and peace in your faith that the power of the Holy Spirit will remove all bounds to hope!" (Rm. 15:13)

Mark these words: "...in your faith!" Everything depends on the faith which inspires your life as priests.

WITNESSING CHANGES

2. Your bishops and particularly those of Quebec, when they came for their *ad limina* visit—and this in addition of course to all the reports or letters I received before this trip—have made me familiar with your religious and social situation, that situation which has existed now for twenty years or so and which continues to evolve. Relatively speaking there are still large numbers of priests here in spite of a recent reduction in the number of ordinations. Like your predecessors, who have left such a strong impression on the life of the Church in Canada, you have been working in faithful union with your bishops. At this time, and in conformity with the

general directions indicated by Vatican II, you are seeking for ways to meet the "crisis" facing your Christian people.

You have been witnessing, in fact, a deep-seated process of change, one which heralds the appearance of a new culture, of a new society, but which poses too a number of questions about the meaning of life. You are facing as well a crisis of values: values of faith, of prayer, of religious practice, moral values, family values, a more materialistic, more selfish attitude to life. The Church is no longer alone in suggesting answers or attitudes; it sometimes feels on the margin of things, some go so far as to speak of being "in exile."

In the face of this new situation most Canadian pastors do not seem discouraged. They are inclined to see here a test, an opportunity for sacrifice, purification, reconstruction, and all this in humility and hope.

RISE TO THE CHALLENGE

3. The Successor of Peter says to you: You must rise to the challenge; do not allow yourselves to be paralyzed; recover your freedom and the dynamism of your faith.

In no way should a sense of realism and meekness of spirit lead to resignation. You cannot allow Christianity to be removed, even temporarily, from the convictions or daily concerns of your compatriots. The novelty of this cultural situation presents in a sense some positive aspects, if one understands by that, that faith can now express itself more freely;

that it depends less on social pressures and more on personal convictions; that it more easily goes beyond formalism and hypocrisy; that it is able to deal better with new scientific questions, with the possibilities of technological progress or social communications; that it fosters a more active and responsible form of participation in more flexible communities; that it may more readily engage in dialogue with others while respecting both their moral convictions and the jurisdiction of civil authorities.

But when we turn to essentials—the sense of a living God, the acceptance of the Gospel of Jesus Christ, salvation through faith, the basic practices of religious life by which faith is expressed and nourished, such as the sacraments of the Eucharist and Reconciliation, the sense of human love in marriage, the theology of the body, respect for life, sharing with the poor and weak, and generally speaking the beatitudes—no Christian, let alone a priest, can be content with silence, or with standing meekly aside on the grounds that ours is a pluralistic society, crossed and recrossed by various currents of thoughts, many of which are inspired by scientism, materialism, even atheism. True, the Gospel does speak of the seed that must die so that it may rise again in a new life (cf. Jn. 12:24-25), yet this death is not one of fear or withdrawal, but one rather of a life totally offered in witness in the very midst of persecution.

In other words we must, more than ever, see to it that the voice of Christianity has a right to be heard in this country, that it might be freely accepted into the mentality of men and women, that its witness be expressed, at all levels, in convincing fashion, so that the developing culture may at the very least feel challenged by Christian values and take them into account. Christ became man, sacrificed His life and rose from the dead so that His light could shine in the eyes of the world, so that His leaven might cause the bread to rise; incorporated in the dough it must be constantly renewing it, on condition, however, that it retains its quality as leaven.

GREATER FAITH NEEDED

4. My dear brother priests, the challenge of secularization calls for greater faith among Christians, first of all among priests. To that world, our world, Christ offers salvation, truth, authentic liberation: the Holy Spirit pursues His work of sanctification; the Good News retains its force; conversion is possible, is necessary. Yes, as I said recently to your Swiss confreres in another context, but one which is not dissimilar to yours—their society, like yours, is an affluent one—the more a society becomes dechristianized, the more it is touched by uncertainty or indifference, the more it needs to find in the person of priests that radical faith which is like a beacon in the night or like a rock on which it can stand (cf. Address to Priests, Einsiedeln, June 15, 1984, no. 7).

I know that you have this faith within you. But it must bring about a new pastoral zeal, in all areas, a zeal like that which moved the founding priests and those who, with so many devout religious and members of the laity, have labored to the point that

French Canada has drawn its inspiration from Christian and Catholic convictions. Yes we must speak of supernatural lucidity and courage of faith which make it possible to resist winds contrary to the Gospel, currents destructive of all that is great in humankind. We must be bold enough to undertake a new effort for the formation of consciences.

With zeal, confident in the Spirit's gift of discernment, encourage those who have managed to renew their faith and their prayer, those who have so generously devoted themselves to apostolic works in the Church and in society. But you will also be careful not to allow the Christian people to remain in a kind of spiritual vacuum or fatal religious ignorance. Should you find your people in confusion with new things, remember that they need, more than ever in these days of change, "visible signs of the Church, props, helps, points of reference..." and community support, as I was saying to your Bishops. When he sees members of his flock disconcerted, the humble pastor must always be ready to welcome them, to listen to them, to understand them. He should on occasion show himself to be receptive to criticism directed at what might well be questionable practices in regard to liturgy, catechesis or education. In all cases he will try to lead his people to a positive attitude and a deepening of their faith.

CHURCH'S SOCIAL RULE

5. You are putting a great hope on the coresponsibility of laity and priests, not only to assist the clergy—whose members have been reduced—but

because it is the role of baptized and confirmed lay persons to participate as living members, unreservedly and fully, in the progress of the Church and its sanctification (cf. *Lumen gentium*, no. 33). They must share in its witness, especially in regard to temporal realities. If the Church is to have a special role, that role must of necessity be played by the laity, united with their pastors and inspired by the Magisterium. Along with your Bishops I urge you to continue along this road to which you have committed yourselves so very much since the Council. The fields of activity are many. In addition to the various forms of the apostolate, there are charisms exercised for others, ecclesial tasks, even formally instituted ministries. In the latter case the presupposition is that the lay person be committed with a certain stability to an important service of the Church.

However, this morning, I will not be dealing with the role of the laity. I will be doing so later, with those that I shall be meeting, notably in Halifax. Because of the lack of time, I would like to turn immediately to your specific role, there being no substitute for the ordained ministry.

GRACE OF ORDINATION

6. "The role of priests," says Vatican II, "to the extent that they are associated with the episcopal order, participates in that authority by which Christ Himself builds up, sanctifies and governs His Church" (cf. *Presbyterorum ordinis*, no. 2). You have been chosen from the Christian community, and you have been chosen to be at its service. To be a priest is

a grace for the whole community. But your role does not derive from the community; you are not delegated by it. To be a priest is to participate in that very act by which the risen Christ builds up His Church which is His Body. Christ the Good Shepherd continues to act in His Church. By your ministry you represent in a very real and efficacious way the Good Shepherd who gives His life for His sheep. You act in the name of Christ the Head who builds up His Church.

The grace of ordination, which has shaped you in the likeness of Christ the Priest and Good Shepherd, permits you to exercise the ministry of the word and of the sacraments. It also enables you to act as an animator of the community thus making manifest the initiative and kindness that Christ has for His Church. Your ministry invariably reminds the community that the word comes from God, that the sacraments are acts of the risen Christ, that the Church is assembled by and in the Spirit. Indeed, nothing can replace your ministry as a sign and means of gathering the faithful into the Body of Christ. May God increase your faith so that you may fulfill the ministry He has entrusted to you!

By your ministry you have been put in charge of Christian communities for which you are responsible. Such is the mandate you have received from your Bishop. This is the basis for the responsible obedience you owe him, for your well-advised and confident cooperation with him. You cannot build the Church of God without him, while, conversely, it is with you and through you that your Bishop discharges his own responsibility as pastor of a particular Church, in unfailing communion with Peter's Successor.

REDISCOVERING PRAYER

7. Among all those acts of the ministry associated with the triple sacerdotal function, may I point out a few that have special relevance to the spiritual needs of your fellow countrymen at this time?

A certain number of young people have rediscovered prayer. But many have forgotten how or dare not pray. As it is, our secularized world will be open to faith and conversion only if it prays as it hears the Gospel. "That kind of devil can be cast out only by prayer and fasting" (cf. Mk. 9:29 and Mt. 17:21). The world needs teachers of prayer and spontaneously turns to the priest whom it sees praying in the name of the Church. But it is impossible to teach others to pray unless prayer is at the very center of our own life, unless it accompanies all our pastoral efforts!

The daily celebration of the Eucharist, with suitable dignity and with a consciousness of entering into the redemptive act of Christ, remains obviously at the center and the summit of your priestly lives.

When Christian people abstain from asking for the forgiveness of their sins, in a personal way, possibly prepared in common, is that not cause for concern? Must we not ask ourselves what importance we attach to this ministry? How available are we in this regard? Do we educate people sufficiently in regard to a sense of sin and of the mercy of God?

The increase in knowledge of mundane matters is matched, in contrast, by an increase in religious ignorance. How are we facing up to this fact in our catechesis of the young? What facilities for education have we provided for adults, in addition to homilies of real substance and serious, in-depth preparation for the sacraments? The proper exposition of the faith is extremely demanding; it must be done in terms that reach both heart and mind while yet remaining faithful to the tenets of the Creed.

My dear friends, you have been entrusted with the task of guiding consciences and therefore of answering in unequivocal terms, and with courage, the innumerable questions posed by contemporary events and discoveries.

All areas of life require this kind of illumination, as they require appropriate reflection. I have in mind, among other things, all that could help families, the young, engaged couples and the newly married, to better grasp God's plan in regard to love, to the meaning of the marriage bond, to responsible parenthood, to faithfulness, not only from a moral point of view, but from a theological and spiritual one as well.

I know that you have the task of educating people in the spirit of the Beatitudes very much at heart, that you are concerned with respect for the human person, with justice, with sharing, with the dignity of the poor, with handicapped people, with the isolation of the old, with solidarity with the hungry masses. And this you must be concerned about in a society where excessive consumption co-exists with the insecurity of unemployment.

Living your daily lives alongside our separated brethren has helped you develop ecumenical relationships. But these still require more thorough theological investigation in conformity with the directives of the Secretariat for Unity.

And how could one not wish to see cultivated that missionary spirit which, in this very century, has so generously flourished in Canada?

I underline finally two points whose urgency cannot have escaped you. Vocations to the priesthood and to religious life must be awakened, through the radiance of your zeal and of your joy in being priests. But it must be associated as well with a pressing invitation to follow Christ who still calls us.

Generally speaking, it can be said that these young people, whom I am to meet this evening and who give evidence of so much good will in spite of their trials, need to find you attentive and able to inspire confidence. And you must be an example to them of disciples of Christ happy to be following His ways.

8. In my meetings with priests around the world, I have seen that they wish to live an intense spiritual life adapted to their vocation. It is from your ministry, fulfilled with conviction, and centered on the Eucharist, that there develops your spiritual vitality, which it is necessary for you to maintain also in moments of personal prayer. As servants of the Word of God, may you yourselves be challenged, refreshed and revived by it. You who assemble communities and are responsible for unity, allow yourselves to stand in wonder at the works which

God accomplishes in His people. As ministers of sacraments, let yourselves be converted by what they celebrate. One cannot baptize without being invited himself to be born again. One cannot preside over a marriage without questioning one's own way of giving oneself in love to the Lord and to one's brothers and sisters: celibacy is a sign of this freedom with a view to service. One cannot celebrate the sacrament of pardon without whispering at the bottom of one's heart: Lord, I too am a sinner who needs to be pardoned. One cannot celebrate the Eucharist without letting oneself be overcome by the love of Jesus who has surrendered His life for the many. In the exercise of your ministry, let yourselves be seized by the power of the Spirit.

Does not the Bishop say to the new deacon when handing him the Book of the Gospels: "Believe what you read, teach what you believe, and practice what you teach"? And to the priest: *"Imitamini quod tractatis."* All your ministry must be situated in a climate of prayer and of sacrifice that unites you to Christ the Mediator and establishes you in His peace and His joy.

The quality of your mission depends also on the fraternity and unity which you priests will establish among yourselves, with respect for legitimate differences of sensibility and charism, but in the impassioned quest of the same proclamation of the Gospel, in faithfulness to the Church.

Remember the priests who, across the world today, risk their freedom and even their lives in order to be faithful to their priesthood and to continue to sustain the faith of their people.

9. I would have liked to address myself at greater length to the permanent deacons. Dear friends, I simply wish to repeat here that your ordained ministry is connected to that of the priests; it prepares for it and effectively prolongs it; or else it shares in it when it is a question of Baptism or of preaching. The Church counts on your actions, for, according to your own vocation, you play your part in accomplishing her mission.

I greet in a special way the seminarians present at this meeting. You have heard me speak of the beauty and the demands of the priestly ministry. This is what must keep you in the joy of being called by God to cooperate in this ministry, with the determination to prepare yourselves for it with all your strength: put prayer at the center of your formation; study thoroughly all the doctrines of the Church on the scriptural, dogmatic and moral planes. From this moment on, live in pastoral availability to the faithful, and maintain fraternal ties with your fellow students and trust in your Bishop. The future of the Church in Quebec will depend on your fervor in following Christ.

Here, in this Oratory, where so many graces have been granted, we pray for the intercession of St. Joseph. In the lives of Mary and Jesus he had a humble role to play, that of a servant, in intimate and continuous contact with the Son of God. Above all else, we are servants of the Son of God.

We pray too for the intercession of Mary, associated in an incomparable fashion with the work of her Son.

Be men of faith and hope! And I, in the name of the Father, of the Son and of the Holy Spirit, give you, with all my heart, my apostolic blessing.

From the English edition of L'Osservatore Romano

We Honor Her as One of the Founders of Montreal and of the Church in Canada

On Tuesday, September 11, on his way to Jarry Park for the Mass of the Beatification of Sr. Marie Léonie Paradis, the Holy Father paid a brief visit to the motherhouse of the Congregation of Notre Dame in Montreal to pray at the tomb of St. Marguerite Bourgeoys, the foundress of the Congregation, whom he canonized on October 31, 1982. Following is the Holy Father's address to the Notre Dame Sisters.

Dear Sisters of the Congregation of Notre Dame,

Time does not permit me, before the Mass that will bring together the whole Christian community of Montreal, to share with you all the thoughts that fill my heart here before the tomb of your holy foundress. It was my honor to canonize her on October 31, 1982. On that date, I spoke of her spirituality, of her admirable apostolate with the young and with families and of the interest her initiatives continue to have for the pastoral ministry today. We honor this saintly woman as one of the founders of Montreal and of the Church in Canada.

Today to you and to all teaching sisters, her dear spiritual daughters, in this country as well as to all others involved in the education of youth and in the promotion of the family, I say simply: look at the zeal, the realism, the audacious love of St. Marguerite Bourgeoys. Think of the value she attached to the soul of every little girl: be she a colonial or an Indian, she was like "a drop of the blood of Jesus Christ"! Consider her devotion and her capability as a teacher, opening schools where they were needed, near the families and working with them. Appreciate her concern for giving complete training to youth, emphasizing faith, prayer, apostolic sense and the cultural and practical abilities necessary to take on the task of an adult woman. Admire her pastoral imagination and tenacity in preparing young men and young women to establish stable homes, and in forming cultivated, hard-working and radiant Christian wives and mothers. Note the concrete support she continued to offer families and married women in associations. You know the faith, the firmness and the tenderness that marked all her work.

Today, the children and young people, like those whom I am going to see this afternoon and this evening, need educators like her to help them discover the meaning of life and to give of themselves generously. And, above all, those families in distress have a greater need than ever of a specific apostolate in their favor (cf. *Familiaris consortio*). Women who rightly desire their advancement have a reason to contemplate this valiant woman who wanted the women of her time to be worthy of their vocation.

Let us pray for all these intentions to St. Marguerite Bourgeoys. And you, dear sisters, continue to draw light and strength from her example. With all my heart, I bless your Congregation.

From the English edition of L'Osservatore Romano

A Message to Women: Bring to the Heart of This Society the God-given Human and Christian Gifts of Your Femininity

On Tuesday, September 11, Pope John Paul II celebrated Mass in Jarry Park, Montreal, for the beatification of Sr. Marie Léonie Paradis, the foundress of the Institute of the Little Sisters of the Holy Family, dedicated especially to the service of priests in the parishes. This was the first beatification ever on Canadian soil.

Following is the translation of the homily the Holy Father delivered to the immense gathering at the Mass.

Beloved brothers and sisters in Christ,

I am happy to be with you today in Montreal, and I thank the Lord for this opportunity. I come among you as a pilgrim of faith and as Bishop of Rome, as someone who has received the mission once confided to Peter to strengthen his brethren in the faith. To each and every one of you I say: "Grace and peace in abundance, through the true knowledge of God and of our Lord Jesus Christ" (2 Pt. 1:2).

May you have "more and more grace and peace through knowing God and Jesus our Lord."

In seeing you all gathered here I think of the founders of Ville Marie. They planted a seed here at the foot of Mount Royal and near the shores of the St. Lawrence, a seed which has become a great tree. It is with joy that I join you in celebrating the faith which has so profoundly marked your history, the faith that it is up to you to maintain and to intensify following the example of Sr. Marie Léonie whom we are going to beatify.

In the course of my journeys around the world I discover the joys and the concerns of all the Churches. To all of the faithful of Canada I bring their greetings.

I bring you great tidings from the young and dynamic Churches of Asia and Africa.

I bring you the echo of the valiant faith of your brothers and sisters in Latin America who are exposed to the violence of underdevelopment and arms.

The brothers and sisters of the Church of Rome and of Italy greet you.

I also bring to you greetings from your brothers and sisters in the faith living in Poland.

May these indications of the tenacious faith of your Christian sisters and brothers throughout the world stimulate you and strengthen you in your own faith.

1. "For the place on which you stand is holy ground" (Ex. 3:5).

These were the words spoken to Moses from the burning bush. He was looking after the flock and had come to Horeb, the mountain of God. The bush was blazing but was not being burnt up. And so Moses wondered: "What is the meaning of this fire that does not destroy the bush and yet burns and gives light?"

The answer came from the midst of the wonderful sight, a more than human answer: "Take off your shoes, for the place on which you stand is holy ground!" (Ex. 3:5).

Why is this place holy? Because it is the place of the presence of God, the place of the revelation of God, of the theophany. "I am the God of your father, the God of Abraham, the God of Isaac and the God of Jacob" (Ex. 3:6).

Moses covered his face, afraid to look at the fire where the living God was revealing Himself.

2. Dear brothers and sisters of Quebec and Canada, what of your meeting with the living God? Sometimes today's world seems to conceal Him, seems to make you forget Him. This apparent spiritual desert stands in sharp contrast with a period, not far removed in time, when the presence of God was highly visible here in social life and in the existence of many and varied religious institutions. And you hear repeated around you: "Where is your God?" (Ps. 42:4).

For the human heart, however, there is no way to become accustomed to the absence of God. Like Moses' compatriots, it suffers when removed from His presence. But He is never far from each one of us (Acts 17:27). He is mysteriously present, like the fire that cannot be grasped, like the gentle breeze that cannot be seen (cf. 1 Kgs. 19:12-13). He beckons to us. He calls us by name to charge us with a mission.

To replace God is an impossible task. Nothing can fill the emptiness of His absence, neither abundant material wealth which does not satisfy the heart, nor easy and permissive lifestyles which do not quench our thirst for happiness, nor the exclusive search for success or power for their own sake—not even technology which makes it possible to change the world but brings no real answer to the mystery of our destiny. All this may prove to be attractive for a time, but it leaves an aftertaste of illusion and a void in the heart (if we have moved away from the burning bush).

It is at this point that we may see appearing, by a kind of reversal, hunger for things spiritual, attraction for the Absolute, thirst for the living God (Ps. 42:3). Paradoxically, the time "of the absence of God" may become the time of the rediscovery of God, as in the approach to Mount Horeb.

3. Yes, God continues to beckon to us, through our own personal history and that of the world we live in, as He called Moses through the sufferings of His people. Is there any one of us who, at one time or another, has not known experiences of light and peace? "God has entered my life!" This might be a sudden experience or the result of a slow maturing process. His mysterious presence can be felt on occasions of all kinds: the wondrous birth of a child, the beginning of authentic love, the meeting with death in the case of loved ones, the confrontation with failure or with the mystery of evil, compassion felt for the sufferings of others, the grace of having

escaped an accident or of recovering from a sickness, the creation of a work of art, the silent contemplation of nature, the meeting with a person in whom God dwells, participation in a praying community.... All these are sparks which light up the road to God, events which open the door to Him. But revelation itself comes from God, from the heart of the burning bush. It is His Word, read and meditated upon in prayer, it is the sacred history of the People of God, which make it possible for us to decipher these signs, to recognize the name and the face of the living God, to discover that He transcends all experience and all creatures. As one of your poets has said, our God is "like the deepest spring of the deepest waters" (Anne Héber, *Présence*, 1944).

4. God reveals Himself to Moses in order to give him a mission. He must lead Israel out of Egypt, out of its bondage under the Pharaohs.

Moses experiences the presence of God. He knows who the God of his fathers is, but as he is charged with this mission, he poses a question: "But if they ask me what his name is, what am I to tell them?" (cf. Ex. 3:13) This matter of the name is of fundamental importance. Moses' question relates to the essence of God, to what constitutes His absolutely unique reality.

And the answer came, "I am who I am" (Ex. 3:14). The essence of God is to be, to exist. All that exists, the whole cosmos, has its origin in Him. Everything exists because God gives existence.

Once Saint Catherine of Siena—following Saint Thomas Aquinas—inspired by the same wisdom drawn from the theophany of which Moses had been the witness, said to God: "You are the One who is; I am the one who is not."

Between the "I am" of God and the "I am" of a human being—as indeed of all creatures—the relationship is the same: God is the One who is; the creature, the human being, is the one who is not.... It is called into existence from nothingness. It is from God that we receive life, movement and being (cf. Acts 17:28).

5. Today in this great city of Montreal, we want to praise the One who is. We want to praise Him along with all creation, we who exist only because He exists.

We exist and we pass away, whereas He alone does not pass away. He alone is Existence itself.

And that is why we say with the Psalm in today's liturgy: "The Lord is great, loud must be his praise; give the Lord the glory of his name...worship the Lord..." (Ps. 95[96]:4-9) as Moses did when he "covered his face, afraid to look at God" (Ex. 3:6).

Prostrate yourselves, men and women of today!

You know the mysteries of creation far better than Moses did! Do they no longer speak to you of God?

Prostrate yourselves. Read again and read thoroughly the witness of creation!

6. God is above every creature; He is absolute transcendence. Where the evidence of creation ends, there begins the Word of God, the Word: "In the beginning he was with God.... Through him all things came to be, no one thing had its being but through him..." (Jn. 1:1-3).

"In him was life,

And the life was the light of men...."

But listen to what follows: "The Word was made flesh, and dwelt among us.... To all who accepted him he gave the power to become children of God; to those who believe in his name, those...who are born of God" (Jn. 1:1-14).

Yes, God who is above all creatures, who is absolute transcendence. God has become a creature, a man. The Word was made flesh. In Him, human beings, born of human beings, are born of God. They become sons and daughters through divine filiation, sons and daughters in the Son.

On this day, in this great city of Montreal, we wish to pay tribute to God made man.

"A holy day has risen for us...

the light has shone on the earth...

Glory be to you, O Christ,

proclaimed among the people;

glory be to you, O Christ,

greeted in this world by faith" (cf. 1 Tm. 3:16), Alleluia!

7. We give thanks for all those who have welcomed this light here, on Canadian soil.

We give thanks especially for those who have become, through Christ, the light of the Church and of the whole of mankind.

The Church has officially recognized the holiness of some of them; several came from abroad, especially from France, but it is here that they completed their lives and attained their measure of holiness. They are familiar to you. I am referring to the holy Jesuit Martyrs, founders of the Church in Canada;

St. Marguerite Bourgeoys; and the blessed: Bishop François de Montmorency-Laval, Mother Marie de l'Incarnation, the young Iroquois woman Kateri Tekakwitha, Mother Marguerite d'Youville, Father André Grasset, Mother Marie-Rose Durocher, and Brother André Bèssette.

I personally had the joy of celebrating in Rome the beatification of five of these and the canonization of one. But I know that other cases are under consideration and I hope the decision will be positive. I am thinking particularly of Mother Catherine de Saint Augustin, the heroic quality of whose virtues was recently recognized.

Beyond those who have been officially canonized or beatified, there are surely many whose faith has grown into an admirable, constant and often discreet love of God and of neighbor. If the few traces they left behind prevent the Church from examining their lives in detail, they are most certainly known to God; they answered His call, as Moses did. They increased His glory and His kingdom on this Canadian soil.

In the face of all these men and women, we must repeat the words of the great Irenaeus, in the second century: "the glory of God is the human person fully alive," the person who lives the fullness of life, the life that comes from God in Jesus Christ.

8. Today, to this living record of the saints and the blessed which has been in this land for centuries, a new name is being added, that of Sr. Marie Léonie Paradis.

This woman is one of you, humble among the humble, and today she takes her place among those whom God has lifted up to glory. I am happy that for the first time, this beatification is taking place in Canada, her homeland.

Born of simple, poor and virtuous parents, she soon grasped the beauty of religious life and committed herself to it through her vows with the Marist Order of the Holy Cross. She never once questioned that gift to God, not even during the difficult periods of community life in New York and in Indiana. When she was appointed to serve in a college in Memramcook in Acadia, the richness of her religious life drew to her young women who also wanted to dedicate their life to God. With them and thanks to the understanding of Bishop Larocque of Sherbrooke, she founded the Congregation of the Little Sisters of the Holy Family which is still thriving and is still very much appreciated.

Never doubting her call, she often asked: "Lord, show me Your ways," so that she would know the concrete form of her service in the Church. She found and proposed to her spiritual daughters a special kind of commitment: the service of educational institutions, seminaries and priests' homes. She never shied away from the various forms of manual work which is the lot of so many people today and which held a special place in the Holy Family and in the life of Jesus of Nazareth Himself. It is there that she saw the will of God for her life. It was in carrying out these tasks that she found God. In the sacrifices which were required and which she offered in love, she experienced a profound joy and peace. She knew that she was one with Christ's fundamental attitude; He had "come not to be served, but to serve." She was filled with the greatness of the Eucharist and with the greatness of the priesthood at the service of the Eucharist. That is one of the secrets of her spiritual motivation.

Yes, God looked upon the holiness of His humble servant Marie Léonie, who had been inspired by Mary's openness and receptivity. And henceforth, from age to age, her Congregation and the Church will call her blessed (cf. Lk. 1:48).

9. This new beatification of a Canadian nun reminds us how much religious communities in every sector of ecclesial and social life have contributed to Canada. They have done this through contemplative prayer, education, assistance to the poor, work in hospitals and apostolic involvement of all kinds. It is a great gift. And if, today, the concrete forms of service can be different and evolve according to need, the religious vocation as such remains a marvelous gift of God. It is a witness without parallel, a prophetic charism essential to the Church, not only because of the immeasurable services for which the sisters are responsible, but because first of all it signifies the gratuity of love in a spousal gift to Christ, in a total consecration to His redemptive work (cf. my letter *Redemptionis donum*). I would ask this of all the Christians gathered here: Are the Canadian people still able to appreciate this gift? Do they help religious women to find and to strengthen their vocation? And you, dear sisters, do you appreciate the greatness of the call of God and the fundamentally evangelical lifestyle which corresponds to that gift?

10. Women religious, turned towards the Burning Bush, have a particular experience of the living

God. But I address myself in this Mass to all the Christian people of Montreal, Quebec and Canada. Brothers and sisters: seek the Lord; seek His will; listen to the One who calls each of you by name in order to entrust a mission to you, so that you can bear His light within the Church and society.

You are the Christian laity, baptized and confirmed. And you wish to live as sons and daughters of God. In the Body of the Church there are many charisms, many forms of activity for developing your talents in the service of others. God sends you to serve your brothers and sisters who are suffering, in distress, in search of Him. By your prayers and deeds each day may the love of God, the justice of God and hope find their place in the earthly city, in all your places of work, leisure and research. Having had the experience of God yourselves, contribute to building a fraternal world which is open to God. I address this message to all people; but since I am beatifying a woman today, I address it especially to women. Like all the baptized, you are called to holiness in order to sanctify the world according to your vocation in the plan of God, who created humanity as "man and woman." Together with men, bring into the heart of your families, bring into the heart of this society, the human and Christian capacities with which God has endowed your femininity and which you will be able to develop according to your rights and duties to the very degree that you are united with Christ, the source of holiness.

The Lord counts on you so that human relations may be permeated with the love that God desires. The ways of accomplishing this service may differ from that chosen by Blessed Sister Marie Léonie. But—in the most evangelical sense which transcends the opinions of this world—it is always a question of service, which is indispensable for humanity and the Church.

11. The saints and the blessed, and all those guided by the Spirit of God, can make their own the words of the Letter to the Ephesians which we have heard: "Blessed be God the Father of our Lord Jesus Christ, who has blessed us with all the spiritual blessings of heaven in Christ" (Eph. 1:3).

Yes, the names of the saints confirm in a special way the truth of our existence in Jesus Christ. The truth and the call to holiness, that is, union with God through Christ.

Let us again listen to this Letter to the Ephesians:

—God "before the world was made, chose us, he chose us in Christ,"

—out of love He determined that we "should become his adopted sons through Jesus Christ,"

—in Him, "through his blood, we gain our freedom, the forgiveness of our sins," and this, through "the richness of his grace,"

—He has united everything "under Christ, as head, everything in the heavens and everything on earth,"

—in Him, we too have been made heirs,

—in Him, we have been stamped "with the seal of the Holy Spirit...the pledge of our inheritance which brings freedom for those whom God has taken for his own, to make his glory praised" (Eph. 1:4-14).

12. "For the place on which you stand is holy ground!"

In the period in which we live, what we see on earth makes sin more obvious to us than holiness. There are many reasons why, in the different countries and continents, we should see more often the unfortunate results of sin than the light of holiness. Despite a growing tendency no longer to call a sin a sin, the human family lives in fear of what is finally the product of human intelligence and will be at odds with the will of the Creator and the Redeemer. All of us here are aware of the perils that threaten our planet and we recognize man's hand in those threats.

And yet...

Yet this earth, the place where we live, is holy ground.

It has been marked by the presence of the living God, whose fullness is in Christ. And that presence remains on earth and produces the fruits of holiness.

That presence is reality.

It is grace.

The presence will always be a call and a light.

"The light shines in the dark, but the darkness cannot overcome it" (Jn. 1:5).

Amen.

From the English edition of L'Osservatore Romano

Friendship Consists in Giving Happiness to Others Every Day

On Tuesday, September 11, the Holy Father met about 3,000 elementary school children in Notre Dame Basilica, Montreal, and spoke to them as follows.

Dear young people,

First, let us observe a moment's silence to thank God from the bottom of our hearts for the joy of this meeting!

You are happy to be so close to the Pope! Well, I can assure you that the Pope is also very happy to be among you!

You know as well as I that when people, young people like you or older people like me, take the time to meet one another and to show their friendship, simply and sincerely, to help one another as best they can, that is *happiness* on earth! It is this fraternity among all the inhabitants of the earth that the Lord desires so strongly. You know that Jesus came and that He remains, mysteriously but truly, among us.

He continues to seek this universal brotherhood with us, He brings us together to make us members of His Body.

Of course, no one individual alone can realize this plan for friendship in the world and unity within each country and among all the peoples of the earth. But everyone has to make his or her contribution a personal, irreplaceable contribution. I know you understand me for I can see it in your young faces.

There are almost three thousand of you young people gathered here in the house of the Lord, and you are all different. Some are quiet, others a little more restless; some of you like music and art, others prefer sports; many of you work with all your heart at school while there are others who have less interest and less courage for study; some of you have health problems, while others enjoy good health. Different, yes, but each and every one of you has a place—a unique place—in the heart of the Lord, a role in the vast plan the Lord has for the world.

If Jesus were to meet you here today...but He is here in one way, in the person of the Bishop of Rome, me, the Successor of the Apostle Peter—He would say to you again: you must, above all, love one another; that is how you will be recognized as my disciples, as my true friends! Yes, always love one another more.

I am happy to have seen with my own eyes your symbolic gestures of friendship and mutual aid and to have heard you sing your desire to love the other as he is, to love others as they are. I have every confidence that each one of you will, here in Canada and throughout the world, promote friendship in the way Jesus meant it to be: by giving happiness to others every day…by giving one's life. Through your personal and collective efforts, this is happening and will continue to happen. Jesus is always helping you: in prayer; you are very close to Him. You meet Him in the sacraments He gave to His Church: since Baptism you are tied to Him; you seek His pardon through Confession and you like to receive Him and share His life in the joy of Communion; the Sacrament of Confirmation assures you of the gift of the Holy Spirit who bestows His light and strength on you so that you may grow with the Spirit of Christ in you and take your active place in His Church.

I would like to add one more thing. I know that you all have your place in a family, in a community specially adapted to you, as well as in Christian action movements. Your parents and your teachers give you what you need to live, to grow and to build your future. They understand you, they support you and they give you their affection. So I would ask you to show more confidence, respect and consideration for those who take such good care of you. Thus you will be their joy and thus every day you will know, not only the joy of being loved, but the joy of loving. Is that not a great thing?

That is what I wanted to say to you here. Dear young people, to help you live like brothers and sisters, like friends, and that with as many people as possible, I bless you in the name of the Father and of the Son and of the Holy Spirit.

From the English edition of L'Osservatore Romano

With Christ
You Shall Love Life

The Pope's last engagement of Tuesday, September 11, was a meeting with youth in the Olympic Stadium of Montreal. About 70,000 were present and they came from the 21 dioceses of Quebec. The Holy Father addressed them as follows:

My dear young people,

1. As part of my visit to Quebec it is a great joy for me to be with you. In a country that is alive, in a vibrant Church, it is you who determine the shape of the future. And this evening in the Olympic Stadium, a scene of human endeavor and accomplishment, it is good to hear and see you express the faith and concerns, the hope and the questions of your generation as you examine with great frankness all that constitutes your life.

You have chosen that fundamental text that begins the Gospel of John. And so you place our meeting under the sign of the life that is stronger than death, under the sign of the light that darkness cannot overcome, under the sign of the Word, the eternal Word of God, who comes to dwell among us

The Holy Father was greeted at the Quebec
City Airport.

Pope John Paul II received a warm welcome at the Laval University campus.

The Eucharistic celebration at Laval University named for François de Laval, the first Bishop of Quebec.

At the Shrine of Saint Anne de Beaupré, His
Holiness was welcomed by Amerindian and Innuit
representatives from Quebec.

Pope John Paul II celebrated Mass for a large crowd at the Sanctuary of Notre Dame du Cap de la Madeleine, despite inclement weather.

Jarry Park in Montreal was the scene of a Eucharistic celebration in which the Pope beatified the French-Canadian Sister Marie Léonie Paradis.

At Flatrock in St. John's, Newfoundland, His Holiness blessed the fishing fleet.

The Holy Father celebrated an open air Mass at Moncton, New Brunswick. Flowing down from under the altar was a waterfall symbolizing the graces of Christ given in Baptism and the Eucharist.

The Pope had a very warm meeting with the children and handicapped at Izaak Walton Killam Hospital in Halifax.

Meeting with the Ukrainians in the Cathedral of Sts. Vladimir and Olga, Winnipeg.

During a ceremony in Midland, Ontario, an
Iroquois chief offers to Pope John Paul II an eagle
feather, which symbolizes the "Great Spirit."

In Winnipeg, Ukrainian Catholics gave a
colorful welcome to His Holiness at the Cathedral
of Sts. Vladimir and Olga.

His Holiness attended a special program for children, senior citizens, and the disabled in Vancouver, British Columbia.

The Pope was welcomed to Ottawa by over
350,000 people who lined Rideau Canal as the
Papal Barge passed.

"You have been told that my visit among you is that of a Shepherd. The shepherd is one who gathers together. We gather together to celebrate our Faith."

in Christ. May this act of faith guide us, may this light permeate us as your questions resound.

For your questions are numerous. You have just expressed some of the more serious ones among them. They can be added to those which were sent to me with confidence and simplicity by several thousand of you before I even came to visit you. I would dare to say to you that these questions often seem to me to have been formulated in a kind of shadow zone where humanity fears its future, mapping its path without seeing the light which is offered it, without recognizing the true light which enlightens every one.

I COME AS A WITNESS

2. One of you, a young girl from Quebec, wrote to me: "Give us your secret of responding to love and of having confidence in Jesus." I have not come to reveal a secret to you. I have come as a witness, as John the Baptist came, to witness to the light. I have come to invite you to open your eyes to the light of life, to Christ Jesus. If we listen to His word, if we follow Him, if we discover the greatness of His love for all men and all women of every age, then we will know that life is worth living, and better still, that it is worth giving.

In the passage of the Gospel which has been your inspiration this evening, John tells us that Jesus is the Word, that He is the life and that He is the light of men. Certainly, no one has ever seen God but the Son can reveal Him to us (Jn. 1:18). The Son is the Word who expresses perfectly the will of the Father, who calls us all to share the unparalleled beauty and purity of His infinite love through the inexhaustible generosity of His creation. In one of the prayers of the Mass we say: "You, the God of goodness, the source of life, have created all things...in order to lead all people to the joyful vision of your light" (Eucharistic Prayer IV).

3. However, there is darkness: when life disappoints us, when life wounds us, when one does not find happiness, when the heart hardens and when brothers and sisters are divided and fight one another. Darkness overcomes the light: humanity sets up, as it were, a screen, and experiences in anguish the difficulties of life. The world no longer recognizes the one who has called it to life, a life that should blossom in a universal fraternal union. Darkness brings a chilly closing in on oneself; it makes one incapable of loving freely and generously, and truth is lost in falsehood. In the darkness, our blinded gaze can no longer perceive the Father, whose love remains faithful in spite of the estrangement of His sons and daughters, in spite of all breaches of friendship.

"In him, there is no darkness" (1 Jn. 1:5).
"The light shines on in the darkness, a darkness that did not overcome it." The Word was "the true light which gives light to all men." "The Word became flesh and made his dwelling among us" (cf. Jn. 1:5, 9, 14).

In regard to the dark side of your questions, I would like to say to you, "Stand erect and hold your heads high, for your deliverance is near at hand" (Lk. 21:28). Jesus, the Son of God, "true God from true

God, light from light," lives among us. "In him was life and the life was the light of men."

GIFT OF NEW LIFE

4. These words are the introduction to the whole of the Good News: Jesus of Nazareth, the Son resplendent in the glory of the Father, became one of us: He begins an amazing contest with the forces of darkness: a contest in which the powers of darkness cannot overcome the strength of Christ, which is of a totally different order, for He is only strong in the gift of Himself to His Father for His brothers and sisters. It is a struggle in which He accepts to share our weakness and our loneliness, to endure the hostility of men to the point where He cries out: "It is now the hour of the power of darkness" (Lk. 23:53). But the darkness will not overcome Him; He fights with the arms of peace.

Over against the excess of power, Jesus sets unselfishness: He chose to be the Servant.

Over against the excess of pride, Jesus sets humility: "I am not seeking my own will, but the will of him who sent me" (Jn. 5:30).

Over against hatred which rejects and kills, Jesus sets forgiveness: "Father, forgive them, they do not know what they are doing" (Lk. 23:24).

Over against the blind power of death, Jesus sets the love of Him who gives Himself: "No one takes my life from me, I lay it down freely" (Jn. 10:18).

Over against the absurd watch over His body in the tomb, Jesus sets the freedom of the resurrection.

"The Son of man in his day will be like the lightning which flashes from one end of the sky to the other" (Lk. 17:24).

To those who despair of life and experience the threat of nothingness, Jesus offers the gift of new life: "This is the will of my Father, that everyone who looks on the Son and believes in him shall have eternal life. Him I will raise up" (Jn. 6:40).

SEEKERS AFTER TRUTH

5. My friends, in the letters I have received from you, I see two series of questions: on the one hand you say: "Speak to us of Jesus Christ, of hope and of faith," and on the other hand you write: "Help us to resolve the difficulties that overshadow our personal, social and religious life."

I wanted first of all to speak to you about the light of Christ, because it is as a witness to the Redeemer that I have come among you. The passage of the Gospel which you chose corresponded to this wish. Seek nowhere else an inspiration for answers to your questions. Listen to Him who says to you: "I am the light of the world. Whoever follows me will not walk in darkness; he will have the light of life" (Jn. 8:12).

You must remember this in moments of doubt. If you follow Christ, you will develop your full potential. You will be seekers after truth because it alone makes us free. I appeal to your inner dynamism: you will know how to move toward the solution of your problems by listening to the whole Gospel, by reflecting on it with your elders, and in your various Christian youth groups. Mobilize together your energies: be clear about what constitutes the foundation of your life; recognize the light of Christ—it will show you how to escape from the circles in which you might enclose yourselves. With Him, you will love life.

6. In times of darkness, do not seek an escape. Have the courage to resist the dealers in deception who make capital of your hunger for happiness and who make you pay dearly for a moment of "artificial paradise"—a whiff of smoke, a bout of drinking or drugs. What claims to be a shortcut to happiness leads nowhere. It turns you away from that intelligent self-discipline which builds up the person. Have the courage not to take the easy path; have the courage to reverse directions if you have taken it. And know how to lend a helping hand to those of your companions who are haunted by despair when the darkness of the world is too cruel for them.

Many of you have been affected by unemployment. Here it is the whole problem of a changing society that touches you. There are economic solutions, difficult and long-term: they remain to be found. The leaders of society must devote themselves to this issue with a primary concern that the condition of everyone be reasonably acceptable and that there be observed the first demand of justice which is respect for the individual, however destitute, however young. But as for you, do not allow the difficulties to destroy the resilience of your own personality; take your future in hand.

Ask yourselves, too, what you expect from professional life, you who are preparing for it, you who are already beginning it and you who are prevented from blossoming in it. Be creative! Do not be conspicuous by your absence when the future of the world is being shaped! You already share responsibility for it.

You are often critical, and rightly so, of a society so hungry for consumer goods that it destroys nature and lays waste its resources. But you ask yourselves what value you put on gain, on the possession of riches. Are you free in regard to money? How far are you prepared to share? Remember Jesus the day He went into Zacchaeus' house: His presence transformed an entire lifestyle; not only did Zacchaeus rediscover justice in promising to repay the money he had acquired unjustly, but he also discovered generosity in sharing his wealth.

Broaden your vision beyond your usual milieu and your own country. Your brothers and sisters in vast regions of the world are without even the necessities of life, wounded in their dignity and oppressed in their freedom and their faith. Christ loves all His own and He identifies lovingly with the poorest. May He share with you His love for all His brothers and sisters! May He help you to live in that true solidarity which crosses frontiers and overcomes prejudices!

You are citizens of a country that enjoys peace but you are concerned about the future of humanity. You long for peace from the depths of your heart. Let this longing reverberate! I want your concern for world peace to make of you workers for peace. Begin with where you are. Repeat with sincerity the prayer of Francis of Assisi, a builder of peace in his own city: "Lord, make me an instrument of Your peace. Where there is hatred, let me bring love...." And, as Madame Jeanne Sauvé said recently, "Peace must become a state of soul—a way of being and of working."

RELATIONSHIP WITH GOD

7. Before evoking some other questions that you asked me, I would like to return to the Gospel passage which is our inspiration this evening. "He came unto his own.... To all those who received him, to those who believe in this name, he gave power to become children of God!"

It is an unimaginable, unhoped for relationship with the living and true God that Jesus makes possible because He is near us. "The Word became flesh and dwelt among us." In giving His life for the many, He promises to remain among us for all generations. Faithful to His mission, He became one of us and remains present, a light which enlightens all people, "the way, the truth and the life" (Jn. 14:16).

For the majority of you, the intimate meeting with Christ was consecrated through Baptism. Jesus has offered us the riches of life in God. Peter said: "He has called us from darkness into his marvelous light" (1 Pt. 2:9).

IF HE CALLS, LISTEN

8. Today, often enough you do not find it easy to take your place in the community of the baptized. Some of you say that you do not see the Church as the place where it is natural to be united with one

another by the Christ of the Gospel. The building seems to you to be too big, built by others in a style different from your own. The "light that enlightens," you find blocked by too many shadows.

It is true that the community is still far from being the perfect mirror that would reflect the whole face of Christ. It is true that unity remains a goal too often contradicted. It is true, in a word, that the Church called by our Savior to be assembled in Him, is on the path of conversion and that there is still a long way to go.

Nevertheless, you the young, remember that Jesus asked us not to set ourselves up as judges (cf. Mt. 7:1-5). Do not remain either on the threshold, or outside. Do not let yourselves be tempted to expect the Church to be just a reflection of yourselves. As baptized persons, you are members of the Body of Christ. Only the whole Body will be able to reflect for humanity the luminous face of Christ.

You rightly expect your elders to accept you with tolerance and to respect you for what you are. You must do the same for them.

The Church is the community in which we inherit the gifts given to the Apostles and handed on by them without interruption to us: the one, holy, catholic and apostolic Church. It is for everyone the place to encounter Him who dwells among us; it is the place of the gift of the Spirit and of His grace; it is the place where we are given a rule of life; it is the place where all are called to share, to give thanks, to join in the Eucharistic offering of the life given by Christ, to receive the gift of forgiveness, to accept the mission of proclaiming the truth and spreading love.

Take your place in the life of this Body, however imperfect it remains. Bring to it your exigency, your enthusiasm. Contribute to the expression of faith and prayer, with your poetic gift and your desire to commit yourself.

And if there should arise in you the desire to consecrate your life to the service of God and of your brothers and sisters in the ministry of the Church, in the religious life, know how to recognize in it the call of Christ and respond with the boundless generosity of youth.

Take the time necessary to discern your vocation, allow it to be tested by prayer and reflection, consecrate yourselves to a solid formation. Speak with confidence to the pastor and superiors whose duty it is to confirm your call. You will know the joy of serving in the footsteps of Christ in the Church in which He lives, of surrendering your life, in freedom and poverty, to share His love for His brothers and sisters.

COMMITMENT TO LOVE

9. There is one last point that I wish to address, because you are deeply interested in it. It concerns your questions about marriage and about the love of a couple and love in marriage.

In reading your letters I have been impressed in seeing that they express much pain. Too many of you suffer because of the breakdown of family life, because of separation and divorce; and you have been wounded to the point of sometimes doubting whether a faithful and lasting love is possible.

It is not ours to judge those who have been hurt by the upheaval affecting morals and society. But I say to you: do not doubt; you can build a home on the rock of fidelity, because you can count totally on the fidelity of God, who is love.

Prepare yourselves for the worthwhile and true commitment of marriage. React against false illusions and do not confuse a premature experience of pleasure with the giving of oneself in love, deliberately consented to, and forever. When, as man and woman, you bind your lives together, decide to do so with complete generosity, each one desiring first the well-being of the other, together desiring to communicate life and to ensure the welfare of your children. Prepare yourselves for the one commitment that is worthy of human love, the commitment of marriage, in order to build something that deserves and requires the whole of one's life. And for this, too, may the words of Christ give you light: "A man can have no greater love than to lay down his life for his friends" (Jn. 15:13).

THE LIGHT OF HOPE

10. Dear young people: in all the questions that deeply interest you, there is a dark side that worries you—and there is a light of hope. This hope—and you have shared it with me—rightly leads you to question yourselves about your future, about the future of the world and the future of the Church.

In the name of Christ, I ask you: when you are overcome by weariness or seized by doubt, break out of the bonds of your loneliness, find Him who is the light of all people, join with your brothers and sisters in order to walk together, seek the support of your elders.

Remain seekers after truth. Use with courage the rich gifts that are within you. Give yourselves without reserve to the service of justice, of peace, of freedom and of love, in the light of Christ.

Quebec, like your powerful river, you are a country with a generous nature. You know how to channel your rivers. Do you know how to channel the energies of your youth for the service of the whole human person and of all humanity loved by God?

Turn, my dear young friends, at each stage of your journey towards Him in whom dwells the fullness of God (cf. Col. 2:9). Following Peter, put your trust in Him: "Lord, to whom shall we go? You have the words of eternal life" (Jn. 6:68).

From the English edition of L'Osservatore Romano

The Primacy of Man in the Factors of Production

On Wednesday, September 12, the Pope went by air to St. John's, Newfoundland, and from there he went to the fishing port at Flatrock, where he prayed before the Grotto of Our Lady of Lourdes, and then blessed the fishermen and their boats. Before giving his blessing he addressed them as follows.

Dear brothers and sisters, dear people of Newfoundland,

1. It was from their fishing boats on the Sea of Galilee that Jesus called Simon Peter and James and John to share His mission. As the Gospel reminds us, Jesus spent much of His time in the ordinary circumstances of daily life, sharing the hopes and hardships of the people. This is why I am immensely pleased to be with you, the members of the fishing community. I extend a special greeting to you, Archbishop Penney, and to those of you who are the spiritual leaders of the other churches and communions represented here. The joyful event that unites us is the blessing of the Fishing Fleet here at Flatrock.

It is in this context that I have come today to express my solidarity with you, and to profess with you faith in our Lord Jesus Christ. This faith of ours, in the Eternal Son of God made man, offers an uplifting message for the whole human community. Our faith in Jesus Christ, true God and true Man, opens up before us a vision of great hope and, at the same time, it speaks to all of us about Christ's commandment to love and serve one another.

IN PAIN AND HOPE

2. Long before they settled on these shores, Europeans fished these banks. From fishing villages along these coasts you and your ancestors have set out in all kinds of weather to wrest a living from the sea, often at the risk of your lives. Your wives and families have shared the uncertainty and fear that your way of life involves. In Christian pain and hope they have mourned the loss of many loved ones that did not return. As a Newfoundland poet wrote:

"It took the sea a thousand years,
A thousand years to trace the granite features
    of this cliff,
In crag and scarp and base.
It took the sea an hour one night,
An hour of storm to place
The sculpture of these granite seams
Upon a woman's face."

CHANGING CONDITIONS

3. Today your lives are touched by another kind of insecurity, coming not from the sea but from the changed conditions in the fishing industry and in the world economy. Not even Canada with its immense natural resources and limited population has escaped the effects of worldwide economic uncertainty. Here in Newfoundland, even more than in other parts of

Canada, you feel the heavy burden of unemployment, which has settled like a blight on the hopes of so many, especially the young, who experience in their own lives how the absence of rewarding employment affects the many aspects of their existence and of society, destroying prospects for the future, affecting the livelihood of families and *disturbing the social fabric of the community.*

In my Encyclical *Laborem exercens,* I have emphasized "the fact that human work is a key, probably the essential key, to the whole social question" (no. 3). Men and women are meant to contribute by their work to the building up of the human community, and so to realize their full human stature as co-creators with God and co-builders of His kingdom. Prolonged failure to find meaningful employment represents an affront to the dignity of the individual, for which no social assistance can fully compensate. The human cost of such unemployment, especially the havoc it brings to family life, have frequently been deplored by the Canadian Bishops. I join with them in appealing to those in positions of responsibility, and to all involved, to work together to find appropriate solutions to the problems at hand, including a restructuring of the economy, so that human needs be put before mere financial gain. The social doctrine of the Church requires us to emphasize the primacy of the human person in the productive process, the primacy of people over things.

A CRUEL PARADOX

4. Canada has been called the breadbasket of the world, and it was one of the world's largest exporters

of fish before the recent recession. It is a cruel paradox that many of you who could be engaged in the production of food are in financial distress here, while at the same time hunger, chronic malnutrition and the threat of starvation afflict millions of people elsewhere in the world.

With careful stewardship, the sea will continue to offer its harvest. However, during the last few years the means of processing and distributing food have become more technically sophisticated. The fishing industry has also been concentrated more and more in the hands of fewer and fewer people. Around the globe more and more small or family fishing concerns lose their financial independence to the larger and capital intensive enterprises. Large industrial fishing companies run the risk of losing contact with the fishermen and their personal and family needs. They are exposed to the temptation of responding only to the forces of the marketplace, thus lacking at times sufficient financial incentive to maintain production. Such a development would put the security and distribution of the world's food supply into ever greater jeopardy, if food production becomes controlled by the profit motive of a few rather than by the needs of the many.

CURRENT SITUATION

5. The current economic situation, especially with regard to fishing, demands courageous decisions in order to overcome all negative consequences. Our Christian view of man and what constitutes his good must be the guiding principles in looking for

alternate solutions. The promotion of cooperatives of fishermen, collective agreements between workers and management, some form of joint ownership or partnership—these are some of the possible solutions that would aim at ensuring that the workers have a voice in the decision-making affecting their own lives and the lives of their families.

In a world of growing interdependence, the responsible stewardship of all the earth's resources, and especially food, requires long-range planning at the different levels of government, in cooperation with industry and workers. It also requires effective international agreements on trade. It must take into account the problem of food-aid and aid to development, and be responsive to those in need.

YOUR CHRISTIAN LIVES

6. My dear friends: hard work and a strong sense of family and community have sustained you in the past in your upright Christian lives. Above all, your faith in Jesus Christ and the hope that it generates in you are at the basis of all your aspirations for a better future. For this reason, in the efforts and struggles of daily living you can say with Saint Paul: "To this end we toil and strive, because we have our hope set on the living God" (1 Tm. 4:10).

Together with your spiritual leaders gathered here with me, I pray for all of you and your families. May God our Father grant success to the work of your hands. May His divine Son, our Lord Jesus Christ, who multiplied the loaves and fishes to feed the hungry multitudes, expand the horizon of your fraternal concern to embrace all His brothers and sisters. May the Holy Spirit live in your hearts and fill you with His peace, today and forever.

Let us never forget, dear people of Newfoundland, the values that Christ taught from Peter's boat on the sea of Galilee and throughout all his life. And let us heed the words of the Apostle Paul: "Let everything you do be done in love" (1 Cor. 16:14).

Vatican Translation

You Are Called
To Share Fully
in the Church's Mission
in the World

The Pope's second meeting in St. John's, Wednesday, September 12, was with handicapped, sick, and elderly persons in Memorial Stadium. Following is the original English text of the Holy Father's address.

Dear brothers and sisters,

As I visit the province of Newfoundland, I am pleased to have this special meeting with handicapped and disabled persons. I greet you in the joy and peace of our risen Savior. I extend greetings, too, to your families and friends who are with you today and to all who are close to you through their prayers and concern.

1. In recent years, I have had the opportunity to meet large numbers of handicapped and disabled persons: pilgrims who have come to Rome, groups such as this one today whom I have met on my

pastoral journeys, and many special groups such as handicapped children on the occasion of their First Communion or Confirmation. I have always welcomed these meetings, for they have afforded me the opportunity of getting to know you better and of coming to understand your struggles and achievements, your sorrows and joys. Such meetings have made me even more aware of how effectively you participate in the life of the community, and of how you must not be relegated to some marginal place in society. In the Church, too, you have an important part to play. You are called to share fully in her life and mission in the world.

2. Each of you, through Baptism, enjoys the gift of new life in Christ and the dignity of an adopted son or daughter of our Father in heaven. In Baptism, you have also been given a share in the priestly, prophetic and kingly functions of our Lord Jesus Christ; and you are called to exercise your role in order to build up Christ's Body, the Church, and to further the kingdom of God in this world. Your personal call to holiness and to loving service of others is not separate from your daily life. Rather, your patient acceptance of your disabilities and your joyful hope in the face of difficulties are in their own way a proclamation of the Gospel, for they bear silent witness to the saving power of God at work in your lives.

"Try then," as St. Paul said, "to imitate God, as children of his that he loves, and follow Christ by loving as he loved you" (Eph. 5:1-2). Seek to accept all things in a spirit of faith and in the light of the cross. And may you find in the Eucharist and in prayer the strength needed to overcome any obstacle—the liberating power of Christ's love that has conquered the world.

3. Dear brothers and sisters in Christ: be assured that you are never alone. God loves you and has given you a special place in the Church. And the Pope loves you, too, and blesses you with all his heart. He is also close to your families and all your dear ones. May Christ fill you with His peace.

Vatican Translation

Let Us Thank the Lord for the Christian Families of Canada

In the early afternoon of Wednesday, September 12, at Quidi Vidi Lake in St. John's, the Holy Father celebrated Mass with some fifty thousand faithful in attendance, despite the heavy rains.

Following is the original English text of the homily His Holiness delivered after the proclamation of the Gospel.

Dear brothers and sisters in Christ,

1. Let us give thanks to the Lord our God!

These words we take from the very heart of the Eucharistic liturgy. Eucharist means thanksgiving. Today, as we meet around this altar, our first desire is to give thanks—to give thanks with the Archdiocese of St. John's and with the whole Church throughout Newfoundland, as it celebrates the two-hundredth anniversary of its establishment on the island. In this way we wish to express what is the most characteristic element of the Eucharistic liturgy.

Our sacrifice and our prayer in union with the Sacrifice of Jesus Christ—in the sacramental identification with Him—is above all a great act of thanksgiving by the Church.

This thanksgiving has shaped the spiritual life of those who have been the disciples and confessors of the Redeemer in Canada from the very foundations, from the very roots.

The liturgy that we are celebrating is meant in a special way to express the fact that the sons and daughters of Newfoundland, Labrador and all of this land, rooted as they are in the mystery of Christ, cry aloud to God with full hearts: "Let us give thanks to the Lord our God."

PRAISE GOD FOR CANADA

2. We give thanks for all the richness of creation —in particular for the richness that has been shared in by the succeeding generations in Canada. Both by the generations that lived here in the past, according to the principles of their original culture, and also by the generations that have come here from beyond the sea, gradually building up the structures of a new civilization and Canadian culture. We give thanks to the Lord for the opportunities that countless families have found here over the years, and for the freedom and hope that they have enjoyed.

And so we cry aloud with the psalmist:
"How good is the Lord to all,
compassionate to all his creatures.
All your creatures shall thank you, O Lord,
and your friends shall repeat their blessing.
They shall speak of the glory of your reign
and declare your might, O God"
    (Ps. 145[144]:9-11).

And as we praise God for the beauty of nature found in this island and throughout all Canada let us reread with eyes of faith the testimony borne by created things: in this way our minds and hearts turn to Him who on the seventh day saw what He had made and "it was very good" (Gn. 1:31).

THANKS TO THE TRINITY

3. Our thanksgiving rises from created things to God Himself.

We thank God for His existence: for the fact that He is God, for His Godhead, for His omnipotence and holiness, for His truth and love, for His eternal plan for the salvation of man and the world.

We thank the Father for the Son and the Holy Spirit. We thank the Son for the Father. We thank the Holy Spirit because through the love of the Father and the Son He is the uncreated Gift: the Source of all the gifts of created grace.

The Apostle Paul writes: "This is what I pray, kneeling before the Father, from whom every family whether spiritual or natural, takes its name: Out of his infinite glory may he give you the power through his Spirit for your hidden self to grow strong" (Eph. 3:14-16).

Man looks into his own heart, into "the hidden self," and he offers up thanksgiving to the very mystery of the Godhead. For he, man, has been created "in the image and likeness of God" (cf. Gn. 1:26), and he is now called for this reason to give particular thanksgiving. We give thanks to God for the fact that He is God in whom is found the eternal

Model of our human essence. We thank Him for the Godhead, for the inscrutable mystery of the Trinity, for the Father, the Son and the Holy Spirit.

THANKS FOR EVERYTHING

4. We give thanks for everything that is the work and fruit of grace, whereby human hearts share in the intimate life of God Himself.

For this is how Paul continues to write: "...so that Christ may live in your hearts through faith, and then, planted in love and built on love, you will with all the saints have strength to grasp the breadth and length, the height and depth; until, knowing the love of Christ, which is beyond all knowledge, you are filled with all the fullness of God" (Eph. 3:17-19).

We give thanks to God for the fact that He is God: for this absolute fullness that He is.

And we also give thanks for this dimension of our humanity, which is our sharing in God's nature, in the intimate life of God.

We give thanks for grace and holiness. In a particular way for the grace and holiness that in the course of the centuries has been shared in and continues to be shared in by the sons and daughters of this land:

"Bless the God of all things,
the doer of great deeds everywhere,
who has exalted our days from the womb
and acted toward us according to his mercy"
   (Sir. 50:22).

VOCATION IN JESUS CHRIST

5. Indeed, we give thanks for the fact that He, God, allows us, human beings, to share in the messianic mission of Jesus Christ, His eternal Son who became man. We thank Him for the fact that He has made us the People of God and has sealed our mission on earth with the priestly, prophetic and royal seal through our sharing in the mission of Christ Himself.

Christ says to us in today's Gospel: "You are the salt of the earth. But if salt becomes tasteless, what can make it salty again? ...You are the light of the world. A city built on a hilltop cannot be hidden. No one lights a lamp to put it under a tub; they put it on the lampstand where it shines for everyone in the house" (Mt. 5:13-15).

These are eloquent words, demanding words. And in the light of these words we give thanks for our Christian vocation.

We wish to understand this vocation in all its different forms, and to penetrate it with the light of faith and of our lifeblood. We want to fulfill it. We truly want to fulfill it!

How else can we express our thanks for the gift of our vocation in Jesus Christ?

FOR CHRISTIAN FAMILIES

6. We offer a very special act of thanksgiving at this time for our Christian families. In union with His Son, Jesus Christ our Lord, we thank the Father "from whom every family takes its name." We thank Him:

—For all those many families throughout Canada whose lives reflect "the beauty and grandeur of the vocation to love and the service of life" (*Familiaris consortio*, no. 1).

—For the deep love that Christian spouses communicate to each other in the communion of married life, as they keep alive in the world an altogether special image of God's love.

—For the lives of mutual fidelity lived by countless couples through the power of sacramental grace.

—For all those couples who generously endeavor to follow God's plan for human love as expressed in the Church's teaching in *Humanae vitae* and *Familiaris consortio*, and whose marriage is always open to new life; and for all those who help educate couples in Natural Family Planning.

—For the great and unique service given by parents in providing new members for the Mystical Body of Christ.

—For the day-in and day-out efforts made by fathers and mothers in educating their children to Christian maturity.

—For the families who amid pain, sorrow and economic distress live lives of Christian hope.

—For the commitment of families, in accordance with the teaching of the Second Vatican Council, to share actively in the mission of the Church, as a believing and evangelizing community and as a community in dialogue with God and in the service of man.

—For the efforts made by Christian families to help young people understand the dignity of marriage and to prepare themselves adequately for this vocation.

—For the renewed commitment of the Church to uphold and explain the sanctity and unity of the family, and for the generous love with which so many priests and religious expend their energies for the building up of family life.

—For the efforts of families who have experienced problems and difficulties, but who have persevered, being convinced that God's everlasting and unbreakable love is expressed in the indissoluble covenant of their own sacramental marriage.

—For the special witness given to Christ's teaching on the indissolubility of marriage by all spouses who suffer the pain of separation, abandonment or rejection.

—For the transmission of the Gospel message in Christian homes, and for the evangelization carried out by Christian families in their neighborhoods and places of work.

—For those many families that pray together and find strength in worshiping God.

—For the families that embrace the cross and, in Christian joy, live their share in the Paschal Mystery of the Lord Jesus.

—Yes, we give thanks and praise to God our Father for all the Christian families—and they are a mighty legion—who listen to those lifegiving words of Jesus Christ His Son: "Your light must shine in the sight of men, so that, seeing your good works, they may give praise to your Father in heaven'' (Mt. 5:16).

7. May all the Christian families of the world, and all of us, fulfill our Christian vocation, each one in accordance with the gift he has received. Each one of us, by the testimony of our good works. Each one of us caught up by the call to give glory to our Father who is in heaven, to give thanks to the Lord our God.

Thanksgiving is the manifestation of God's glory in everyone. Man, whom God has placed in the midst of the visible world—man whom God has made a sharer in the mystery of creation and in the mystery of the Redemption through grace—this man is called to glory. As he manifests—through thanksgiving— the glory of God that is in all things, man receives in himself the pledge of the future glory that will be revealed in him.

Beloved brothers and sisters of Newfoundland, Labrador and all Canada: Let us give thanks to the Lord our God!

It is right to give Him thanks and praise. Amen.

Vatican Translation

Christ Needs You
To Bring Salvation
to the World

On September 12, the Holy Father met the youth of Newfoundland, on the grounds of Memorial University of St. John's, and spoke to them as follows.

Dear young people, brothers and sisters in our Lord Jesus Christ,

1. I thank you for your warm welcome here today in Newfoundland. It is a great joy for me to join you as you celebrate your faith in Jesus Christ at this festival of youth. I thank God for you and for young people everywhere, for the special gifts of your youth, and for the part you play among us in building a more just, peaceful and loving world. In the words of St. Paul: "I thank my God whenever I think of you, and every time I pray for all of you, I pray with joy" (Phil. 1:3).

2. To live in this immense country, which has been blessed with peace and freedom, is cause for thanksgiving. You have freedom of speech, of wor-

ship and movement—and you have political options. And yet you are not without your problems. I know that many of you young people have no jobs and look to the future with deep anxiety. You are challenged by chronic and painful unemployment to keep alive a spirit of hope, to try to use creatively the enforced leisure which joblessness creates. Others among you are in school, where there is also uncertainty. You are sometimes tempted to give up and to ask: What is the use of all this effort? What is the meaning of human life? Where is it all leading?

These are questions that are being asked by young people all over the world. They are being asked by young men and women who, in many countries, do not have enough to eat and have no chance for a formal education. They are being asked by young people who live in the midst of injustice, violence and persecution. They are being asked by young people who are searching for peace, craving for justice and longing for God. They were asked this year by the young people who came to Rome to celebrate with me the Holy Year of the Redemption.

TO SEE LIFE
AS GOD'S PRECIOUS GIFT

3. As a pastor and as a brother, I wish to offer you today a powerful reason to hope and to see life as a great and precious gift of God. And this reason is Jesus Christ, the Son of God who came into the world to teach us the full meaning of human life. Through the power of His Spirit, the same Jesus who died on

the cross and rose from the dead is alive in His Church; He is alive in you who bear His name as Christians and who strive to listen to His words of life.

I am here to proclaim this presence of Jesus in your lives and the power of His love working in your hearts. Because of this presence and this power you can do great things. This is your life's call, a call of God to serve your community and your Church. Perhaps you will be called to serve as a husband or wife, a parent, a single person, a religious or a priest. But in every case it is a call to a personal conversion, a call to open your hearts to the message of Christ and to His power in your lives. Every economic, social or political structure in the world that needs reform can be adequately changed only when our hearts are purified, because the source of all injustice is the human heart.

Young people of Newfoundland and of all Canada, you are invited by Christ to a conversion of heart, to a life lived in union with Him. For this reason you must not let yourselves be overwhelmed by anxiety, by the painful sense of helplessness, or by the temptation to revolt or drop out. No one can deny that much of the world is in frightening disorder: the inhumanity of many persons and the injustice of certain systems cause unspeakable human misery; the possibility of nuclear confrontation creates anxiety and fear. But you are in a position to face all problems with a new attitude, a new heart, a new power: your faith in Jesus Christ who is alive in you. In the words of St. John: "This is the victory that overcomes the world, our faith" (1 Jn. 5:4).

NOT MEANT TO INHERIT
A BROKEN WORLD

4. In God's plan you were not meant to inherit a broken world. It is the responsibility of all of us to change the dangerous course of events on which human beings have embarked. You, the youth of this country, are called to play a special part in shaping and building a better world. Your efforts can succeed, bu. you must make them in union with the Christ who is powerful within you and who speaks to your hearts.

In union with the Lord begin your task by looking critically at yourselves and then at the society in which you live. To do this you have to know how to judge and with what set of rules. You need the right scale of values, a clear vision of the world, of human work, of human life, of love. How, you may ask, do you acquire all this?

Every day the media and the example of people around you present certain models of life. Very often these show selfishness winning over generosity. Today I invite you to look at another model of humanity—one which can fully satisfy your thirst for meaning. The person that I present over and over again to the youth of the world is the Jesus about whom we are speaking. Although He is the Son of God, He is also Mary's Son and He shares completely in our human nature. He experienced joy and suffering, hunger and pain; He knew the beauty of nature and the love of friendship. Forever He remains the true image of what it is to be human. He is Jesus of

Nazareth and we get to know Him in the pages of the Gospels. He was put to death for having cast His lot with the poor and exploited, for having come to serve and not to be served. But God His Father raised Him from the dead. Through His Holy Spirit He remains in our midst and within us: He is the source of strength in the daily struggle to uplift our world. This is our Christian faith: with His help, we can carry out the program He left us, so simple and yet so all-embracing: "Love one another as I have loved you" (Jn. 15:12).

NEVER DESPAIR

5. On every page of the Gospel, Jesus keeps telling us that we must never despair, that love triumphs over every obstacle, over every failure, over suffering and hatred, even over death itself. This love, dear young people, and the peace that it brings, will anchor you firmly amid the chaos of the world; it will also lead you into deeper involvement with that world. Jesus invites you to love and to serve.

Begin by doing something concrete in your own situation. Do not look too far afield. Begin now where you work or study, in your youth groups, in your family circle, in your parish. Never allow anyone among your acquaintances to be deprived of his or her rights, or put down by others because he or she is not of your social milieu, or your color, or does not speak your language or share your faith. Refuse to build barriers between yourselves and older people. Be present also in their situations, because there your voice is needed and you will contribute and learn.

Give your enthusiastic support to those local groups which are seeking to build a more human world, and then broaden your horizons and work with the joyful energy of youth for the cause of justice everywhere. Learn to deprive yourselves, in order to share with the hungry and with young people who have received less than you. In solidarity with your brothers and sisters of different nations and races and cultures, it is possible for you to change the world and to shape a better future for all—a future in which persons are more important than profits; in which the world's resources are justly shared, and in which peaceful negotiations replace threats of war.

NEED OF GOD'S HELP

6. But in order to do this you need God's help. And God's help comes to you through prayer. Your union with Christ will be the secret of your effectiveness, and it is strengthened by your prayer, your conversation with God, the lifting up of your heart to Him. But Jesus has also provided for your needs through the sacraments of the Church, particularly the Eucharist and the Sacrament of Penance. The conversion of your hearts is brought about by Christ's action and Christ reaches out to you in His sacraments, which will always be for you an expression and celebration of your faith and your life in Christ. Sin is a human reality and we all need to experience forgiveness, reconciliation and peace in a personal encounter with Christ. God's providence supplies this opportunity for us in Confession, and makes

available in the Eucharist an access to His love that responds to our deepest yearning for an interpersonal relationship.

Yes, to build a civilization based on love and truth and justice is surely a gigantic task. But you are equal to it! Why? Because of Christ, living in you, because of His sacraments, because of your union with Him through prayer. Take courage then, dear young people, for we are celebrating together our faith in Jesus Christ, the Son of God and Savior of the world. As we approach the end of this millennium, remember that Christ needs you, the youth of Newfoundland, of Canada and the world. He needs you with pure hearts and generous love to help Him in His mission of uplifting humanity and bringing His salvation to the world. This is Christ's mission and He shares it with you!

Vatican Translation

Exalting and Satisfying Challenges in the Instruction and Guidance of Youth

On Wednesday evening, September 12, in the basilica-cathedral in St. John's, Newfoundland, Pope John Paul II met with Catholic educators. After an entrance hymn and a prayer for educators, the Holy Father delivered the following address in English.

Dear brothers and sisters in Christ,

1. This evening in this basilica dedicated to Saint John the Baptist I feel very close to all of you. I feel that I belong very much to Newfoundland.

It is indeed a joy and privilege to join this gathering of educators, to speak to those who carry out one of the most important tasks of the Church and of society. The task of the teacher and the school is indeed a sacred trust conveyed to them by parents and families. As Catholic educators you have accepted a special responsibility given by parents. These parents and families have invested in you their precious confidence. On her part the Church looks upon you as co-workers, with an important measure of shared responsibility, in helping to fulfill Christ's mandate transmitted through the Apostles: "Go therefore and make disciples of all nations...teaching them to observe all that I have commanded you" (Mt. 28:20).

To you it is given to create the future and give it direction by offering to your students a set of values with which to assess their newly-discovered knowledge. Few challenges are more exalting and rewarding than the instruction and guidance of young people, and few more difficult. You are preparing for adulthood and Christian maturity a generation of Newfoundlanders, of Canadians, who will build the Church and the society of tomorrow.

COPING WITH CHANGES

2. As you pursue your professional and spiritual goals as teachers, or as educational administrators, you experience the ambiguities and conflicts which characterize our contemporary society. In the span of a single lifetime, we have seen enormous changes in social values, in economic circumstances, and in technological innovation. As educators you must cope with these changes since they are the daily experience and fare of your students.

At the same time as a teacher and a school system seek to adapt continually to the new, they must affirm and preserve the meaning and importance of perennial truths and values. Educators must be ready to grasp firmly the challenge of providing a kind of education whose curriculum will be inspired more by reflection than by technique, more by the search for wisdom than the accumulation of information.

In the same way, the radically different cultural expressions and activities of our time, especially those which catch the popular attention of young people, demand that educators be open to new cultural influences and be capable of interpreting them for young people in the light of the Christian faith and of Christ's universal command of love.

It has always been difficult to be a Christian, and even more difficult to be a truly Christian teacher, especially if that teacher is called to bear witness from within a secular system. Every age presents a new set of problems as well as fresh opportunities to witness to the redemptive love of Jesus Christ.

You are called to bring professional competence and a high standard of excellence to your teaching. To influence your students at this juncture of history to grow in faith and in love, you must be aware of the pressures upon them and at once respect the natural stages of their growth toward maturity. But your responsibilities make demands upon you which go far beyond the need for professional skills and competence.

WHAT IT MEANS TO TEACH

3. An extremely important aspect of your role is that you are called to lead the young to Christ, to inspire them to follow Him, to show them His boundless love and concern for them, through the example of your own life. Through you, as through a clear window on a sunny day, students must come to

see and know the richness and the joy of a life lived in accordance with His teaching, in response to His challenging demands. To teach means not only to impart what we know, but also to reveal who we are by living what we believe. It is this latter lesson which tends to last the longest. *En masse*, the students of the world are today repeating to their Catholic teachers those words recorded in the Gospel of St. John and originally addressed to the Apostle Philip: "We wish to see Jesus" (Jn. 12:21). This is indeed a vital task of the Catholic teacher: to show Jesus to the young. St. Paul looked upon his own ministry as a prolonged travail in forming Christ in those whom he was called to serve (cf. Gal. 4:19).

4. As teachers and educators, you also share in the proclamation of the word in the service of truth. You seek to liberate the mind and spirit of those whom you teach, guiding them to maturity in faith, knowledge and understanding. By offering your students the truth of Christ you are likewise helping them to experience His freedom. You are thus engaged in the authentic liberation of this generation of students, to whom Jesus Christ, who calls Himself the "Truth," repeats His Gospel promise: "If the Son makes you free, you will be free indeed" (Jn. 8:36). You are called to serve and spread Christ's liberating truth.

YOUTH IS SEEKING

5. Young people today are buffeted in every direction by loud and competing claims upon their attention and allegiance. From around the world, they hear daily messages of conflict and hostility, of

greed and injustice, of poverty and despair. Amid this social turmoil, young people are eager to find solid and enduring values which can give meaning and purpose to their lives. They are searching for a firm place—a high ground—on which to stand. They seek a sense of direction, a goal which will give meaning and purpose to their lives.

The Gospel tells us where the high ground is to be found. It is beside our Lord, sharing in His strength and love, responding eagerly and generously to His challenge to love and serve Him, as He has loved and served us. Who can show young people the way to that secure place, to that dynamic and fulfilling life, better than the teachers to whom they look for guidance? No one else will ever be where you are. No one else will ever have the opportunity you have to accompany students in the search for truth, to foster in them a thirst for justice, and an appreciation of the goodness of God, to lead them patiently and lovingly in their journey of faith.

6. Young people are hungry today for truth and justice because they are hungry for God. To respond to that hunger is the highest calling of the Christian educator. In partnership with the parents, who bear the primary responsibility for the education of their children, the teacher is called upon to reflect, in faithful and discerning fashion, God's presence in the world.

Teachers and parents must strive for a mature spirituality in their own lives, a strength and relevance of faith which can withstand the assault of conflicting values upon the home and the school. If the teaching of the Gospel is visible in your daily lives, it will have visible influence upon the young whom you teach. When young people see their teachers and parents, whom they love, as people committed to Jesus Christ, people whose lives are inspired by that commitment, the meaning and the message of Faith is spontaneously communicated to them and the Good News is announced once again in and to the world.

CHRISTIAN EDUCATION

7. The specific goals of Christian education as described by the Second Vatican Council take into account the many needs of the young. These goals are a constant challenge to you and spell out your lofty work: "Christian education...aims above all at ensuring that the baptized...may grow evermore conscious of the gift of Faith which they have received; that they may learn to adore God the Father in spirit and in truth (cf. Jn. 4:23), especially through liturgical worship; and that they may be prepared to live their personal lives according to a new nature in justice and holiness of truth (Eph. 4:22-24), so that they may reach perfect maturity, the measure of the fullness of Christ (Eph. 4:13) and make their contribution to the increase of the Mystical Body" (*Gravissimum educationis*, no. 2).

PRECIOUS HERITAGE

8. Here in the province of Newfoundland and in other provinces throughout Canada, your forebears struggled over the years to have a Catholic educational system where these ideals for Catholic teachers

and principles of Catholic education might best be applied. It is a precious heritage which has been confided to you, a heritage which makes a positive and valued contribution not only to the Church but to society as well.

Catholic schools can provide young people with insights and spiritual incentives badly needed in a materialistic and fragmented world. Catholic schools speak of the meaning of life, of values and of faith that make for a meaningful life. Similarly, since individualism is often alienating, Catholic schools must hand on and reinforce a sense of community, of social concern and the acceptance of difference and diversity in pluralistic societies. While professing an institutional commitment to the word of God as proclaimed by the Catholic Church, they must inculcate an attitude of profound respect for the conscience of others and a deep desire for Christian unity.

While striving for excellence in the areas of professional and technical training, Catholic schools must never forget that their ultimate purpose is to prepare young people to take up, in Christian freedom, their personal and social responsibility for the pilgrimage of all humanity to eternal life.

For these same reasons Catholic schools, while always committed to intellectual development, will also heed the Gospel imperative of serving all students and not only those who are the brightest and most promising. Indeed, in accord with the spirit of the Gospel, and its option for the poor, they will turn their attention particularly to those most in need.

RIGHT TO EDUCATION

9. All men and women—and all children—have a right to education. Closely linked to this right to education is the right of parents, of families, to choose according to their convictions the kind of education and the model of school which they wish for their children *(Universal Declaration of Human Rights,* Art. 26). Related as well is the no less sacred right of religious freedom.

In a society such as Canada's, people's freedom to associate and enter into certain group or institutional endeavors with the aim of fulfilling their expectations according to their own values is a fundamental democratic right. This right implies that parents have a real possibility to choose, without undue financial burden placed upon them, appropriate schools and educational systems for their children. Here in Newfoundland I note that you view education as a partnership between the Church and the province. Fortunately, in other parts of Canada similar cooperation between Church and government exists. I realize that this varies from province to province.

Society is called to provide for and support with public funding those types of schools that correspond to the deepest aspirations of its citizens. The role of the modern state is to respond to these expectations within the limits of the common good. A state thereby promotes harmony, and, in a pluralistic situation such as Canada, this effectively fosters respect for the wide diversity of this land. To ignore this diversity and the legitimate claims of the people within various groups would be to deny a fundamental right to parents.

Governments have the responsibility, therefore, to ensure the freedom of ecclesial communions to have appropriate educational services with all that such a freedom implies: teacher training, buildings, research funding, adequate financing and so forth.

In a pluralistic society it is surely a challenge to provide all citizens with satisfactory educational services. In dealing with this complex challenge one must not ignore the centrality of God in the believer's outlook on life. A totally secular school system would not be a way of meeting this challenge. We cannot leave God at the schoolhouse door.

PRIVILEGED PLACE

10. Dear teachers and parents, the Catholic school is in your hands. It is a reflection of your convictions. Its very existence depends on you. It is one of those privileged places, together with the family and the parish community, where our faith is handed on. The Catholic school is a community effort, one that cannot succeed without the cooperation of all concerned—the students, the parents, the teachers, the principals and pastors. As parents, you claim a special responsibility and privilege. You are the first witnesses and artisans of the awakening in your children of the sense of God. You bear the first responsibility of bringing them to the sacraments of Christian initiation. In this work you are assisted and helped by the school and the parish.

Our world searches for a new sense of meaning and coherence. A Catholic school through the ministry of Catholic teachers is a privileged place for the development and communication of a world-view rooted in the meaning of creation and Redemption. You are called, dear educators and parents, to create those schools which will transmit the values which you would hand on to those who will come after you. And always remember that it is Christ who says: Go and teach!

Vatican Translation

Our Lady Has Ensured that the Well-rooted Faith of the Acadian People Can Weather All Storms

In the morning and early afternoon of Thursday, September 13, Pope John Paul II visited Moncton, New Brunswick. His first stop was at the cathedral dedicated to Our Lady of the Assumption, the patroness of the Acadian people, where he presided at a Marian celebration. During the course of the prayer meeting, the Holy Father delivered the following address, partly in French and partly in English.

Dear brothers and sisters,

1. Praised be Jesus Christ! I give thanks to God for allowing me to come and visit this province of New Brunswick which is celebrating this year its second centenary. With joy I greet the Church of God in Moncton, the metropolitan See, and its Archbishop, the Most Reverend Donat Chiasson. I also greet St. John, the oldest diocese, established in 1842, with the Most Reverend Arthur Gilbert; the diocese of Bathurst with the Most Reverend Edgar Godin;

and that of Edmundston with the Most Reverend
Gérard Dionne. I greet those who have come from
other provinces of Canada and even from the United
States because they are neighbors or because their
ancestors came from Acadia.

The Lord is in the midst of us who are gathered
in His name. We who have put our faith in the risen
Christ have been given the task to reflect as a mirror
the glory of the Lord and to be transformed by the
Holy Spirit (cf. 2 Cor. 3:18). It is as if we were seeing
Jesus *"ut videntes Jesum,"* according to the beautiful
motto of this diocese. And it is Mary, who, through
the Holy Spirit, has given us the Savior Jesus. It is she
who leads us to Him.

2. This cathedral reminds us of the role of Mary
in the Church. The Acadians have always had a great
devotion for Mary, their mother in heaven.

In 1881, at their first national congress, they
chose her as their patron saint under the title of Our
Lady of the Assumption, and they adopted
August 15 as their national feast day. They even
founded the Society of the Assumption. And so the
star of Mary shines bright on their flag with its French
and papal colors, and the "Ave Maris Stella" rings
out like a national anthem. The first Acadian parish
here, in Moncton, was dedicated to Our Lady of the
Assumption and it is on the site of its chapel that the
first Archbishop of Moncton, Most Reverend Arthur
Mélanson, had this cathedral built and inaugurated
in 1940.

Dear brothers and sisters, how your century-old
devotion to Mary fills me with joy! I am sure that you
fully intend to be faithful to it, to intensify it, along

the lines which Vatican II suggested at the end of the Constitution on the Church. Our Lady of the Assumption is truly "the sign of assured hope and consolation for the People of God in pilgrimage on earth" (*Lumen gentium,* no. 68). And I think that she has already allowed this deeply-rooted faith of the Acadian people to weather all storms.

3. The Church which welcomes the Pope here today is the magnificent outcome of a laborious beginning of a tormented history, in which we admire your ancestors' tenacity.

It was here, in 1604, that the first French colony in America was founded. In this region of Acadia, thanks to the zeal of many groups of missionaries, the Catholic Faith took deep root among the population and among all the Amerindians of the maritime provinces, who have shown since then a marvelous fidelity. Yes, despite the trials of deportation and even the threat of annihilation because of political vicissitudes, the Acadians remained faithful to their Faith, faithful to their culture, faithful to their land to which they continuously strove to return, in the greatest poverty deprived of the ministry of their priests, of the means of education and of political rights. For a time, lay people saw to prayer meetings and sustained the Faith, until a few priests and religious could come to exercise their apostolate among them. Since then, during the past hundred years, the Acadian people have been able to lift up their heads again and the Catholic Faith has flourished. I am thinking, among other things, of the many profoundly Christian families, of the numerous vocations to the priesthood and to the religious life.

How could one forget that a place not far from here, Memramcook, was the cradle of the Congregation founded by Blessed Sister Marie Léonie? Cultural growth took place too as the French-speaking university and the means of social communication bear witness.

At the beginning of this century, the Acadians came to Rome in the person of Father François-Michel Richard to see my Predecessor, Pope Pius X, to bear witness to their heroic history and to explain their need for an Acadian Bishop. The saintly Pope, so devoted to the mystery of the Eucharist, gave them a gold chalice as a pledge of his concern and of his promise. Today, it is the Bishop of Rome who comes to you. He gives thanks for the fidelity and strength of your faith through trials that remind him of those of his own country in the course of the centuries, and of those which are known today by our brothers and sisters around the world who are persecuted for their faith, harassed for their cultural and national attachments in which their faith is deeply rooted. It is not without emotion that I will celebrate Mass with the chalice given by St. Pius X. All this suffering will be united in it with the blood of Christ in the hope that it will be transfigured into the glorious life of the Lord.

4. But the Church here does not limit herself to the people of Acadian origin. She embraces all those who, united to the Successor of Peter, share the same Catholic Faith; and she invites them to live as brothers and sisters, respectful of their different spiritual and cultural riches, and joined together in the same mission of evangelizing this contemporary world. Other waves of immigrants, in fact, particu-

larly from Ireland, came to join them during about the last century and a half. The vitality of the Church in New Brunswick owes them much, and I greet with affection these English-speaking families.

I likewise greet all our brothers and sisters of this region who originally came from other countries, from other cultures and from other Christian confessions. They too place their faith in Jesus Christ the Savior; they participate in one and the same Baptism; and they are called to the same charity, without yet being able to share the same Eucharist because full unity in the faith has not yet been reached. As I said in Switzerland, in another context, to our Protestant brothers and sisters: "The purification of the memory is an important element of ecumenical progress." It is necessary for us "to entrust the past without reticence to the mercy of God and, in all liberty, to strain forward to the future in order to make it more conformed to His will." God wills that His own people should have a single heart and soul and welcome the salvation of which He always gives us the grace (cf. Discourse at Kehrsatz, June 14, 1984, no. 2).

May the Holy Spirit guide us on this arduous but necessary road of ecumenical efforts in order that we may constantly go towards full unity! God wants us to be faithful to the authenticity of our Faith, to our culture, to our history, to our land, with respect for others and, also, in fraternal love, in real solidarity in the face of the present human needs, and in the sincere search for His truth.

5. Dear brothers and sisters: we shall meet again this afternoon for the Eucharistic celebration, on a site

of natural beauty which is part of the charm of this area. But let us look again at this beautiful cathedral of granite. It is the house of God, built with care by your forefathers as a sign of the divine presence, visible from afar, and in witness of their own gratitude to Mary. It is the eminently fitting place for the Eucharistic assembly, around the bishop; and in the person of the bishop assisted by his priests, it is the Lord Jesus Christ, the Supreme Pontiff, who is present in the midst of the faithful (cf. *Lumen gentium*, no. 21). This cathedral is also the place for the personal reconciliation of sinners with God. It is permanently the house of prayer, community prayer and also the silent prayer of adoration.

It is, at the same time, the symbol of the Church which is in Moncton, built of living stones, of you yourselves who are its members. Each of you has your place here, your specific role according to ordination, vocation or charism. You, the bishops, priests and deacons, who are ordained to represent Christ the Head in the service of the community. You, the religious, brothers and sisters, who are consecrated to give to the world an appreciation of the kingdom of God, present and to come, in its radical evangelical character. And all of you, the baptized and confirmed laity. You, the Christian families, the incarnation of love; you, fathers and mothers in charge of your families. You, the members of movements of spirituality. And so many of you here who represent the youth. You who are engaged in the service of the liturgy, of catechetics, of charity, of the sick, of the aged, or of those on the margin of society. You, the educators, and those of you in charge of culture and the media. You, the laity of Catholic action movements or of professional associations of fishermen, farmers or workers.

The one universal Church is necessarily present in this particular Church. And I myself—whom Christ has asked, as He asked Peter, to be the shepherd of the "sheep" and of the "lambs," and to confirm my brethren in the faith—come to strengthen each one of you in your mission. We shall meditate this afternoon on the ecclesial community.

The only foundation of our Church is Jesus Christ. The mortar that binds its stones is the love that comes from His Holy Spirit. The sign it must give to all passers-by is a witness of the theological virtues, virtues which derive from God and which consist in believing unconditionally in Christ, in hoping in the very depth of our trials, in loving without limits. We are a pilgrim people, making our way towards a fullness that surpasses our earthly horizons. And Mary is our star in this turbulent sea.

Ave Maris Stella! (Hail, Star of the Sea!)

From the English edition of L'Osservatore Romano

The Crisis of Values Demands Authentic Witnesses

On September 13, in the afternoon, the Holy Father celebrated Mass at Front Mountain Road, Moncton, and preached the following homily.

"If our life in Christ means anything to you, if love can persuade at all, or the spirit that we have in common, or any tenderness and sympathy, then be united in your convictions and united in your love.... That is one thing which would make me completely happy. There must be no competition among you... so that nobody thinks of his own interests first but everybody thinks of other people's interests instead. In your minds you must be the same as Christ Jesus" (Phil. 2:1-5).

These words, originally addressed by St. Paul to the Christians of Philippi, are also addressed to you, dear brothers and sisters of Moncton, of Acadia and of the entire Province of New Brunswick. I encourage you to form human communities that will be examples in their practice of solidarity. I urge you to maintain in your Church communities the dignity vested in them by Christ. Draw your inspiration in this from the Gospel; look for what is just in the eyes of God. Have the courage of faith, the dynamism of charity and the strength of Christian hope, whatever be your trials. Yes, open your communities to the spirit of Christ.

ST. JOHN CHRYSOSTOM

1. To deepen this appeal I commend to you the example and the words of the holy bishop whom we are celebrating today, one of the most famous bishops of the first centuries of the Christian East. The text of the psalm admirably expresses his soul:

"My God, I have always loved your law from the depths of my being. I have always proclaimed your righteousness in the great assembly; nor do I mean to stop proclaiming, as you know well" (Ps. 39[40]:9-10).

This great pastor spoke again and again in order to enlighten his people, to educate them, to incite them to follow their Christian vocation. They called him "Chrysostom," which means "golden mouth." His teaching, steeped in the Word of God and the contemplation of Christ's mystery, was expressed in clear, convincing, concrete terms, challenging Christians of all centuries to make those choices essential to their salvation and to the bringing about of "justice."

POWER OF HIS FAITH

2. At the end of the fourth century, at a time when the Church was in full growth, John lived in

Antioch of Syria. He would undoubtedly have been successful in the world of the courts, of the theater, of literature, but following his Baptism, around the age of twenty, he preferred to devote himself to the study of Sacred Scripture and to the service of the Church. He experienced a life of contemplation and asceticism in remote mountain wildernesses. Then, for eleven years, as deacon and then priest, he tirelessly preached the Gospel to the crowds in Antioch. He was called in 397 to become the Patriarch of Constantinople but was able to exercise his epis-copal responsibilities freely for only six years. The milieu was a believing one and sensitive to piety, but it was also given over to passion, to courtly intrigue, to worldly manifestations, to the pursuit of luxury and to the neglect of priestly and monastic duties. But he refused to reduce in any way the vigor and clarity of the Gospel, the requirements of Christian Baptism and of the Eucharist, of the priesthood, of charity, of the dignity of the poor. In truth, "he never ceased to proclaim justice." Nor did he do so when twice he was deposed and driven into exile by the Empress Eudoxia. She made his lot even more difficult on the second occasion on the road to the Caucasus, on which he died on September 14, 407. We can indeed consider him a martyr of pastoral courage. But what we will remember above all is that he succeeded in forming a Christian people, Christian communities worthy of the name.

ALWAYS LOYAL TO CHRIST

3. His "golden mouth" drew its eloquence from the power of his faith. He could repeat after St. Paul:

"I believed and therefore I spoke" (2 Cor. 4:13). And his faith, filled with love, called forth his apostolic zeal: "You see, all this is for your benefit, so that the more grace is multiplied among people, the more thanksgiving there will be to the glory of God" (2 Cor. 4:15).

In fact, his pastoral zeal was based on union with Christ. This relationship was particularly close when the great Bishop of Constantinople was exposed to suffering and persecution. He too could say following St. Paul: "We carry with us in our body the death of Jesus, so that the life of Jesus, too, may always be seen in our body" (2 Cor. 4:10). This union to Christ's suffering and dying on the cross made his apostolic service efficacious and a source of supernatural life for others: "So death is at work in us, but life in you" (2 Cor. 4:12).

4. John Chrysostom had no fear of unjust judgments, of harassment, of defamation, of persecution. These merely made him more firm in his proclamation of the requirements of the Gospel, both because of his loyalty to Christ and because of his love for those he wished to convert. Yet, unshakable as his strength was, it never caused him to go against charity. He truly lived the words of Christ recorded in the Gospel of Luke and which we have just heard: "Love your enemies, do good to those who hate you, bless those who curse you, pray for those who treat you badly" (Lk. 6:27-28). His eloquence made him popular with the crowds in Antioch, in Constantinople, even in exile in Asia Minor; his frankness, however, drew down upon him the hatred of some. He had devoted his gift of speech entirely to the

service of justice and charity, for which he paid dearly, in heart and body. Yet he did not allow this to turn him away from loving others and from seeking to do them good. He gave them no thought of return. "Do good and lend without hoping for anything in return.... Give and it will be given to you" (Lk. 6:35-38). Rather than see his followers spill the blood of his fellow citizens, he chose to surrender himself to the soldiers.

This is the pastor, dear brothers and sisters, who formed a generation of Christians in a large part of the East, through his preaching and by the example of his life. This is the witness that is presented to you today as you seek to strengthen your Church communities.

CHRISTIAN COMMUNITY

5. Vatican II spoke of the "Christian community" as a sign of the presence of God in the world. "By the Eucharistic sacrifice it is on the way to the Father with Christ; carefully nourished by the Word of God, it bears witness to Christ; it walks in love and glows with an apostolic spirit" (Decree on the Missionary Activity of the Church, no. 15). May your parishes and your various communities carry out this program! But that it may be done according to the Gospel, it might be well to listen once again to John Chrysostom expressing his faith: "Am I relying on my own strength? I possess His word; that is my support, my security and my harbor of peace" (cf. homily delivered before his departure into exile, 1-3; PG 52, 427-430). Steep yourself in this word. He added, "You must continually find your strength in

the Scriptures." He also asks us to pray unceasingly, everywhere, in that temple of God which is the human heart.

John Chrysostom took great care in preparing candidates for Baptism and above all in helping the baptized to understand the greatness of the gift given them by God in the sacrament. He speaks in enthusiastic terms of the Eucharist by which we share in the victory of Easter. But he never forgets that "the first road to conversion is the condemnation of our faults. Begin by confessing your faults in order to be justified" (cf. PG 49, 263-264).

MEANING OF LOVE

6. This insistence of John Chrysostom on the gift of grace, on faith, prayer and the sacraments, invariably issues in a statement of the requirements for Christian living; if not, we would be faced with a lack of logic or with hypocrisy. And it is in this connection that he speaks with surprising vigor of charity, of the love of neighbor.

This love is reconciliation: "Let no one who has an enemy come to the holy table.... Go first and be reconciled, then receive the sacrament" (cf. homily to the people of Antioch).

This love is will for unity and for fraternity. "The Church does not exist so that we will remain divided when we come to it, but rather so that our divisions will be overcome there—that is the meaning of the assembly. If we come for the Eucharist, let us do nothing that contradicts the Eucharist" (cf. homily Cor. 24:2; 27:3-5).

This love is respect and welcome for the poor. "You wish to honor the body of Christ? Do not hold it in contempt when it is naked. Do not honor it here, in the Church, by wearing silken robes while you allow it to remain outside suffering from the cold and lack of clothes.... God needs no chalices of gold, but golden souls.... Begin by feeding the hungry, and with what is left, you may decorate the altar" (cf. PG 619-622).

Love is a search for what is useful for our neighbor. "Nothing is colder than a Christian indifferent to the salvation of others" (cf. PG 60, 162-164). "We neglect the salvation of our children. We are looking for nothing but profit. We are more concerned with asses and horses than with our children.... What is comparable to the art of shaping a soul?" (PG 58, 580-584)

Love involves apostolic work; it is missionary zeal that extends to the ends of the earth. "God does not ask us to succeed, but to work.... If Christ, that model of pastors, worked until the very end to convert a man in despair (Judas), what must we not do for those for whom we have been commanded to hope?" (cf. homily on the Canaanite woman, 10-11) "As the leaven is absorbed into the mass, it loses none of its strength; on the contrary, it communicates it little by little.... It is Christ alone who invests the leaven with its power...and when the dough has risen it becomes leaven in its turn, for all that remains" (cf. homily on Mt. 2-3).

These few strong words from St. John Chrysostom are evidence of the faith, charity, apostolic courage and hope which he sought to share with his brothers and sisters.

7. Dear brothers and sisters of New Brunswick: is it still necessary for the progress of your communities for these exhortations to be articulated in terms of challenges adapted to our times?

I know that your community spirit already allowed you to overcome many early difficulties in Acadia: still today you are known for your sense of fraternity, cordial hospitality and sharing. But your region, like many others, is undergoing a profound transformation which is a new test. Urban life is developing, an economic crisis affects the local communities, and likewise a spiritual crisis, a crisis of values. Meanwhile, you can look to the future with serenity if you stand firm in the faith of the risen Christ, if you allow His Spirit to form within you the responses to the new challenges, if you show solidarity with one another, if you accept being a leaven in the Church and in society.

And your Christian communities will immediately take up the challenge if they are able to form and deepen the faith of their members through the catechesis of youth and of students, through the continuing formation of adults, through courses or retreats. It is a question of a faith that is a personal attachment to the living God and takes account of the whole creed. Do not allow religious ignorance to stand side by side with the prestige of secular knowledge! Your communities will progress and be renewed if you accord greater place to meditation on the Gospel, to prayer, to the Sacraments of the Eucharist and of Penance.

Efforts in sharing, justice and charity—which one can call "social love"—run the risk of becoming simple philanthropy, if they are not rooted in the spiritual energy to which I have made reference in the writings of St. John Chrysostom. And yet, he was speaking to a group of believers who had forgotten the ethical consequences of the Faith. Today it is necessary in the first place to revive the Faith which, for a certain number, has been shaken and questioned.

COMMITMENTS OF CHARITY

8. But it is evident that a well-understood faith involves all the commitments of charity of which the pastor of Constantinople spoke and which today might be called:

—respect for persons, of their freedom, of their dignity, so that they may not be crushed by the new social constraints;

—respect for human rights, according to the charters already well known, and including the right to life from the moment of conception, the right to one's reputation, the right to development, the right to freedom of conscience;

—the refusal of violence and torture;

—concern for the less fortunate categories, for women, for laborers, for the unemployed, for immigrants;

—establishment of social measures for greater equality and justice, for all men and women, regardless of individual interests or privileges;

—the will to live a simple life and to share, in contrast with the present race for profit, consumption and artificial gratification, in such a way as not to be deprived of what is essential for oneself, while also permitting the poor, whoever they may be, to lead a dignified life;

—a more universal openness towards the basic needs of the less fortunate countries, in particular those that are referred to as the "South," the regions where each day thousands of human beings die because of the lack of peace or elementary care given to them; and hence concern to inaugurate, at the international level, effective solutions for a more equitable distribution of goods and opportunities on the earth;

—missionary zeal for help among the Churches.

Thus your communities will be able to provide a generous sharing that begins in the immediate neighborhood and that then opens up, without boundaries, to the world. You will not wait to settle your own social problems—that are certainly most real, and I am thinking in particular of unemployment—before living that fullness of charity described by St. John Chrysostom.

All this activity of solidarity you will accomplish individually, or by your Christian associations, and also taking part in the initiative of the institutions of civil society (cf. *Gaudium et spes*, nos. 42-43). And with the Christian motivation which sees in the other person a brother or sister in God and a member of Christ, you will be the leaven that raises the dough to a level of greater justice, fraternal solidarity and social love.

9. Your ecclesial communities will be so much more stable and dynamic if everyone plays his or her

own role, according to his or her vocation and charisms, as I said this morning in the cathedral: bishops, priests, religious, laity.

It is necessary without doubt that there be formed what you call the *groupes-relais* in order to manifest better the vitality of the Church in allowing specialized activities and truly human action. But all must be vigilant for unity within the common mission of evangelization, and here the parish plays a unique role. For all groups the parish's vocation "is to be a fraternal and welcoming family home, where those who have been baptized and confirmed become aware of forming the people of God.... From that home they are sent out day by day to their apostolic mission in all the centers of activity of the life of the world" (cf. *Catechesi tradendae,* no. 67).

A PILGRIM PEOPLE

10. Dear brothers and sisters: we are a people on a journey. We toil here below with courage and strong love to construct a new world more open to God and more fraternal, one that offers some sketch of the world to come (cf. *Gaudium et spes,* no. 39). Let us take care not to forget the fullness to which God calls us!

St. John Chrysostom, a disciple of the Lord, a successor of the Apostles, was strengthened during the whole course of his toilsome and difficult life by an eschatological hope—the hope of what lies beyond, of the new life promised by God—which St. Paul announced in his letter to the Corinthians: "Yes, the troubles which are soon over, though they weigh little, train us for the carrying of a weight of eternal glory which is out of all proportion to them.

And so we have no eyes for things that are visible, but only for things that are invisible; for visible things last only for a time, and the invisible things are eternal" (2 Cor. 4:17-18).

Let the voice of St. Paul, let the voice of the great saint of Constantinople continue to echo in your hearts, together with the voice of your own pastors united with the Successor of Peter!

Through the intercession of Our Lady of the Assumption, Our Lady of Acadia, may the Church of Moncton and of the other dioceses grow, be strengthened and shine forth, in conformity with its eternal destiny. "Our regard is focused on the invisible, on what is eternal!"

Amen!

From the English edition of L'Osservatore Romano

To the World in 1984 and Beyond We Must Bring the Gifts of Communion and Love

On Thursday afternoon, September 13, the Holy Father arrived in Halifax, the capital of the province of Nova Scotia. The pastoral visit began with a meeting with the youth of the city and the province in the Central Commons. At the heart of the meeting was the recitation of the Angelus, before which the Holy Father offered the young people the following reflections in English.

Dear young people,

1. I greet you in the peace of Christ! It is a great joy to be with you this evening at Central Commons in Halifax. As you know I am always happy to meet with young people, whether in Rome or during my travels throughout the world. It is a pleasure to be with you because I see in your faces an openness to learn and an eagerness to serve. I know of the great desire you have for peace and unity throughout the world. I am well aware, too, that the future belongs to you, that the decisions you make will shape the Church and the world of tomorrow.

2. As we gather this evening to pray the Angelus, there is a common spirit of faith and joy which unites us. It is only right that we should feel this way since we are gathered as friends, as brothers and sisters in Christ. We know, too, that the Church is a communion of persons—men, women and children of different ages and races, different backgrounds and cultures, people who, while so diverse, are all made one by the love of Christ and the gift of the Holy Spirit.

This communion of persons which is the Church is really a mystery, in that it is more wonderful than we could imagine, greater than our minds could ever comprehend. As members of the one Body of Christ, we share in the very life of the Most Holy Trinity, united with one another as children of a loving Father, as brothers and sisters in Jesus Christ, coheirs of the kingdom of heaven.

3. What we have received as a gift, however, we must give as a gift (cf. Mt. 10:8). The great gift of communion with God must be shared with others. Our modern world is torn apart by prejudice and violence, while our families are threatened by divorce, pornography, alcohol and drug abuse and many other evils. To the world in 1984 and beyond, to our families and to our cities, we must bring the gifts of communion and love. We must forge the bonds of justice and peace. You who are young and full of enthusiasm have a special part to play in the mission of the Church.

Try, then, to create a communion of Christian love at home and in your schools, in your parishes and neighborhoods, among your friends and with people of all ages. Recall the words of St. Paul: "Lead a life worthy of your vocation. Bear with one another charitably, in complete selflessness, gentleness and patience. Do all you can to preserve the unity of the Spirit by the peace that binds you together" (Eph. 4:1-3).

Dear young people of Halifax: The Lord Jesus is counting on you!

4. Each evening, in countries throughout the world, church bells ring out, inviting people to recite the Angelus. As we turn in prayer to the Mother of God this evening, we recall how she, already as a young woman, was closely united to the mystery of Christ, fully devoted to His work of salvation. From her example of faith and prayer, we learn how to meet God in the deep recesses of our hearts; we learn how to listen to God's word that it may bear fruit in our lives.

Let us, then, turn to Mary with great confidence and hope, bringing to her our petition for a communion of love and harmony in our homes and for peace and unity in the world. Mary, Mother of God and Queen of Peace, pray for us.

Vatican Translation

Consistency Between Conduct and Faith

On September 13, the Holy Father went to St. Mary's Cathedral in Halifax to meet with priests, religious and lay people involved in the apostolate. The meeting took the form of a Celebration of the Word with a reading taken from the Gospel of St. Luke. After the singing of the Magnificat, Pope John Paul II delivered the following homily.

Dear brothers and sisters in Christ,

1. The visitation of Mary to her cousin Elizabeth is a very beautiful episode in the Gospel of St. Luke. It is the dramatic encounter of two expectant mothers, two women whose hearts are filled with joy in anticipation of the "human miracle" which is unfolding within their bodies. The account also has an important theological message: it shows how John the Baptist, the greatest of the Old Testament prophets, bore witness to Jesus already from within his mother's womb. It likewise focuses attention on Mary's faith: "Blessed is she who believed that the promise made her by the Lord would be fulfilled" (Lk. 1:45).

Together with these reflections we are brought to realize yet another meaning that this Gospel has for us. We are drawn to appreciate the touching human gesture of Mary as she reaches out in love to her cousin Elizabeth. She provides us with a model of service to others, an example of how we, as her spiritual sons and daughters, should open our hearts in compassion to those who yearn for Christ to come to them through us.

For the idea of service, dear brothers and sisters, is essential to the lay apostolate and to all ministry. Service is at the very core of every vocation in the Church: the service of God and our neighbor which is at once zealous and humble, always motivated by a desire to fulfill God's will as it is manifested through the guiding action of the Holy Spirit at work in the Church.

HALIFAX BASILICA

2. I wish to tell you how happy I am to be with you this evening. You have come from the farms, villages, towns and cities of Nova Scotia and Prince Edward Island. By the grace of God each of you has been called to bear witness to Christ in a particular way. You have heard this call and have responded generously to it. I thank you for your active commitment to the Church, and I greet you in the name of our Lord Jesus Christ and in the name of Mary His Mother in this Halifax Basilica dedicated to her.

ACTIVE PARTICIPATION

3. We read in the Gospel: "God loved the world so much that he gave his only Son so that everyone who believes in him may not be lost but may have

eternal life" (Jn. 3:16). Jesus Christ, the Son of God, took on human flesh not "to be served but to serve and to give his life as a ransom for many" (Mk. 10:45). After His Resurrection Christ appeared to His disciples, breathing His Spirit into them and sending them to continue His own mission: "As the Father sent me, so am I sending you" (Jn. 20:21).

Thus we understand that the Church was founded on the Apostles to continue Christ's mission, which is to lead all humanity through faith to eternal life. Every activity undertaken by the Church for this purpose forms part of her apostolate, and this apostolate is her response to the mission entrusted to her by Christ.

4. Through Baptism and Confirmation everyone is called to share in the saving mission of the Church. As a member of the living organism which is the Mystical Body of Christ, no Christian can play a purely passive part. Each person must participate actively in the life of the Church. For the Christian vocation is, of its nature, a vocation to the apostolate.

It is Christ the Head of the Body who personally commissions His members to the apostolate. By sharing in the Church's mission, all the faithful share in Christ's mission. Their effective contribution requires that they live by the faith, hope and charity that is poured into their hearts by the Holy Spirit. And the precept of charity, which is the Lord's greatest commandment, urges everyone to work for the glory of God and for the communication of eternal life to all people, so that all may know the only true God and Jesus Christ whom He has sent (cf. Jn. 17:3).

Among the members of the Church there exists a diversity of services within a unity of mission. To the Apostles and their successors Christ has entrusted the ministry of teaching, sanctifying and governing in His name and by His power. But the laity have been given a share in the priestly, prophetic and kingly functions of Christ (cf. *Lumen gentium,* no. 31). To fulfill the role proper to them, they must join their efforts to the ministry of the entire People of God and work in union with those whom the Holy Spirit has appointed to govern the whole Church (cf. Acts 20:28). At the same time, on all Christians rests the obligation of working to bring the divine message of salvation to all people throughout the world.

As lay people you are called to bear witness to Christ within the context of your homes, neighborhoods, towns and cities. You contribute to the Church's mission first of all by showing consistency between your conduct and your faith. In word and deed you must proclaim Christ the Light of the world. This is the general call to the apostolate which all Christians have received. As laity you also have the specific task of renewing the temporal order, by permeating it with the spirit of the Gospel.

Coming as you do from different cultural and social backgrounds, you are able to infuse the Christian spirit into the mentality and behavior, the laws and structures of the community in which you live. Likewise, you exercise a special work and responsibility by engaging in the apostolate of "like towards like": families evangelizing families, students evangelizing students, young people leading young people to Christ. Especially here the witness of your lives is completed by the witness of your word (cf. *Apostolicam actuositatem*, no. 13). Through lives which manifest deep integrity and by your persevering practice of fraternal charity in dealing with others, those whom you encounter in your work and with whom you associate on various levels of social life can be profoundly influenced.

You have the very special mission of speaking to the world in a practical way: to manifest truth and justice in your own lives; to proclaim by action your respect for life, your social concern, your rejection of materialism and consumerism. You are called to exemplify purity of life and, if you are married, to be living signs of conjugal fidelity and of the indissolubility of marriage, just as Christ preached them. Never doubt, dear friends, that the word of God has power to bring this about in you: "You are the salt of the earth.... You are the light of the world" (Mt. 5:13-14).

ROLE OF THE FAMILY IN SPREADING THE WORD

5. But more than that, to each of you has been given a charism, the gift of the Holy Spirit, enabling you to have a special aptitude for a particular service within the Church. As St. Paul tells us, the Holy Spirit is given in a particular way to each person: "Our gifts differ according to the grace given us. If

your gift is prophecy, then use it as your faith suggests; if administration, then use it for administration; if teaching, then use it for teaching" (Rom. 12:6-7).

This exercise of the Christian apostolate may be done as individuals or as members of groups of people who work together for the same particular aim. Within the vast variety of the apostolate some are called to proclaim God's word as catechists, teachers or as those who lead adults through the Rite of Christian Initiation. Some will minister to families, the sick, the imprisoned, the disabled, youth or the aged. Some will assist in the area of social justice or health care or ecumenism. Others exercise administrative talents in diocesan or parish councils, or in the various organisms needed to involve the wider Christian community. Specialized movements of spiritual renewal for individuals and groups, especially for families, are able to contribute greatly to the Church's mission.

The role played by the family in the service of the Gospel is held in special honor by the Church. In my Apostolic Exhortation on the Role of the Christian Family in the Modern World, I emphasized that "the ministry of evangelization carried out by Christian parents is original and irreplaceable" (Familiaris consortio, no. 53). In this regard, children too have a role to play and they should be encouraged to make their contribution. In the words of the Second Vatican Council: "They have their own apostolic work to do" (Apostolicam actuositatem, no. 12).

UNITED WITNESS
IN THE SERVICE OF CHRIST

6. Since the primary aim of the Church's apostolate is to announce to the world by word and action the message of Christ and to communicate to it the saving grace of Christ, the principal means of bringing this about is the ministry of the word and of the sacraments. This task is fulfilled in a specific way through the ordained ministries conferred by the Sacrament of Orders. Christ Himself has instituted the ministerial priesthood to make available to the whole People of God the Eucharistic Sacrifice, which is "the source and summit of the whole Christian life" (Lumen gentium, no. 11). Hence all ministry is directed to this Sacrifice as to its goal and center.

Some lay people are called to be associated in a particular way with the activities of the Bishops, priests and deacons, or to exercise certain pastoral or ministerial tasks in a stable manner. When there is a shortage of clergy, this aspect of lay ministry is particularly providential. Yet all the laity are permanently assigned by Christ Himself to the service of His Gospel within the unity of His Church. The Church rejoices when clergy, religious and laity work together, each group according to its specific calling, to give a united witness to the world of a common mission—the mission of Christ.

7. There is so much to be done. There are whole areas of human life which seem to be withdrawn from any ethical or religious influences. In this situation we are reminded of Jesus: "When he saw the crowds he felt sorry for them because they were

harassed and dejected, like sheep without a shepherd. Then he said to his disciples, 'The harvest is rich but the laborers are few, so ask the Lord of the harvest to send laborers to his harvest'" (Mt. 9:36-37). The true disciple is eager to announce Christ by word, either to unbelievers so as to draw them to the faith, or to the faithful in order to instruct them, strengthen them and incite them to more fervent Christian lives (cf. *Apostolicam actuositatem*, no. 6). There is truly an urgent need in the Church today for more lay people engaged in teaching Christian doctrine to the young.

The diversities of human needs require a diversity of response on the part of the Church. The Church is one, as is her saving Gospel and her Eucharist, but she counts on the diligence of her members to discover effective ways to face new problems and new needs. Paul VI has clearly stated the Church's stand: "We cannot but experience a great inner joy when we see so many pastors, religious and lay people, fired with their mission to evangelize, seeking ever more suitable ways of proclaiming the Gospel effectively" (*Evangelii nuntiandi*, no. 73).

PRAY FOR ONE ANOTHER

8. We know that the foundation and the fruitfulness of every apostolate and ministry in the Church depends on our living union with Christ our Lord and Master. This life of intimate union with Christ is maintained and nourished by prayer. In a very real sense we can say that the apostolate is the

unfolding of Jesus' love for others from within ourselves. However, without that union with Christ which is fostered through prayer our energy flags, we lose fervor and we run the risk of becoming as "a sounding brass or tinkling cymbal" (1 Cor. 13:1).

Moreover, all ministry requires the support of the whole Christian community, especially through our perseverance in prayer for each other. How we need to pray for each other! How I appreciate and need your prayers! How your Bishops, priests and deacons count on your prayerful support! They know how much you contribute to the well-being of the entire Church, how much you do to promote the saving mission of the Church to the world.

9. We find a model of this apostolic spiritual life in the humble Virgin of Nazareth, the Mother of Jesus, Queen of the Apostles. As the Second Vatican Council says of her: "While on earth Mary's life was like that of any other, filled with labors and the cares of the home; always, however, she remained intimately united to her Son and cooperated in an entirely unique way in the Savior's work. And now, assumed into heaven, 'her motherly care keeps her attentive to her Son's brothers and sisters, still on pilgrimage amid the dangers and difficulties of life, until they arrive at the happiness of their homeland'" (*Apostolicam actuositatem*, no. 4).

10. My brothers and sisters: be thankful to God for the opportunity to serve Christ and His Church. Serve with gratitude and joy! Be thankful to God for the faith you have found in your maritime homes and

communities which has spread to every corner of this country, and even around the world. Be thankful for all those who have served before you, for all who have preached the Gospel of our Lord Jesus Christ along these Atlantic shores. Be thankful for your parents, teachers and pastors who first presented you with the Gospel.

As a servant of Christ who loves you all, I urge you, my companions in the faith, fellow pilgrims in our journey to the Father, to listen again to the words which St. Peter wrote to the early Christian community:

"Each of you has received a special grace, so, like good stewards responsible for all these different graces of God, put yourselves at the service of others. If you are a speaker, speak in words which seem to come from God; if you are a helper, help as though every action was done at God's orders; so that in everything God may receive the glory, through Jesus Christ, since to him alone belong all glory and power, for ever and ever. Amen" (1 Pt. 4:10-11).

I Come as a Pastor and Friend To Tell You of the Church's Great Affection for You

On September 14, in Halifax (capital of Nova Scotia), the Holy Father visited the I. W. Killam Hospital for children and disabled persons, and spoke to them as follows.

Dear friends, and beloved children at Izaak Walton Killam Hospital,

1. As we begin this new day, a day when the Church throughout the world celebrates the Triumph of the Holy Cross, I am very pleased to pay you a visit at this hospital. I greet you all in the name of Jesus Christ. I greet the doctors, nurses and staff, the pastoral care workers, the handicapped and the sick, the children and their families. I am grateful to God for the opportunity of being with you. I come as a pastor and friend, wishing to assure you of the great affection which the Church has for you. You have a special place in my heart. And my prayers and the prayers of the whole Church are with you, particularly when you feel most helpless and weak.

2. I would like to recall, at this time, the special love which Jesus has for the handicapped and the sick, for children and all who suffer. For example, we find the following passage in the Gospel according to St. Mark: "People were bringing little children to him, for him to touch them. The disciples turned them away, but when Jesus saw this he was indignant and said to them, 'Let the little children come to me; do not stop them; for it is to such as these that the kingdom of God belongs. I tell you solemnly, anyone who does not welcome the kingdom of God like a little child will never enter it.' Then he put his arms around them, laid his hands on them and gave them his blessing" (Mk. 10:13-16).

What a striking illustration of the tender love of Jesus for children! And at the same time, a model of loving service which we, the Church, seek to imitate in our own day. We, too, wish to assure all children, and all those who are sick or handicapped, of our deep concern and support. We wish to bless them and lift them up to the Lord in prayer.

3. And now, I would address a few words to the doctors, nurses, the pastoral care workers, parents and all who care for the sick and handicapped. I wish to thank you first of all, and commend you for your dedicated labors, for the countless hours of care and concern which you direct to these, God's little ones in need.

Jesus, during His life on earth, not only had a special love for children and for those who are ill or disabled. He even identified Himself with them when He said: "I was sick and you visited me.... As you did it to one of the least of these my brethren, you did it to me" (Mt. 25:36, 40). These words recorded by Saint Matthew show the dignity and value of your work on behalf of these little ones. Your loving devotion, your generous service, your medical and professional expertise—all these are acts of love for the child or the patient, and are acts of love for Christ who is mysteriously present in them. And your charity and devoted care bear witness to the dignity and worth of every human being, even the tiniest and most helpless baby. May God bless you and sustain you with His grace.

With these few words, then, I assure all of you of the love and concern of the Church and of my own pastoral affection in Christ. And I ask God to bless you with His gifts of peace and joy. May the Lord of Life be with you all.

I Proclaim Yet Again the Absolute Value of the Missionary Vocation

On the morning of September 14, Feast of the Triumph of the Cross, John Paul II celebrated Mass in Central Commons, Halifax, and preached the following homily.

We adore You, O Christ, and we praise You, because by Your cross You have redeemed the world. Alleluia!

Dear brothers and sisters,

1. As representatives of the People of God in the Archdiocese of Halifax, Cape Breton, all of Nova Scotia and Prince Edward Island, you are united in this acclamation of the liturgy with Archbishop Hayes and your other Bishops, and with the Church throughout the world. The Catholic Church celebrates today the feast of the Triumph of the Cross of Christ. Thus the crucified Christ is lifted up by faith in the hearts of all who believe, and He too lifts up those same hearts with a hope that cannot be destroyed. For the cross is the sign of the Redemption, and in the Redemption is

contained the pledge of resurrection and the beginning of new life: the lifting up of human hearts.

At the very beginning of my service in the See of St. Peter I endeavored to proclaim this truth through the Encyclical *Redemptor hominis.* In this same truth I desire to be united with all of you today in the adoration of the cross of Christ:

"Never forget the deeds of the Lord"
(cf. Ps. 77[78]:7).

2. To comply with this acclamation of today's liturgy let us follow attentively the path traced out by these holy words in which the mystery of the Triumph of the Cross is announced to us.

In the first place, the meaning of the Old Testament is contained in these words. According to St. Augustine, the Old Testament conceals within itself what is fully revealed in the New. Here we have the image of the bronze serpent to which Jesus referred in His conversation with Nicodemus. The Lord Himself revealed the meaning of this image, saying: "The Son of Man must be lifted up as Moses lifted up the serpent in the desert, so that everyone who believes may have eternal life in him" (Jn. 3:14-15).

During Israel's march from Egypt to the Promised Land, God permitted—because of the murmuring of the people—a plague of poisonous snakes, as a result of which many died. When the others understood their sin they asked Moses to intercede before God: "Intercede for us with the Lord to save us from these serpents" (Nm. 21:7).

Moses prayed and received the following order from the Lord: "Make a fiery serpent and put it on a standard. If anyone is bitten and looks at it, he shall live" (Nm. 21:8). Moses obeyed the order. The bronze serpent set upon the standard became salvation from death for anyone who was bitten by the serpents.

In the book of Genesis the serpent was a symbol of the spirit of evil. But now, by a startling reversal, the bronze serpent lifted up in the desert is a figure of Christ lifted up on the cross.

The feast of the Triumph of the Cross recalls to our minds, and in a certain sense makes present, the lifting up of Christ on the cross. This feast is the lifting up of the saving Christ: whoever believes in the Crucified One has eternal life.

The lifting up of Christ on the cross gives a beginning to the lifting up of humanity through the cross. And the final measure of this lifting up is eternal life.

3. This Old Testament event is recalled in the central theme of John's Gospel.

Why are the cross and the Crucified One the doorway to eternal life?

Because in Him—Christ crucified—is manifested to the full the love of God for the world, for man.

In the same conversation with Nicodemus Christ says: "God loved the world so much that he gave his only Son, so that everyone who believes in him may not be lost but may have eternal life. For God sent his Son into the world, not to condemn the world, but so that through him the world might be saved" (Jn. 3:16-17).

The salvific lifting up of the Son of God on the cross has its eternal source in love. This is the love of the Father that sends the Son; He gives His Son for the salvation of the world. And at the same time it is the love of the Son who does not "judge" the world, but gives Himself for the love of the Father and for the salvation of the world. Giving Himself to the Father through the Sacrifice of the cross, He gives Himself at the same time to the world: to each person and to the whole of humanity.

The cross contains in itself the mystery of salvation, because, in the cross, Love is lifted up. This is the lifting up of Love to the supreme point in the history of the world: in the cross Love is lifted up and the cross is at the same time lifted up through Love. And from the height of the cross, love comes down to us. Yes: "The cross is the most profound condescension of God to man.... The cross is like a touch of eternal love upon the most painful wounds of man's existence" *(Dives in misericordia,* no. 8).

4. To the event of John's Gospel the liturgy of today's feast adds the presentation made by Paul in his letter to the Philippians. The Apostle speaks of an emptying of Christ through the cross; and at the same time of Christ's being lifted up above all things—and this too had its beginning in the same cross:

"Christ Jesus...emptied himself to assume the condition of a slave, and became as men are; and being as all men are, he was humbler yet, even to accepting death, death on a cross. But God raised him high and gave him the name which is above all other names, so that all beings in the heavens, on earth and in the underworld, should bend the knee at the name of Jesus, and that every tongue should acclaim Jesus Christ as Lord, to the glory of God the Father'' (Phil. 2:6-11).

The cross is the sign of the deepest humiliation of Christ. In the eyes of the people of that time it was the sign of an infamous death. Free men could not be punished with such a death, only slaves. Christ willingly accepts this death, death on the cross. Yet this death becomes the beginning of the resurrection. In the Resurrection the crucified Servant of Yahweh is lifted up: He is lifted up before the whole of creation.

At the same time the cross is also lifted up. It ceases to be the sign of infamous death and becomes the sign of resurrection, that is, of life. Through the sign of the cross it is not the servant or the slave who is speaking, but the Lord of all creation.

5. These three elements of today's liturgy—the Old Testament, the Christological hymn of Paul and the Gospel of John—form together the great wealth of the mystery of the Triumph of the Cross.

Finding ourselves immersed in this mystery with the Church, which throughout the world celebrates today the Triumph of the Holy Cross, I wish to share in a special way its riches with you, dear brothers and sisters of the Archdiocese of Halifax, dear people of Nova Scotia, Prince Edward Island and all Canada.

Yes, I wish to share with all of you the riches of that holy cross—that standard of salvation which was implanted on your soil 450 years ago. Since that time the cross has triumphed in this land; and, through the collaboration of thousands of Canadians, the liberating and saving message of the cross has been spread to the ends of the earth.

HOMAGE TO MISSIONARIES

6. At this time I wish to pay homage to the missionary contribution of the sons and daughters of Canada who have given their lives so "that the Lord's message may spread quickly, and be received with honor as it was among you" (2 Thes. 3:1). I pay homage to the faith and love that motivated them, and to the power of the cross that gave them strength to go out and fulfill Christ's command: "Make disciples of all nations; baptize them in the name of the Father and of the Son and of the Holy Spirit" (Mt. 28:20).

And in paying homage to your missionaries, I pay homage likewise to the communities throughout the world who have embraced their message and marked their graves with the cross of Christ. The Church is grateful for the hospitality of a final resting place given to the missionaries, whence they await the definitive Triumph of the Holy Cross in the glory of resurrection and eternal life.

I express profound gratitude for the zeal that has characterized the Church in Canada, and I thank you for the prayers and contributions and various activities through which you support the missionary cause. In particular I thank you for your generosity to the mission aid societies of the Holy See.

7. Evangelization remains for all time the sacred heritage of Canada, which has indeed such a proud history of missionary activity at home and abroad.

Evangelization must continue to be exercised through personal witness, by preaching hope in the promises of Jesus and by proclaiming fraternal love. It will forever be connected with the implantation and building up of the Church and have a deep relationship with development and liberation as expressions of human advancement. At the center of the message, however, is an explicit proclamation of salvation in Jesus Christ—that salvation brought about on the cross. In the words of Paul VI: "Evangelization will also always contain—as the foundation, center and at the same time summit of its dynamism—a clear proclamation that, in Jesus Christ, the Son of God made man, who died and rose from the dead, salvation is offered to all people, as a gift of God's grace and mercy" (*Evangelii nuntiandi*, no. 27).

The Church in Canada will be herself to the extent that in all her members she proclaims in word and deed the Triumph of the Cross—to the extent that she is at home and abroad an evangelizing Church.

Even as I speak these words there is Another who is speaking to the hearts of young people everywhere. It is the Holy Spirit Himself and He is urging each one, as a member of Christ, to embrace and to speak the Good News of God's love. But to some the Spirit is proposing the command of Jesus in its specific missionary form: Go and make disciples of all nations. Before the whole Church, I, John Paul II, proclaim once again the excelling value of the missionary vocation. And I assure all those called to the priesthood and religious life that our Lord Jesus

Christ is ready to accept and make fruitful the special sacrifice of their lives, in celibacy, for the triumph of the cross.

8. Today the evangelizing Church returns in a certain sense to relive the whole period that begins on Ash Wednesday, reaches its height in Holy Week and Easter, and extends through the following weeks until Pentecost. The feast of the Triumph of the Holy Cross is like a concise summary of the whole Paschal Mystery of our Lord Jesus Christ.

The cross "triumphs" because on it Christ is lifted up.

Through it Christ has "lifted up" man. On the cross every person is definitively lifted up to his or her full dignity—to the dignity of final destiny in God.

In the cross the power of love that elevates man, that exalts him, is also revealed.

Indeed the whole plan of Christian life, of human life is summarized and reconfirmed here in a marvelous way: the plan and its meaning! Let us accept this plan—and its meaning! Let us once again find a place for the cross in our lives and in our society.

Let us speak of it in a special way to all those who suffer, and hand on its message of hope to the young. And let us continue to proclaim to the ends of the earth its saving power: *Exaltatio crucis!* The Triumph of the Holy Cross!

Brothers and sisters: "Never forget the deeds of the Lord"! Amen.

Vatican Translation

The Meaning and Scope of the Priestly Life Come from the Mystery of Christ's Cross

On Friday, September 14, Pope John Paul II met with the clergy of Ontario in St. Michael's Basilica in Toronto and addressed the priests in English and French.

Dear brother priests,

1. I am pleased that the first major meeting of my pastoral visit to the Church in Toronto finds me here with you. I want you to know the joy I experience and how much I appreciate all that you do for God's holy people. Happily our gathering occurs on the feast of the Triumph of the Cross. The significance of this celebration is outlined for us in today's liturgy. Here we find a rich source of inspiration for reflecting on the meaning which the cross has for the priesthood of Jesus and, consequently, the meaning that it has for our own priestly lives.

2. The cross represents the culmination of Jesus' priestly service. On it He offers Himself as the perfect

sacrifice of reparation to the Father for the sins of humanity; thereby He establishes a new and lasting covenant between God and man. This wonderful covenant is renewed in every Eucharist that we celebrate; and in every Eucharist, the Church reaffirms her identity and her calling as the Body of Christ.

In turning to the Gospel passage from St. John which we have just listened to, we find Jesus in discussion with Nicodemus, a ranking Jewish leader of his time, who "came by night," under the cover of darkness, to be enlightened by Him who is "the light of the world." By his questions Nicodemus indicates that he is in search of the truth about God and that he desires to know the right direction that his life should take. Jesus does not disappoint him. His response is clear and direct. In answering Nicodemus, Jesus goes to the very core of the Gospel message:

"God loved the world so much that he gave his only Son, so that everyone who believes in him may not perish, but may have eternal life" (Jn. 3:16).

The lifting up of the Son of Man on the cross is a sign of the Father's love. Jesus confirms this when He says: "The Father loves me because I lay down my life in order to take it up again" (Jn. 10:17). At the same time the cross demonstrates Jesus' loving filial obedience to the Father's will: "My food is to do the will of the one who sent me, and to complete his work" (Jn. 4:34). The cross is truly a sign of divine love—but a divine love that the Son shares with humanity.

This love symbolized by the cross is profoundly pastoral, for by it everyone who believes in Christ gains eternal life. Upon the cross the Good Shepherd "lays down his life for the sheep" (Jn. 10:11). Jesus' act of dying on the cross is the supreme *ministerium*, the highest act of service to the community of believers. The sacrifice of Jesus expresses more eloquently than human words the pastoral nature of the love that Christ has for His people.

The cross represents the will of the Father to reconcile the world through His Son. St. Paul summarizes for us the reconciling mission of Christ when he writes:

"God wanted all perfection to be found in him and all things to be reconciled through him and for him, everything in heaven and everything on earth, when he made peace by his death on the cross" (Col. 1:19-20).

The cross not only stands over the ecclesial community that is gathered in faith, but its sphere of influence extends to "everything in heaven and on earth." The power of the cross is the reconciling force that directs the destiny of the whole of creation. Our Lord reveals the center of that reconciling power when He says: "And when I am lifted up from the earth, I shall draw all men to myself" (Jn. 12:32). The reality of the cross profoundly affects our contemporary society with all its technological skills and scientific achievements. It is through the priesthood of Christ that this society will reach its ultimate destiny in God.

3. As the meaning of Christ's priesthood is discovered in the mystery of the cross, so too the life of the priest derives its sense and purpose from this

same mystery. Since we share in the priesthood of the Crucified Jesus, we must realize more and more each day that our service is marked by the sign of the cross.

The cross reminds us priests of God's great love for humanity and of God's personal love for us. The greatness of that love is communicated first of all in the gift of new life that each Christian receives through the saving waters of Baptism. This wonderful expression of divine love continually fills the believer with gratitude and joy.

And how marvelous is that gift which Jesus offers to certain men—for the benefit of all—of sharing in His ministerial priesthood. Which of us priests cannot but find in that call an expression of God's deep and personal love for Him and for the whole Church that He is called to build up through a specific ministry of word and sacrament?

Knowing that we have been called to join our lives to the redeeming mission of Jesus, each of us senses his own unworthiness in being ordained a "man of God" for others. This realization leads us to seek a greater dependence on God in prayer. In union with Christ in prayer, we find the strength to accept the Father's will, to respond joyfully to Christ's love and thereby to grow in holiness. In this process, the shadow of the cross falls across our whole existence as priests, urging us to imitate Christ Himself with ever greater generosity. Throughout this struggle, the words of St. Paul constantly echo in our hearts: "Life to me, of course, is Christ" (Phil. 1:21).

4. As priests we also see in the cross a symbol of our own pastoral service to others. Like the High Priest in whose name we act, we are called "not to be served but to serve" (Mt. 20:28). We are charged with shepherding the flock of Christ, to lead it "in paths of righteousness for his name's sake" (Ps. 23:3).

Our primary service as priests is to proclaim the Good News of salvation in Jesus Christ. We communicate this message, however, not "in terms of philosophy in which the crucifixion of Christ cannot be expressed," but through "the language of the cross," which is "God's power to save" (1 Cor. 1:17-18). Effective preaching requires that we be imbued with the mystery of the cross through study and through daily reflection on God's word.

Our priestly service finds its most sublime expression in the offering of the Eucharistic Sacrifice. Indeed, the Eucharistic Sacrifice is the sacramental proclamation of the mystery of salvation. In this sacred action we make present, for the glory of the Most Holy Trinity and for the sanctification of the people, Christ's sacrifice on the cross. The Eucharist brings the power of Christ's death on the cross into the lives of the faithful: "Until the Lord comes, therefore, every time you eat this bread and drink this cup you are proclaiming his death" (1 Cor. 11:26).

The Eucharist is the very reason for the priesthood. The priest exists in order to celebrate the Eucharist. In the Eucharist we find meaning for everything else we do. We must, therefore, be attentive to this great gift entrusted to us for the good of our brothers and sisters. We must reflect deeply on what it is we do as we celebrate the Eucharist, and how this action affects our whole lives.

For Holy Thursday 1980, I shared this thought with the Bishops of the Church in a letter addressed to them: "The priest fulfills his principal mission and is manifested in all his fullness when he celebrates the Eucharist, and this manifestation is more complete when he himself allows the depth of that mystery to become visible, so that it alone shines forth in people's hearts and minds through his ministry" (no. 2).

Through his love for the Eucharist the priest inspires the laity to exercise their own distinctive and important role in liturgical worship. He also makes this possible by actuating the charism of his own ordination. In his pastoral letter on the priesthood, Cardinal Carter describes this aspect of the priest's role: "Its function is to summon the People of God to their own high responsibility...to offer that sacrifice of praise which should leaven their lives and through them the world. This the priest must do *in persona Christi*" (Pastoral Letter, V, 7).

In a word, priests lift up Christ in the midst of the assembly so that, under the sign of the cross, the assembly may be built up in unity and in love and give witness to the world of Christ's redeeming love.

5. Under the sign of the cross, we know that certain sacrifices will be demanded of us. This does not surprise us because Christ's way of performing pastoral service is the way of the cross. At times we may encounter discouragement, loneliness, even

rejection. We may be asked to give of ourselves to a point that we feel completely depleted of our energy. We are regularly asked to be understanding, patient and compassionate with those with whom we may disagree and with everyone we encounter. Yet we accept these demands, with whatever sacrifices they may involve, in order to be "all things to all men in order to save some at any cost" (1 Cor. 9:23). And we accept what is demanded, not begrudgingly, but willingly—yes, joyfully.

Our priestly commitment to live a celibate life "for the sake of the kingdom of heaven" is likewise embraced for the benefit of others. Allow me to repeat what I wrote to the priests of the world in my Holy Thursday letter of 1979: "Through his celibacy, the priest becomes the 'man for others,' in a different way from the man who, by binding himself in conjugal union with a woman, also becomes, as husband and father, a man 'for others....' The priest, by renouncing this fatherhood proper to married men, seeks another fatherhood and, as it were, even another motherhood, recalling the words of the Apostle about the children whom he begets in suffering. These are children of his spirit, people entrusted to his solicitude by the Good Shepherd.... The pastoral vocation of the priests is great.... The heart of the priest, in order that it may be available for this service, must be free. Celibacy is a sign of a freedom that exists for the sake of service" (no. 8).

6. Moreover, we priests find in the mystery of the cross the reconciling power of Christ over all creation. We believe that Christ's cross offers contem-

porary society—with its scientific discoveries and technological advancement, and with its alienation and despair—a message of reconciliation and hope. As leaders of the Eucharistic assembly, which is the source of reconciliation and hope for the Church, we bear the responsibility of assisting the people to humanize the world through the power of the crucified and risen Lord.

Dear brother priests: we are called to proclaim Christ's message of reconciliation and hope in a very special way, in a way that God's Providence has reserved to us alone. To proclaim reconciliation and hope means not only insisting on the greatness of God's pardon and compassionate love in the face of sin, but also making available Christ's forgiving action in the Sacrament of Penance.

Over and over again I have asked my brother priests and bishops to give special priority to this sacrament, so that Christ may meet His brothers and sisters in a personal encounter of love. Our sacramental ministry is an act of close collaboration with the Savior of the world in bringing His Redemption into the lives of the faithful. It is through personal conversion effected and sealed by the Blood of Jesus that renewal and reconciliation will finally permeate all creation.

At this time I would like to recall what I said last September to a group of Canadian Bishops in Rome. It was an appeal made in the context of the preparation for my pastoral visit. Hoping that it will now serve also as a follow-up to my visit, I make this same appeal to you: "to invite all the faithful of Canada to conversion and individual confession. For some it will mean experiencing the joy of sacramental forgiveness for the first time in many years; for everyone it will be a challenge of grace.... The call to conversion is also a call to generosity and peace. It is a call to accept the mercy and love of Jesus Christ" (September 23, 1983). Dear brothers: let us proclaim to the world the reconciliation and hope that we ourselves experience in the Sacrament of Penance.

The vocation to which Christ has called us is truly a challenge to our love. In the words of the letter to the Hebrews: "Let us not lose sight of Jesus, who leads us in our faith and brings it to perfection: for the sake of the joy which was still in the future, he endured the cross" (Heb. 12:2).

As we renew our priestly commitment today, let us offer ourselves to Christ along the way of the cross. And let us do so in union with Mary, His Mother and ours.

The Restoration
of Christian Unity
Is of Crucial Importance
for Evangelization

*After meeting the clergy of Ontario in the Toronto Cathedral
on September 14, the Holy Father then went to the Anglican
Cathedral where he had an ecumenical meeting with the representatives of other Christian churches and communions. John Paul II
addressed them as follows.*

Dear friends in Christ,

1. I am deeply pleased to join in the prayer of
praise and petition with all of you who represent
the different churches and Christian communions
throughout Canada. With deep respect and love I
greet you all in the words of the Apostle Paul: "Grace
to you and peace from God the Father and the Lord
Jesus Christ" (2 Thes. 1:2). I also wish to greet with
deep respect the leaders of the other faiths who have
come here today. I thank you for your presence at
this ecumenical service.

In the Gospel according to St. Matthew we are
told that Jesus "went up on the mountain, and when
he sat down his disciples came to him. And he

opened his mouth and taught them" (Mt. 5:1-2). We, too, are disciples of Jesus, and together we go to Him. We go to listen to His word so that He may teach us as He once taught the crowd that gathered round Him on the mountain. We wish to be instructed and inspired by His message of salvation. We also wish to pray together for the gift of unity among all Christians and to unite our hearts in praise of God: the Father, the Son and the Holy Spirit.

2. It is very good to be with you. I want you to know how deeply grateful I am for the *Ecumenical Pastoral Letter* which was addressed to Christian congregations and parishes throughout Canada prior to my pastoral visit. It was heartwarming to be assured of the prayerful support and fraternal interest of so many Christian brothers and sisters. I deeply appreciate the warm welcome which you have extended to me, and I am very pleased that you have seized this opportunity to affirm the necessity of the ecumenical movement, to point out many of the important steps towards full unity which have already been taken, and to encourage fresh initiatives and continued prayer for the achievement of that goal for which we so greatly long.

TWENTY YEARS AGO

3. Exactly twenty years ago today, on September 14, 1964, my Predecessor Paul VI addressed those taking part in the Second Vatican Council as they gathered to begin the Third General Session, which was to promulgate the Constitution on the Church and the Decree on Ecumenism. Towards the end of

his address he spoke directly to the observers from other churches and ecclesial communities, saying: "We wish to assure you once more of our aim and hope to be able one day to remove every obstacle, every misunderstanding, every suspicion that still prevents us from feeling fully 'of one heart and one soul' (Acts 4:22) in Christ and in His Church.... This is something of the greatest importance, having its roots in the mysterious counsels of God, and we shall strive, in humility and piety, to dispose ourselves to be worthy of so great a grace."

In the twenty years that have elapsed since these words were spoken, we can rejoice to see the great strides that have been made, for indeed many obstacles, misunderstandings and suspicions have been removed. For all of this we give thanks to God. At the same time, I am grateful for this occasion, and others such as this, which give us the opportunity to appreciate more fully what God's grace has wrought in our midst, and which give us renewed strength and courage for pursuing together the path which still lies ahead.

REDEMPTOR HOMINIS

4. In my first Encyclical letter, *Redemptor hominis,* written shortly after my election to the See of Peter, I stated: "In the present historical situation of Christianity and the world, the only possibility we see of fulfilling the Church's universal mission with regard to ecumenical questions is that of seeking sincerely, perseveringly, humbly and also courageously the ways of drawing closer and of union. Pope Paul VI gave us his personal example for this. We must

therefore seek unity without being discouraged at the difficulties that can appear or accumulate along that road; otherwise we would be unfaithful to the word of Christ, we would fail to accomplish His testament" (no. 6). The experience of the past six years since my election has confirmed even more in my heart the evangelical obligation "of seeking sincerely, perseveringly, humbly and also courageously the ways of drawing closer and of union."

MESSAGE OF SALVATION

5. We cannot turn back on this difficult but vital task, for it is essentially linked with our mission of proclaiming to all humanity the message of salvation. The restoration of the complete unity of Christians, for which we so greatly yearn and pray, is of crucial importance for the evangelization of the world. Millions of our contemporaries still do not know Christ, and millions more who have heard of Christ are hindered from accepting the Christian faith because of our tragic division. Indeed, the reason Jesus prayed that we might be one was precisely "so that the world might believe" (Jn. 17:21). The proclamation of the Good News of our Lord Jesus Christ is greatly obstructed by doctrinal division among the followers of the Savior. On the other hand, the work of evangelization bears fruit when Christians of different communions, though not yet fully one, collaborate as brothers and sisters in Christ, to the degree possible and with respect for their particular traditions.

As the third millennium of Christianity approaches, we are faced with a rapidly expanding technology which raises numerous opportunities as well as obstacles to evangelization. While it engenders a number of beneficial effects for humanity, it has also ushered in a technological mentality which challenges Gospel values. The temptation exists of pursuing technological development for its own sake, as if it were an autonomous force with built-in imperatives for expansion, instead of seeing it as a resource to be placed at the service of the human family. A second temptation exists which would tie technological development to the logic of profit and constant economic expansion without due regard for the rights of workers or the needs of the poor and helpless. A third temptation is to link technological development to the pursuit or maintenance of power instead of using it as an instrument for freedom.

To avoid these dangers, all such developments need to be examined in terms of the objective demands of the moral order and in the light of the Gospel message. United in the name of Christ, we need to ask critical questions and assert basic moral principles which have a bearing on technological development. For instance, the needs of the poor must take priority over the desires of the rich; the rights of workers over the maximization of profits; the preservation of the environment over uncontrolled industrial expansion; production to meet social needs over production for military purposes. These challenges present us with important areas of ecumenical collaboration and form a vital part of our mission of proclaiming the Gospel of Christ. And before all of this we lift up our hearts to God, the Father of our Lord Jesus Christ.

I know that major efforts of ecumenical collaboration have been taking place in Canada for a number of years; in more recent years there have been an increasing intensity and a growing longing for complete union in Christ. The various theological dialogues between the churches have been very significant, and several inter-church coalitions for social justice and human rights have proven to be particularly important in view of the special problems of our technological age. I deeply admire the Christian spirit which has produced these generous efforts. And I urge you to continue, despite incomplete results, and despite the unfair criticisms which you may at times encounter on the part of those who do not understand the importance of ecumenical activity. I willingly reiterate the position of the Catholic Church that all worthy efforts for promoting unity among Christians are a response to the will of God and the prayer of Christ. They are an essential part of our mission to live the truth in charity and to proclaim the Gospel of Christ.

MANY FORMS OF ECUMENICAL COLLABORATION

6. Ecumenical collaboration, as we have discovered, can take many forms: working together in projects of fraternal service, engaging in theological dialogue and joint ventures to understand our troubled past, cooperative actions for justice and for the humanizing of the technological society, and many others. All of these are of great value and need to be continued in earnest, especially those which promote the truth and help us grow in fraternal

charity. At the same time, we all need to remember the primacy of the spiritual activities which the Second Vatican Council considered as the very soul of the ecumenical movement (cf. *Unitatis redintegratio*, no. 8). I am referring to the faithful practice of public and private prayer for reconciliation and unity, and to the pursuit of personal conversion and holiness of life. Without these, all other efforts will lack depth and the vitality of faith. We would too quickly forget what St. Paul teaches, namely, that "all this is from God, who through Christ reconciled us to himself and gave us the ministry of reconciliation" (2 Cor. 5:18).

There can be no progress towards unity among us where there is no growth in holiness of life. In the beatitudes, Jesus indicates the way to holiness: "Blessed are the poor in spirit.... Blessed are those who mourn.... Blessed are the meek.... Blessed are those who hunger and thirst for righteousness..." (Mt. 5:3ff.). In seeking to be counted among these "blessed ones," we shall grow in holiness ourselves; but at the same time we shall also be making a contribution to the unity of all followers of Christ, and thus to the reconciliation of the world. True holiness of life, which draws us closer to the heart of the Savior, will strengthen our bonds of charity with all people and especially with other Christians.

Let us, then, strive to be counted among these "blessed ones" of the beatitudes, "hungering and thirsting for righteousness" in a technological age, praying for unity with one another and with all who believe in Christ, yearning in hope for the day when "there will be only one flock and one shepherd" (Jn. 10:16).

Vatican Translation

To Protect the Family from Dangers Is a Great Task of the Whole Church

On Friday, September 14, the sixth day of his journey to Canada, the Holy Father spoke to the Polish community at Varsity Stadium in Toronto, where he was greeted by the President of the Canadian Polish Congress, Jan Kaszuba. The following is our translation of the Pope's speech.

Allow me to greet, as one of you, our guests who are present here: the Cardinals, first of all the Archbishop of Toronto, Cardinal Emmett Carter; and of course also our American compatriot, Cardinal John Krol, Archbishop of Philadelphia; Archbishop Edmund Szoka of Detroit, and all our guest bishops and friends who are with us today!

Dearest brothers and sisters, my compatriots on Canadian soil: Praised be Jesus Christ!

1. I have come to this meeting with feelings of emotion and joy. In fact, the hospitality and cordiality with which the parishes and communities of Poles in Canada received me fifteen years ago, in 1969, is

profoundly impressed in my memory, when for the first time I visited this country as a delegate of the Primate and the Polish Episcopate, having been invited by the Canadian Episcopate and the Congress of Poles in Canada on the occasion of their 25th anniversary.

Our meeting today follows and completes in a certain sense my previous visit.

In the words of St. Paul, "I keep thanking God for all of you and I remember you in my prayers, for I am constantly mindful before our God and Father of the way you are proving your faith, and laboring in love, and showing constancy of hope in our Lord Jesus Christ" (cf. 1 Thes. 1:2-4).

2. I cordially greet each and every one. In you and through you I greet all our dear compatriots who live on Canadian soil from the shores of the Atlantic to the Pacific, who for various reasons cannot be present here. My greeting goes to all the Polish parish communities, the Catholic, social, and youth organizations, to the scientific and assistance centers, and to all the Polish families in Canada. I address a special greeting to the priests, together with your Bishop, Most Reverend Szczepan Wesoly, to the religious communities, to all laborers, to those who are being tested in life, who carry the cross of suffering, to youth and children: to everyone. I embrace all of you from my heart and I send all of you a kiss of peace as a brother and as Pope.

My thoughts go also to those fellow Poles who at one time opened the way for the Poles who were arriving here and who now lie in peace, called by the Father of Light.

3. Dearest brothers and sisters!

Divine Providence has willed that you who come from Poland might live your human and at the same time Christian vocation here in Canada. As Poles, for whom for various reasons Canada has become your second fatherland, you make up an integral part of the Church in this country, and in a certain sense you are writing the continuing pages of that history of salvation whose preceding pages were written in the Church on Polish soil.

In accord with the teachings of the last Council, your spiritual position could be defined as "a singular gift" of the Polish Church to Canada, to the Church and to the Canadian people.

WE MUST RETURN
TO OUR CHRISTIAN ROOTS

For this reason, fifteen years ago, when I visited the Polish centers and churches in Canada in 1969, I left you the relics of the Polish saints. I wanted them to be a visible sign and an expression of the spiritual union between the Polish Church and the Canadian Church and to show to all our compatriots that link with the Church which is the mystery of the Communion of Saints and which constitutes the essential part of our Catholic Faith, and which for us Poles constitutes also the essential part of all our spiritual patrimony (cf. Letter to Priests, September 15, 1969).

We must always return to these roots, Christian roots, from which both you and I come, and from which in a certain sense we must ever continue to grow.

Your ancestors knew this well, those who began the immigration movement. As Sienkiewicz wrote in the novel *Za Chlebem (For Bread)*, "They felt that their family tree was not the places where they went, although the wind drove them there like fallen leaves, but rather the places from which they had left: the Polish soil, full of grain that waved in the fields...a noble land, a mother full of sweetness, so kind and more beloved than all the others in the world" (*Za Chlebem*, Warsaw, 1947, p. 16).

Putting down their roots in the new land, your ancestors still maintained a profound bond with their fatherland and the consciousness of being part of the faith, culture, and tradition of their forefathers, although remaining at the same time in the great community of the universal Church. They built Catholic churches; how can we not remember at this point the first Polish church, built in honor of Our Lady of Czestochowa in the nineteenth century by Polish settlers, which still exists in the town by the name of Wilno, which is so interesting: Wilno in Kaszuby; and also the church consecrated to St. Maximilian Kolbe, which you have erected in the Archdiocese of Toronto. The immigrants also built Catholic schools and they founded Polish and youth organizations, as for example the Polish National Union, the Congress of Poles in Canada, the Union of Polish Scouts. They founded Polish study and research centers, libraries and museums; they published books, newspapers, and periodicals. These centers and institutions arose at various times and are directed toward different purposes, but all of them are imbued with the sense of spiritual unity and communion with the Polish nation and with the Catholic Church.

5. The Catholic family played and still plays an important role in maintaining the spiritual link with the homeland, in keeping the faith of your forefathers, and the Polish tradition and culture, supported in this commitment by the parishes and the schools. We must appreciate the Polish family that lives in the diaspora, because finding itself in a new environment, it has never lost heart, but has preserved its identity and has known how to educate new generations in the spirit of the highest ideals and the most noble Christian virtues.

THE FAMILY AND MATERIALISM

In today's world, filled with materialism, the family must confront many difficulties. The situation in which it lives creates much confusion, perhaps, in the understanding of the authority of the parents and the position of the children, as well as in the transmission of essential human and Christian values.

Dear fellow Poles, let the family be the object of your special diligence, that family which is formed in accord with the sacramental union of a man and a woman who have discovered in themselves a common vocation to matrimonial and family life. To protect the family from the dangers of the contemporary world is a great task of the whole Church, a great task for the pastoral work of Poles abroad, and a great task for all Poles everywhere and for every compatriot. Whatever the family will be, such will be the image of the Polish community in Canada, thus will be the man who grows in Canada from the "Polish tree."

6. During this meeting today, I am thinking in a special way of youth, of the generation of my compatriots in Canada who within a few years will be responsible for the life of the religious and Polish communities. My dearest friends, I address myself to you because I feel the need for it in my heart.

More than ten years ago, at the conclusion of my pastoral visit to this country, I wrote a special letter to those who at that time were the Polish youth in Canada. I believe that the basic thought contained in that letter has not lost its relevance. Accept it today as the Pope's thought. It is centered on the question: who are you?

To be yourselves! How important it is for man, contemporary man, and above all, contemporary youth, who perhaps spend much energy trying to affirm and express themselves in an authentic way. I therefore desire for you youth of today always to remain yourselves, especially knowing how to express your Polish spirit: that particular patrimony of your nationality handed on to you by your parents. For you young people I also wish that you may seek God fervently and live in communion with Him through prayer, that you may discover the true beauty of the world and the ultimate meaning of your humanity. May you know how to read the vocation of your life, that God has written in your hearts, and thanks to which you bring a greater contribution to the life of the country that received your parents and grandparents with so much hospitality. Try not to impoverish that heritage which the previous generations have preserved with so much effort. Young people, do not disappoint the hopes placed in you.

7. You who have come to Canada recently with the intention of staying here always or for a limited time, enter into the life of this society, which is so impressive with its material development, its organization of life, its wealth, its impetus, its civilization. It so often happens that the foreigner finds himself faced with all these accomplishments as the "weakest one" who depends on everyone, like the poorest of all. Such a situation can easily lead to a state of frustration.

Dear compatriots, may you know how to appreciate in the proper way that which is within you and around you! May you know how to evaluate, discern and choose. Know how to appreciate that good that is within you and do not erase the traces that lead to your native country. May you also know how to make use of the rich experience of others. May you know how to participate in a creative, constructive way in the life of this new society with which your destiny is joined. But above all, keep the gift of faith and the living communion with the great community of the People of God that is the Church of Christ in all the earth, whether in Poland or in Canada.

8. When I came here fifteen years ago, I had much time to dedicate to the Polish immigrants in Canada. If I remember correctly, I had two weeks or

even more. We were able to meet, talk, travel, and to visit new Polish centers. Today all this must be reduced to this meeting in Toronto. I think back to those meetings, which gave me so much. I remember especially meeting with the new wave of immigrants, which arrived here after the Second World War and which had found here, not without effort, even more important positions in Canadian society.

The Second World War is a great chapter in the history of Europe and in the history of humanity. It is a great chapter in the history of our fatherland. We know how many victims this Second World War cost us, and how heavy was the price of the independence that Poland regained after the First World War, in 1918. Six million victims. It is a great testimony, a great contribution: at the same time a contribution to the work of the reconstruction of the world, of renewal of the human family.

At the end of the Second World War, the nations—especially those that, more than others, have known cruelty, violence, concentration camps, hatred of man toward his fellow man, and the degradation of man—considered it their duty to make a Declaration of the Rights of Man. This was a great event. Everyone understood that if humanity and the nations were to avoid in the future catastrophes similar to the Second World War, they would have to put the question of man in the center of attention. We spoke much about this fifteen years ago with the organizers of my visit to the Polish immigrants in Canada.

Now for several days I have been traveling through various cities of this country. I have seen many banners with the inscription "*Solidarnosc*" (Solidarity). For this reason I think that, especially after what the President of the Congress of Poles in Canada said at the beginning of this meeting, I should say what is the meaning of these inscriptions, these found in the various cities of Canada, in the various streets during the Pope's visit.

SOLIDARITY AND THE RIGHTS OF MAN

My dear brothers and sisters, my dear fellow Poles, they mean that Poles have always tried to add a logical content to that Declaration of the Rights of Man in the course of these forty years and above all in the 80's. The inscription "*Solidarnosc*" constitutes the symbol of an order in which man is placed in the center. The dignity of man and the rights of man are criteria for the building of the organization of labor and culture, of social life, and of the life of the national community. That is why we honor this word, this symbol, this reality.

I think that on the road of history which our nation is traveling—which is not an easy road, especially for the recent generations—this word adds a certain logical content; it constitutes a stage that is the result of the same premises, which is in the service of the same aspirations, which gives our history its life. Because we want to be ourselves and to live our own life.

9. Dear compatriots, our meeting today coincides with the liturgical feast of the Triumph of the Holy Cross. Through the cross, which was once a sign of dishonor for man, man has been raised "on

high," men of all times and generations, of all nations, tongues, cultures, and races...every man, every one of us.

I ask God that the cross be for you and for future generations the sign of salvation and of the elevation of man, so that man may not lose his way, overtaken completely by the world, but that he may have eternal life in God. That is what the cross means. That is why it is the symbol of salvation. The eternal love of the Father, expressed in the history of humanity by means of the cross, through the sacrifice of the Son, has come close to each one of us, through Mary, the Mother of Christ, who to the end remained at the foot of the cross. And for this reason she knows how to introduce herself fully into the human and divine dimension, the dimension of the mystery of redemption fulfilled through the cross. No one, in fact, has been introduced like Mary into the depth of this mystery by God Himself. Today, the feast of the Triumph of the Cross, and the vigil of the feast of Our Lady of Sorrows, our thoughts and our hearts, as the poet said, turn to her who "defends the Holy Mountain of Czestochowa and reigns at Wilno on the Ostra Gate" (A. Mickiewicz).

Let us place ourselves before her and repeat in spirit the words that the great primate of Poland, Cardinal Stefan Wyszynski taught us: "In the millennium of Christianity: Mary, Queen of Poland, I am near you, I remember, and I keep watch."

Dear brothers and sisters, the cross is the sign of our faith, of our hope, of our love. Let us place at the foot of the cross our prayers that come from our heart, confident that they will be heard.

From the English edition of L'Osservatore Romano

You Hold a Place
of Honor in the Church

On Saturday, September 15, the Holy Father paid a long visit to Huronia, in Midland, where the village of Sainte Marie is located, rebuilt a few years ago. This is a village founded by a group of Jesuit missionaries to bring the Gospel to the Indian peoples of Canada, and is the site of the sanctuary dedicated to eight of those missionaries venerated as the first martyrs of Canada. Here the Pope met with the sick and elderly and addressed them in English as follows.

Dear friends,

1. I am happy to be with you this morning at the Martyrs' Shrine in Huronia. My pastoral visit to Canada would be incomplete without meeting the sick and elderly who are so close to my heart. When I think of you, I am reminded of the words of the Lord spoken through the prophet Isaiah: "You are precious in my eyes, because you are honored and I love you" (Is. 43:4). Indeed you are precious in the eyes of the Lord and in the eyes of the Pope. You hold a place of honor in the Church for, in a particular way, you share in the mystery of the cross of Christ, the cross which in faith we know to be the tree of everlasting life.

2. Suffering and sickness, and death itself, are part of the mystery of life. But while they remain a mystery, they need not be without meaning. In Christ and through His passion and resurrection, all creation has been redeemed, including all human experience. In fact, in His passion Christ used suffering and death to express in the fullest way His obedient love for the Father. And now, in union with Christ our sufferings can become an act of love for the Father, a loving act of surrender to the Providence of God.

3. People often tell me that they are offering their prayers and sacrifices for me and my intentions. I am deeply grateful for this gesture of solidarity and devotion, and I am humbled by the goodness and generous love of those who suffer. May you never doubt that the willing acceptance of your suffering in union with Christ is of great value for the Church. If the salvation of the world was accomplished by the suffering and death of Jesus, then we know that important contributions to the mission of the Church are made by the sick and elderly, by persons confined to hospital beds, by invalids in wheelchairs, by those who fully share in the cross of our saving Lord. As St. Paul said of his own sufferings: "In my flesh I complete what is lacking in Christ's afflictions" (Col. 1:24).

St. Paul's words are especially true of the martyrs whom we honor at this shrine. For these martyrs gladly accepted suffering, and even death, for the sake of our Lord Jesus Christ. Through the shedding of their blood, they bore witness to the power of God's grace shining through our human weakness.

By their prayers and courageous example, we receive inspiration and strength for our lives.

4. Once when Jesus was addressing a large crowd, He said to them: "Come to me, all you who labor and are overburdened, and I will give you rest. Shoulder my yoke and learn from me, for I am gentle and humble of heart, and you will find rest for your souls" (Mt. 11:28-29). These words are intended for all of us, but they have a particular significance for the sick and elderly, for whoever feels "overburdened." We note, with consolation, Jesus' promise that our souls will find rest—not our bodies but our souls. Jesus does not promise to remove all physical suffering from our lives during our earthly pilgrimage, but He does promise to refresh our spirits, to lift up our hearts, to give rest to our souls. Come to the Lord, then, with your weariness and pain, your burdens and sorrows, and "you will find rest for your souls." For Jesus is the Good Shepherd, the shepherd who leads His sheep to green pastures of consolation, to fresh waters of peace.

While I know that you pray for me, I also want you to know that I pray for you. I pray that you will have the spiritual strength to accept your difficult crosses and not to lose courage. Dear brothers and sisters: may the Lord Jesus make you strong in faith and hope and fill your hearts with peace and joy.

Vatican Translation

The Gospel Proclaimed by the Holy Martyrs Enriches the Culture of the Indian Tribes

On Saturday morning, September 15, Pope John Paul II went to Shrine Field in Huronia, Ontario, for a celebration of the Liturgy of the Word and a meeting with about 100,000 faithful, many of whom belong to the Indian peoples. At this martyrs' shrine, the Holy Father addressed the assembly in English and French as follows.

Dear brothers and sisters in Christ,

1. *Chay!* With this traditional Huron word of welcome I greet you all. And I greet you, too, in the name of Jesus Christ who loves you and who has called you out "of every race, language, people and nation" (Rv. 5:9) to be one in His Body, the Church. Truly, Canadians are a people of many races and languages, and thus it gives me great joy to pray with you at this holy place, the martyrs' shrine, which stands as a symbol of the unity of faith in a diversity of cultures. I greet those of you who have come from the far north and the rural areas of Ontario, those

from the cities to the south, those from outside Ontario and from the United States as well. And in a special way I greet the native peoples of Canada, the descendants of the first inhabitants of this land, the North American Indians.

HISTORIC PLACE

2. We are gathered at this site in Midland which is of great importance in the history of Canada and in the history of the Church. Here was once located the Shrine of St. Marie which one of my predecessors, Pope Urban VIII, designated in 1644 as a place of pilgrimage, the first of its kind in North America. Here the first Christians of Huronia found a "house of prayer and a home of peace." And here today stands the martyrs' shrine, a symbol of hope and faith, a symbol of the triumph of the cross. The reading from St. Paul's letter to the Romans, which we have just heard, helps us to understand the meaning of this holy place, and what it was that gave the martyrs the courage to lay down their lives in this land. It helps us to understand the power that attracted the native peoples to the Faith. And this power was "the love of God made visible in Christ Jesus our Lord" (Rom. 8:39).

TRIALS OF MISSIONARIES

3. St. Paul also tells us how firmly he believed in the love of Christ and in its power to overcome all obstacles: "Nothing can come between us and the love of Christ" (Rom. 8:35). These are words which

proceed from the very depths of his being and out of his personal experience as an Apostle. For this great missionary faced many trials and difficulties in his zealous efforts to proclaim the Gospel. To the Corinthians, he writes: "I have been in danger from rivers and in danger from brigands, in danger from my own people and in danger from pagans; in danger in the towns, in danger in the open country, danger at sea and danger from so-called brothers. I have worked and labored, often without sleep; I have been hungry and thirsty and often starving; I have been in the cold without clothes, and, to leave out much more, there is my daily preoccupation: my anxiety for all the churches" (2 Cor. 11:26-28).

And yet, Paul glories in these hardships and says of them, "These are the trials through which we triumph, by the power of him who loved us" (Rom. 8:37). All these hardships he gladly bears because he is convinced of the love of Christ, and that nothing can ever separate him from that love.

NORTH AMERICAN MARTYRS

4. A similar confidence in God's love guided the lives of the martyrs who are honored at this shrine. They, like Paul, had come to consider the love of Christ as the greatest of all treasures. And they, too, believed that the love of Christ was so strong that nothing could separate them from it, not even persecution and death. The North American martyrs, then, gave up their lives for the sake of the Gospel— in order to bring the Faith to the native people whom they served. In fact, we are told that their faith was so

strong that they yearned and prayed for the grace of martyrdom. Let us recall for a moment these heroic saints who are honored in this place and who have left us a precious heritage.

Six of them were Jesuit priests from France: Jean de Brébeuf, Isaac Jogues, Gabriel Lalemant, Antoine Daniel, Charles Garnier and Noël Chabanel. Fired with love for Christ and inspired by St. Ignatius of Loyola, St. Francis Xavier and other great saints of the Society of Jesus, these priests came to the New World to proclaim the Gospel of Jesus Christ to the native peoples of this land. And they persevered to the end despite difficulties of every sort.

Two lay brothers were part of the missionary group: René Goupil and Jean de la Lande. With no less courage and fervor, they assisted the priests in their labors, showed great compassion and care for the Indians, and, laying down their lives, won for themselves the martyr's crown.

And as these missionaries laid down their lives, they looked forward to a day when the native people would enjoy full maturity and exercise leadership in their Church. St. John de Brébeuf dreamed of a Church fully Catholic and fully Huron as well.

BLESSED KATERI

A young woman of Algonquin and Mohawk ancestry also deserves special recognition today: Blessed Kateri Tekakwitha. Who has not heard of her outstanding witness of purity and holiness of life? It was my personal joy, only four years ago, to beatify this woman of great courage and faith, who is known by many as the "Lily of the Mohawks." To those who came to Rome for her beatification I said: "Blessed Kateri stands before us as a symbol of the best of the heritage that is yours as North American Indians" (June 24, 1980).

5. As we are gathered in prayer today at the martyrs' shrine, we remember the many efforts of the Church, beginning three and a half centuries ago, to bring the Gospel of Christ into the lives of the native peoples of North America. The martyrs honored here are only a small representation of the many men and women who took part in this great missionary effort. We wish to pay tribute as well to all those who joyfully embraced the Christian faith, like Blessed Kateri, and who remained faithful despite many trials and difficulties. Of great importance to the Church of Huronia is Joseph Chiwatenwa, who together with his wife Aonnetta, his brother Joseph and other family members lived and witnessed to their Faith in an heroic manner. Their fidelity is yet another testimony to the truth attested to by the Apostle Paul: "Nothing can ever separate us from the love of Christ." A statue now commemorates the life and mission of Joseph Chiwatenwa. Particularly striking is the testimony of St. Charles Garnier on the inscription: "It was in this Christian that we had our hope after God." These men and women not only professed the Faith and embraced Christ's love, but they in turn became evangelizers and provided even today eloquent models for lay ministry.

We also recall how the worthy traditions of the Indian tribes were strengthened and enriched by the

Gospel message. These new Christians knew by instinct that the Gospel, far from destroying their authentic values and customs, had the power to purify and uplift the cultural heritage which they had received. During her long history, the Church herself has been constantly enriched by the new traditions which are added to her life and legacy.

And today we are grateful for the part that the native peoples play, not only in the multi-cultural fabric of Canadian society, but in the life of the Catholic Church. Christ Himself is incarnate in His body, the Church. And through her action, the Church desires to assist all people ''to bring forth from their own living tradition original expressions of Christian life, celebration and thought'' *(Catechesi tradendae,* no. 53).

Thus the one Faith is expressed in different ways. There can be no question of adulterating the word of God or of emptying the cross of its power, but rather of Christ animating the very center of all culture. Thus, not only is Christianity relevant to the Indian peoples, but Christ, in the members of His Body, is Himself Indian.

And the revival of Indian culture will be a revival of those true values which they have inherited and which are purified and ennobled by the Revelation of Jesus Christ. Through His Gospel Christ confirms the native peoples in their belief in God, their awareness of His presence, their ability to discover Him in creation, their dependence on Him, their desire to worship Him, their sense of gratitude for the land, their responsible stewardship of the earth, their reverence for all His great works, their respect for their elders. The world needs to see these values—and so many more that they possess—pursued in the life of the community and made incarnate in a whole people.

Finally, it is in the Eucharistic Sacrifice that Christ, joined with His members, offers up to His Father all that makes up their lives and cultures. In His Sacrifice He consolidates all His people in the unity of His Church and calls us all to reconciliation and peace.

Like the Good Samaritan we are called to bind up the wounds of our neighbors in need. Together with St. Paul we must affirm: "It was God who reconciled us to Himself through Christ and gave us the work of handing on this reconciliation" (2 Cor. 5:18). This is truly the hour for Canadians to heal all the divisions that have developed over the centuries between the original peoples and the newcomers to this continent. This challenge touches all individuals and groups, all churches and ecclesial communities throughout Canada. Once again in the words of St. Paul: "Now is the favorable time; this is the day of salvation" (2 Cor. 6:2).

6. Dear brothers and sisters in Christ, this martyrs' shrine of Huronia bears witness to the rich heritage that has been handed on to the whole Church. At the same time, it is a place of pilgrimage and prayer, a monument to God's blessings in the past, an inspiration as we look to the future. Let us then praise God for His providential care and for all we have inherited from the past.

As we go forward, let us commend ourselves to the intercession of the North American martyrs, to Blessed Kateri Tekakwitha, St. Joseph, patron of Canada, and all the saints, together with Mary the Queen of saints. And in union with the whole Church—in the richness of her diversity and in the power of her unity—let us all proclaim by the witness of our own lives that "neither death nor life...nor any created thing, can ever come between us and the love of God made visible in Christ Jesus our Lord" (Rom. 8:38-39).

Technology Truly
at the Service of Man

*On Saturday afternoon, September 15, the liturgical com-
memoration of Our Lady of Sorrows, Pope John Paul II celebrated
Mass in Toronto's Downsview Airport. More than 600,000
faithful attended, representing the population of the great metropolis of Toronto and the whole province of Ontario.*

*During the Liturgy of the Word, the Holy Father delivered a
homily centered on the theme of technology, particularly apropos
in the city of Toronto, which is considered the economic capital of
Canada.*

"Wisdom speaks her own praises,
in the midst of her people she glories in herself.
I came forth from the mouth of the Most High,
and I covered the earth like mist" (Sir. 24:1, 3).

Dear brothers and sisters in Christ,

1. Today's feast finds us united in this city of
Toronto, together with Cardinal Carter, Bishop
Borecky and the other bishops, to proclaim God's
eternal Wisdom. The liturgical readings of the Mass
lead us in our praise of this eternal Wisdom.

The commemoration of Mary as Our Lady of
Sorrows is linked with yesterday's feast of the
Triumph of the Holy Cross. The mystery of the cross

on Golgotha and the mystery of the cross in the heart of the Mother of the Crucified One cannot be read in any other way: only in the perspective of eternal Wisdom is this mystery clarified for our faith. Indeed it becomes the beam of a special light in human history, in the midst of people's destiny on earth. This light is, first of all, in the heart of Christ lifted up on the cross. This light, reflected by the power of a special love, shines forth in the heart of the sorrowful Mother at the foot of the cross.

For Wisdom also means love. In love is the ripest fruit of Wisdom and, at the same time, its fullest source.

In Christ crucified, man has become a sharer of eternal Wisdom, approaching it through the Heart of the Mother who stood beneath the cross: "Near the cross of Jesus stood his mother and his mother's sister, Mary the wife of Clopas, and Mary of Magdala" (Jn. 19:25).

A CRY FOR SALVATION,
HELP, DELIVERANCE

2. Today—perhaps more than in yesterday's feast of the Triumph of the Holy Cross—the liturgy emphasizes the "human" aspect. This is nothing unusual. For in it there is reflected the human heart of Mary, and beside the Mother is the human heart of the Son, who is God and Man.

In the letter to the Hebrews we read the following words about Christ: "During his life on earth he offered up prayer and entreaty, aloud and in silent tears, to the one who had the power to save him out of death" (Heb. 5:7). Does this not perhaps evoke for us the prayer in Gethsemane when Jesus prayed that the chalice be removed from Him, if possible? (cf. Mt. 26:39)

Dear brothers and sisters: the Christ whom we encounter in our liturgy, alongside His own Mother of Sorrows, the Christ who offers His "prayer and entreaty, aloud and in silent tears," does so as head of humanity—a humanity immersed to a great extent in a unilaterally materialistic conception of being and acting, in the promises and problems connected with technology, and tempted to embrace a materialistic mentality. Christ continues to send forth to His Father His cry for the salvation of the world, for the building of a new earth, one that is more human because it is embraced by the love of a Mother—His Mother and ours.

In this same letter to the Hebrews we read: "Although he was Son, he learned to obey through suffering" (Heb. 5:8). Elsewhere St. Paul will say: He became "obedient unto death" (Phil. 2:8), but here we read: "he learned to obey."

And together with Him, with the Son, His Mother learned obedience—she, who had previously said "Fiat": "I am the handmaid of the Lord...let what you have said be done to me" (Lk. 1:38).

3. This cry of the Son's heart and of His Mother's heart—a cry which from the human standpoint would reject the cross—is expressed even more in the psalm of today's liturgy. This psalm is a cry for salvation, for help, for deliverance from the snare of evil:

"In you, O Lord, I take refuge.
Let me never be put to shame.
In your justice, set me free,
...speedily rescue me.
Be a rock of refuge for me,
a mighty stronghold to save me,
for you are my rock, my stronghold.
Release me from the snares they have hidden....
Deliver me from the hands of those who hate
    me" (Ps. 30[31]:1-3, 5, 16).

Since these words of the psalm reflect the whole
"human" truth of the Hearts of the Son and of the
Mother, they also express an act of absolute entrusting to God—dedication to God. This dedication is
even stronger than the cry for deliverance.

"Into your hands I commend my spirit.
It is you who will redeem me, Lord.
But as for my trust in you, Lord,
I say: 'You are my God'" (Ps. 30 [31]:5, 14).

This awareness—"You are my God. Into your
hands I commend my spirit"—prevails absolutely in
the heart of the Son "lifted up" on the cross, and in
the Mother's heart humanly emptied by the Son's
crucifixion.

TRIUMPH OF THE CROSS

4. We read in the letter to the Hebrews: "He
submitted so humbly that his prayer was heard...but
having been made perfect, he became for all who
obey him the source of eternal salvation" (Heb.
5:7, 9). In this consists the mystery of the "Triumph

of the Cross," on which, together with the whole Church, we meditated yesterday.

Eternal Wisdom has embraced all that the cross of Christ contains.

"I came forth from the mouth of the Most High and I covered the earth like mist" (Sir. 24:3).

So it is: the whole earth has been covered by the mystery of eternal Wisdom, whose real name is Love. "God loved the world so much that he gave his only Son" (Jn. 3:16).

And behold—at the very center of this "giving Himself" through love, from the height of the cross on which the Son is completely united to the Father, and the Father to the Son—the words resound which confirm His Mother's presence and her special sharing in the mystery of eternal Wisdom. Jesus says: "Woman, behold your son!" Beside Mary at the foot of the cross stood John, the disciple whom Jesus loved (cf. Jn. 19:26). And He says to John: "This is your mother!"

These words were written by John himself, as an Evangelist. And he added: "And from that moment the disciple made a place for her in his home" (Jn. 19:27).

BOOK OF SIRACH

5. Eternal Wisdom came into the world and was spoken in the Son who became man and was born of the Virgin Mary.

Eternal Wisdom embraced then from the very beginning also Mary when it assigned the Son's dwelling place on the earth: "Pitch your tent in Jacob, make Israel your inheritance" (Sir. 24:13). For she is the daughter of Israel; she is from the line of Jacob. She is the Mother of the Messiah!

How marvelously are the words of the book of Sirach fulfilled in her—an unknown and hidden Virgin of Nazareth: "From eternity, in the beginning, he created me, and for eternity I shall remain" (Sir. 24:9). You, beloved Daughter of God our Father—you were truly foreseen from eternity in Divine Wisdom, since from eternity by this Wisdom the Son was given to us.

You, beloved Mother of God's Son!

You, Virgin Spouse of the Holy Spirit!

You, who dwell in the tabernacle of the Most Holy Trinity!

Truly, you will never cease to be in the very heart of the divine plan.

And that which Wisdom proclaims further on in Sirach is also true: "I ministered before him in the holy tabernacle, and thus was I established on Zion...and in Jerusalem I wield my authority" (Sir. 24:10-11).

6. Eternal Wisdom caused all this. And in time eternal Wisdom concealed it—to the point of the emptying that took place on the cross of Christ. But right there—at the cross of Christ—eternal Wisdom

revealed both your service and your power! And it did so with the words: "This is your mother!"

The only one who hears these words is John, and yet in him all people hear them—everyone and each one.

Mother, this is your service, your holy service!

Mother, this is your power!

By means of this holy service, the most holy service, through this motherly power you "took root in an honored people, in the portion of the Lord, who is their inheritance" (Sir. 24:13).

All of us desire to have you as a Mother, for as such you were left to us by Christ lifted up on the cross. And this act of His was the fruit of eternal Wisdom. All of us desire your motherly service which conquers hearts, and we long for this power which is the motherly service born from the whole mystery of Christ.

The title Sorrowful Mother means precisely this. *Alma Socia Christi* means precisely this, for you have been associated with Christ in His whole mystery, which eternal Wisdom reveals and in which we desire to share ever more deeply: "They who eat me will hunger for more. They who drink me will thirst for more" (Sir. 24:21).

MARY'S SUFFERINGS

7. Dear brothers and sisters: through the liturgy today, Christ's prayer and entreaty and the love of

His Mother are offered for all those who experience the pains and challenges of this world of technology: increasingly subjected to a materialistic and, in the long-run, totally anti-human view of life:

—For all of you who in your ethnic diversity compose the fabric of this great city, striving to remain faithful to your origins, while working together to express your new moral unity in Canada.

—For all of you who live in Toronto, this heartland of Canada's industrial and technological development.

—For all who in one way or another make up the technological society: for workers in industry; all those engaged in activities of finance, commerce, education, publishing, informatics, medical research, the arts; for the leaders in communities; for the direct and indirect employers of millions of people.

—For the unemployed and all of you who are caught in the coils of an economic crisis and suffer its social effects.

—For the poor, those who experience alienation and all those who hunger and thirst for solidarity.

FOR ALL WHO LIVE IN HOPE

8. Christ's prayer is for all of you who live in hope, beside a cross that rises to the sky and illumines daily existence with the light of eternal Wisdom. And side by side with you, beneath this cross, there is that loving Mother who has experienced sorrow and understands pain, and who, in her

maternity and femininity, offers to all humanity the reassurance of loving care and personal concern for each individual, each human person.

TECHNOLOGY IN THE CAUSE OF HOPE

9. And today I appeal to all of you to view the problems of this world marked by technology within the context of the message of the cross and to do your part so that the power of technology will serve the cause of hope. Technology has contributed so much to the well-being of humanity; it has done so much to uplift the human condition, to serve humanity, and to facilitate and perfect its work. And yet at times technology cannot decide the full measure of its own allegiance: whether it is for humanity or against it. The same technology that has the possibility to help the poor sometimes even contributes to poverty, limits the opportunities for work and removes the possibility of human creativity. In these and other instances technology ceases to be the ally of the human person. Yes, it is more than ever necessary to affirm forcefully, as I did in my first Encyclical, *Redemptor hominis*, the primacy of the person over things and the priority of ethics over technology. In this sense, everything depends on the moral aims and moral norms according to which the material possibilities of technology are utilized.

For this reason my appeal goes to all concerned: to you, labor leaders; to you, business leaders; to you, scientists; to you, political leaders; to everyone who can make a contribution toward ensuring that the technology which has done so much to build Toronto and all Canada will truly serve every man, woman and child throughout this land and the whole world.

And in its final and greatest triumph may technology lead us to proclaim the surpassing magnitude of that Divine Wisdom which makes technology possible, but which from the cross of Christ reveals the very limitations of this technology. And from the cross of Christ, Divine Wisdom portrays that new earth which all technology must serve: the one embraced by a Mother's love. Today we address our prayer to that Mother:

Be a guide to Christ for us, O Mary.

Be for us a Morning Star that shines in the heavens of eternal Wisdom, above the horizons of our human world. Amen.

Relive the Valiant Achievements of Cyril and Methodius

On Saturday evening, September 15, Pope John Paul II visited the cathedral of the diocese of Sts. Cyril and Methodius of Toronto of the Slovaks of the Byzantine Rite, still under construction in Unionville, near Toronto in Ontario. The occasion of the Pope's visit was the blessing of the cornerstone of the new Cathedral of the Transfiguration.

Led by Bishop Michael Rusnak, the large crowd representing Slovaks residing in Canada heard the Holy Father address the following message to them in their own language.

Dear brothers and sisters in Christ,

1. In the joy of the Risen Savior, I greet the Slovak community of the Byzantine Rite of the Eparchy of Sts. Cyril and Methodius of Toronto. I offer fraternal greetings, too, to the ecclesiastical and civil authorities who honor us by their presence here this evening. I am very pleased to be with you to bless the cornerstone of the Cathedral of the Transfiguration and to join you in offering praise and thanks to God for the wonders which He has accomplished in your midst.

2. The marvelous Providence of God has indeed been with you in this land, protecting you and directing your lives since you first came here as immigrants. Among the many signs of His Providential care, we remember how, twenty years ago, in 1964, you were given your own Bishop of the Byzantine Rite. Later, in 1980, the Eparchy of Saints Cyril and Methodius was established. And with the blessing of this new cathedral, we witness another sign of the hand of God directing your destiny and watching over you each day. The same Providence that has sustained your people in the great suffering and sad deprivations which your Church has undergone in Slovakia has brought you to this day.

It is my hope and prayer that the Eparchy of Sts. Cyril and Methodius will continue to flourish and thus become in Christ an ever more effective instrument of evangelization and example of authentic Christian life. May the Lord also hasten a time of peace and total freedom for the Church in the land of your origin, so that "your joy may be complete" (cf. Jn. 15:11).

EVENTS OF 1980

3. Two historic events of 1980 are of special importance to the Byzantine Slovaks of Canada, and both of these render particular homage to the memory of Sts. Cyril and Methodius. On October 13 of that year, I erected the Eparchy of Toronto which bears their names, and on December 31, I declared these two holy brothers to be Patrons of all Europe, together with St. Benedict.

Sts. Cyril and Methodius are rightly known as the Apostles of the Slavs. Motivated by missionary zeal, they left their own homeland to begin to proclaim, in 863, the Gospel of Christ in Moravia and Slovakia. In order to teach the faith to the people, they translated the Gospels and the liturgical books into the Slavonic language. In doing this, they made possible a most successful evangelizing effort. In addition, they laid the foundations for the literary development of the religious and social culture of the Slavs.

These great missionary saints are also remembered for their commitment to the unity of the Church. They were fervent priests of the Byzantine Rite who carried out their pastoral work in union with the Church in Constantinople, which had sent them forth, and with the Church in Rome, which confirmed their mission.

Eleven centuries later we still remember, with great admiration and a deep sense of gratitude to God, the valiant achievements of Cyril and Methodius. The Old Slavonic language of the Sacred Liturgy of the Byzantine Rite stands as a living reminder of their immense influence in the Church. Generations yet to come will not cease to remember their zeal for the Word of God, their dedication to the Slavic culture, their love for the Sacred Liturgy and their commitment to the great cause of unity. For these reasons and others, the Apostles of the Slavs inspire us today, while they support us by their prayers.

BLESSING THE CORNERSTONE

4. It is a great joy for me to bless the cornerstone of the new Cathedral of the Transfiguration. As the

principal church of the Eparchy, this cathedral is a symbol of the light of the Gospel, transmitted through the teaching of the Bishop. It is likewise a symbol of the religious heritage of the Slovak people. Here, the Byzantine liturgy will be celebrated in all its solemn beauty; and here, in a special way, the Bishop will proclaim the Gospel and hand on to you, and to your children and your children's children, the authentic teaching of the Church.

The name of the new cathedral directs our attention to our Savior Jesus Christ and to that moment in human history when He gave Peter, James and John a glimpse of the glory which He shares with the Father. This revelation of Jesus as the beloved Son of God confirmed the Apostles in their faith. And later on it would sustain them during the darkness of Jesus' passion and during the times when they, too, would share in the cross of Christ. The Transfiguration, then, and this cathedral bearing its title, stir up our hope of sharing in this mystery, of being ourselves transfigured by the grace of the Lord, so as to share in His glory.

On this occasion, our thoughts go back to Paul VI, who died on August 6, the day on which the mystery of the Transfiguration is celebrated in both the Byzantine and the Roman Rites. It was he who gave Bishop Rusnak to you in 1964. And this new Cathedral of the Transfiguration is in some part due to the pastoral solicitude of this great Pope for you and for all Slavs. As I bless the cornerstone today, the Church of Rome renews her love and pastoral concern for your people.

UKRAINIAN EPARCHY

5. I would like, now, to extend a particular word of commendation to Bishop Borecky and the entire Ukrainian Eparchy of Toronto for the fraternal support and encouragement which they have been offering to Byzantine Slovaks for a number of years. Their respect for different religious and cultural traditions and their readiness to assist have been a great help in the establishment of the new Eparchy of Sts. Cyril and Methodius. Their collaboration has been a model of harmony and fraternal assistance for other communities.

Before concluding, I wish to tell you how pleased I am by your devotion to Mary the Mother of God. This is evident in your liturgy and is shown by the publication entitled "Maria." This publication, which is a comfort to people far from their homeland, is also a means of fostering true Marian devotion. May you continue in this worthy endeavor, and may Mary assist you on your way.

Dear brothers and sisters in Christ: walk always in the light and power of the Risen Lord; be strong in hope and in the love of God and neighbor; persevere in your worthy Slovak traditions and your heritage of faith. "The grace of our Lord Jesus Christ be with you all" (2 Thes. 3:17).

Through Baptism
We Live in Christ

On the evening of September 15, the Holy Father attended a "Thanksgiving with Pope John Paul II" at the Metro Toronto Convention Center. Following is the Pope's talk to the large crowd of laity gathered there.

Dear brothers and sisters in Christ,

1. It is a joy to meet with such a large and enthusiastic gathering of the laity of the Church. As we assemble this evening in Toronto, we know that Jesus Christ is present in our midst, for He said to His disciples: "Where two or three meet in my name, I shall be there with them" (Mt. 18:20). I embrace you all in the charity of Christ, and I wish through you to extend my prayerful greetings once again to all the laity in Canada: to the young and the old, the sick and the healthy, the handicapped, the poor and those not so poor, to all who by reason of Baptism are my brothers and sisters in Christ.

I want to speak with you this evening about the dignity of the laity. In this way, I wish to remind you of how important you are in the life and mission of the Church. You contribute to both the holiness of the Church and her mission of salvation in the world.

2. Your dignity—and the dignity of all the faithful—is rooted in the Sacrament of Baptism. By Baptism you are incorporated into Jesus Christ, and into His body, which is the Church. By this great sacrament in which original sin is taken away, you have been adopted as sons and daughters of our Father in heaven, and the spirit of truth and love abides in your hearts. Through an act of God's love you have become brothers and sisters of Christ, sharers in His priestly, prophetic and kingly role. And this same sacrament which has accomplished all of this in you has thus made you sharers in the redemption, sharers in the Paschal mystery of our Lord Jesus Christ.

With penetrating insight, St. Paul, in his Letter to the Romans, explains this aspect of Baptism: "When we were baptized in Christ Jesus," he says, "we were baptized in his death; in other words, when we were baptized we went into the tomb with him and joined him in death, so that as Christ was raised from the dead by the Father's glory, we too might live a new life" (Rom. 6:3-4). Baptism brings us into contact with the death and resurrection of Christ. It opens up to us the life that Christ won for us by His Paschal Mystery.

3. Through Baptism we begin to live in Christ, and He lives in us. And in order to explain this union, which is so deep and strong and vital, St. Paul states simply: "Life to me, of course, is Christ" (Phil. 1:20).

This is the meaning and reality of our Baptism: life in Christ—a life that comes to us because Christ died and rose again, and because we have been able to enter into contact with this death and resurrection of the Lord. But because Christ died, because this was the way He entered into His life of glory, we too must share in His death, in order to live the fullness of His life.

Dear brothers and sisters: this life of ours in Christ takes us along the way of the cross—through trials and suffering—to the glory of the resurrection and eternal life. It is our Baptism that introduces us to the cross and to the fullness of life in Christ. And it is Christ Himself who says to us: "Anyone who does not take his cross and follow in my footsteps is not worthy of me" (Mt. 10:38). This too is part of Baptism: to be given a share in the dying and rising of Christ.

4. The work that the Holy Spirit begins in you in Baptism He perfects through Confirmation, calling you to share ever more in the holiness of God. As St. Paul writes: "Your body, you know, is the temple of the Holy Spirit, who is in you since you received him from God" (1 Cor. 6:19). As God's temple, you enjoy the Holy Spirit's special gifts: "love, joy, peace, patience, kindness, goodness, trustfulness, gentleness and self-control" (Gal. 5:22). You must no longer be slaves to earthly passions. Selfishness and sin must not rule your lives. For the victory which Christ won over sin and death is now extended to you. You enjoy the freedom of being children of God, led by the Holy Spirit dwelling in you.

The struggle with evil is not removed from your life, but you have received the pledge of God's grace to conquer temptation and sin. And you find special strength for this struggle through the Sacrament of Penance. It is through this sacrament that your hearts are purified by personal contact with the God of holiness; it is through the power of this sacrament that holiness spreads throughout the entire body of the Church.

5. A temple is a place where God's name is praised.

As temples of the Holy Spirit, you the laity in the Church are called to worship God. You are consecrated for the purpose of giving glory and praise to God. And you fulfill this responsibility above all when you actively take part in the celebration of the Eucharist. The Second Vatican Council tells us: "The liturgy is the summit toward which the activity of the Church is directed; at the same time it is the fountain from which all her power flows. For the goal of apostolic works is that all who are made children of God by faith and baptism should come together to praise God in the midst of His Church, to take part in her sacrifice, and to eat the Lord's supper" (*Sacrosanctum concilium,* no. 10).

It is important to remember that the liturgical life of the Church belongs to all the faithful. And you the laity make up the vast portion of God's people. There are, of course, different roles, different ministries, but everyone is called to active participation in the public worship of God's great majesty. One of the special blessings of the Council—brought about by the call to liturgical renewal—was not only the encouragement for greater involvement by the laity in special liturgical roles, but also the encouragement of active participation by all. The Church rejoices in this development which has enriched her life and made the laity more aware of their Christian dignity and of their vocation to worship God, in union with Christ, in holiness of life.

In the context of the sacred liturgy, I wish to say a word about the unique place that Sunday occupies in the weekly rhythm of life. In a very real sense, this is the Lord's Day, the day when the Church throughout the world commemorates the death and resurrection of Christ. From the beginning, the Church has sought to keep the Lord's Day holy by calling all the faithful together in order to celebrate the Eucharist. All of us need to listen regularly to God's word and be instructed in the teaching of the Church, to give glory and thanks to God, and be nourished with the Bread of Life. And in order that we may enter more easily and fully into the festive nature of the Lord's Day, we need to observe it, as best we can, as a special day of rest.

It is important for society as a whole to recover a renewed sense of the sacredness of Sunday. Even more in the hectic pace of modern life, we need a day set apart, a day to rejoice in God's goodness, a day to worship the Lord together. This worship is an obligation for God's people, yes. But, above all, this worship is an immense privilege: to be able to offer praise and thanksgiving to God, in union with Jesus Christ His Son our Lord.

6. There are many things that you are called to do as Christians. In Halifax I spoke at some length about the various ways in which you the laity are

meant to collaborate in the mission of the Church, about your contribution to building up in justice and holiness of life the Body of Christ. Here this evening I would also offer those observations to your prayerful reflection. But, above all, I wish to call your attention to the great truth that everything you do has meaning because of who you are. And that is why I wish to proclaim to you the dignity that is yours through Baptism and Confirmation, the dignity that is yours as children of God, as brothers and sisters of Christ who live through the power of His death and resurrection. The Lord Jesus lives in you the Catholic laity. He prays in you, acts through you, and communicates to you a share in the holiness of God. This is what my predecessor Leo the Great meant fifteen hundred years ago when he exclaimed: "Recognize, O Christian, your dignity!"

And this gift you must protect and safeguard in yourselves and honor in others. This understanding of your Christian identity—and therefore of your Christian mission—you must pass on with pride to your children. Your Christian dignity must be told and retold through catechesis, because it is the story of God's love revealed in Jesus Christ and kept alive in His Church—kept alive in you, who are called to be God's holy people.

Dear brothers and sisters: "The grace of the Lord Jesus be with you. My love is with you all in Christ Jesus" (1 Cor. 1:23-24).

Always Preserve with Fitting Pride Your Heritage of Faith and Culture

On Sunday, September 16, the Holy Father went by plane to Winnipeg (Manitoba) and there he met the Ukrainian community in the Cathedral of Sts. Vladimir and Olga. After an address by Metropolitan Hermaniuk, the Pope spoke to them in Ukrainian. The following is our translation.

Dear brothers and sisters,

1. It is a joy to be with you today in the Metropolitan Cathedral of Sts. Vladimir and Olga in Winnipeg. I greet you, Archbishop Hermaniuk, my other brothers in the episcopate, and all of you assembled in the name of our Lord Jesus Christ. With joy I note the representations of the Eparchies of Edmonton, Toronto, New Westminster and Saskatoon. Through you I extend cordial greetings to all the faithful of the Ukrainian Catholic Church of the Byzantine Rite and to all the Ukrainian people of Canada. I greet you as a fellow Slav, sharing to a large degree in your spirit and heritage. I am especially happy to be with you as we draw near to the solemn

celebration of the First Millennium of Christianity in the Ukraine. In you I embrace in the charity of Christ all the people of your homeland, together with their history, culture, and the heroism with which they have lived their faith. *Slava Isysy Christy!*

Being here with you, I cannot but recall the great man, the confessor of the faith, Major Archbishop and Cardinal Slipyj, whom God has called to eternity. His death has enveloped us in great sorrow. He was the worthy successor of the holy Metropolitan Andrii Sheptytskyj. In the period of difficulty for the Ukrainian Catholic Church, he underwent considerable sufferings and pain, but he was not crushed. Instead, like a hero, he resisted with dignity. When he became free, he lived in Rome and continued to work with dedication for the good of the Church and his people. As Major Archbishop he visited the various groups of Catholics spread throughout the whole world. He attended to the sciences, founded the San Clemente Center for Higher Studies, and published documents and many other works.

In our prayers let us invoke the Lord to reward him for his sufferings, for his fidelity to God and the Church, and for all the work he carried out.

May he remain in perpetual memory.

A GREAT SPIRITUAL TRADITION IS YOURS

2. As Ukrainian Byzantine Catholics, you have inherited a great spiritual tradition, extending back a thousand years to the time of St. Olga and her grandson St. Vladimir. Who could have known then,

how that faith would grow so organically with your culture, and how it would have such a major impact on your history as it brought the grace of the Redemption into the lives of your ancestors? So much could be said about this history, which not infrequently was linked with that of my own native land, but since time presses on, I must limit myself to recalling only a few important moments of your difficult yet noble past.

Events of every time and place are directed by the loving plan of God, for God is the Lord of history. In a special way God's Providence has guided your development in Canada. The Archeparchy of Winnipeg, which is only the third Metropolitan See in the history of the Ukrainian people, was erected here in 1956, just forty-four years after you were given your first bishop. This ecclesiastical province, like that small mustard seed of the Gospel, has quickly grown and flourished. When Ukrainian immigrants first came to this land, they brought with them a strong Catholic faith and a firm attachment to their religious and cultural traditions. They placed a high priority on the construction of their churches and schools, desiring to preserve this precious heritage and pass it on to their children. They sank deep roots into Canadian soil and quickly became productive and loyal citizens.

At the same time, a number of generous people greatly assisted the new immigrants. As soon as it was possible, the Metropolitan of Lwow, the Servant of God, Andrii Sheptytskyj, sent zealous priests to minister to their needs. He himself came on a visit in 1910 and prepared the way for the appointment of

Bishop Budka, the first of your many zealous bishops in this land. It is important, too, to remember the contributions made by many local Latin Rite bishops and priests, some of whom dedicated as much attention and care to Ukrainians as to the faithful of their own rite. The presence here today of the Latin Rite bishops is a sign of continuing harmony and collaboration. "Behold, how good it is, and how pleasant, when brethren dwell at one" (Ps. 133:1).

Your own Byzantine clergy, together with your men and women religious, contributed greatly to your adjustment and growth in this land. Religious such as the Basilian, Redemptorist and Studite Fathers, and the Sisters Servants of Mary Immaculate have staffed parishes, hospitals, schools and many other institutions. All of these have served to protect and strengthen family life, offer assistance to the sick and needy, and contribute to the betterment of society.

APPRECIATION
OF PRECIOUS HERITAGE

3. Our meeting today, taking place as it does on the threshold of the solemn celebration of the Millennium of Christianity in Kiev and the entire Ukraine, carries our minds and hearts back through the centuries of your glorious history of faith. We feel deep gratitude to God, in a special way, for the grace of fidelity to the Catholic Church and loyalty to the Successor of St. Peter which was bestowed on your forebears. As Archbishop of Krakow I came to

know and appreciate this precious heritage of the Ukrainian people, as seen particularly in the martyrs of Cholm and Pidlassia who followed the example of St. Josaphat, a great apostle of unity, and as seen also in the pastoral zeal of so many of your bishops, down to the present day.

These great men and women of Ukrainian history encourage you today to live your Catholic faith with equal fervor and zeal. They inspire you, too, to work and pray without ceasing for the unity of all Christians. In the many and varied ecumenical efforts of the Church, members of the Byzantine Rite like yourselves have a special role to play in regard to the Eastern Christians who are not in full communion with the See of Peter.

You are in a privileged position to fulfill that request of the Second Vatican Council which is expressed in the Decree on Ecumenism, namely: "Everyone should realize that it is of supreme importance to understand, venerate, preserve and foster the rich liturgical and spiritual heritage of the Eastern Churches in order faithfully to preserve the fullness of Christian tradition, and to bring about reconciliation between Eastern and Western Christians" (*Unitatis redintegratio*, no. 15). Your Ukrainian heritage and your Byzantine spirituality, theology and liturgy prepare you well for this important task of fostering reconciliation and full communion. May the hearts of all Bishops, priests, religious and laity be filled with a burning desire that the prayer of Christ be realized: "May they all be one. Father, may they be one in us, as you are in me and I am in you, so that the world may believe it was you who sent me" (Jn. 17:21).

But this desire for unity will be realized only if it goes hand in hand with a sincere fraternal love towards all, a love like that of Christ which is without limit or exception. Such Christian love will open our hearts to the light of divine truth. It will help to clarify the differences which still divide Christians, foster constructive dialogue and mutual understanding, and thereby further the salvation of souls and the unity of all in Christ. And we must remember that this Christian love is nurtured by prayer and penance.

4. Dear brothers and sisters: It is good to be with you today. I rejoice to see your children dressed in your beautiful national costumes, and to know that your young people are growing up with a grateful awareness of their ethnic origins and religious roots. I join you in thanking God for the many institutions and traditions which aid and strengthen the bonds of your families, which are the foundation of the Church and society. May you always preserve with fitting pride the heritage of faith and culture which is yours. I place this intention, together with all your prayers, before the Immaculate Virgin Mary, Queen of the Ukraine, asking her to protect you with her motherly love and lead you ever closer to her divine Son, Jesus Christ the Redeemer of the world. Beloved friends: in the words of the Apostle Peter: "Peace to all of you who are in Christ" (1 Pt. 5:14).

How Great Is the Need for Forgiveness and Reconciliation in Our World Today

After his visit to the Ukrainian Cathedral of Sts. Vladimir and Olga, Sunday, September 16, the Holy Father went to Saint Mary's Cathedral in Winnipeg for the recitation of the Angelus, before which he offered the following reflections in English.

Dear brothers and sisters,

1. At this midday hour, we gather in the Cathedral of St. Mary to pray the Angelus together. The Lord invites us to pause for a moment, and, in the company of the Blessed Virgin Mary and all the saints, to ponder the mystery of the Redemption and to lift our voices in praise of the Most Holy Trinity. It is a joy to be with you here in Winnipeg, and especially to join in prayer with the local Catholic community. I greet you all in the peace and love of Christ, and I extend cordial greetings to all the beloved people of this city and of the province of Manitoba.

In the Gospel of this Twenty-fourth Sunday of Ordinary Time, Peter asks Jesus the questions: "'Lord, how often shall my brother sin against me, and I forgive him? As many as seven times?' Jesus said to him, 'I do not say to you seven times, but seventy times seven'" (Mt. 18:21-22).

"Seventy times seven": with this reply the Lord wants to make it clear to Peter and to us that we should set no limit to our forgiveness of others. Just as the Lord is always ready to forgive us, so we must always be ready to forgive one another. And how great is the need for forgiveness and reconciliation in our world today—indeed in our communities and families, in our very own hearts! That is why the special sacrament of the Church for forgiveness, the Sacrament of Penance, is such a precious gift from the Lord.

2. In the Sacrament of Penance, God extends His forgiveness to us in a very personal way. Through the ministry of the priest, we come to our loving Savior with the burden of our sins. We confess that we have sinned against God and our neighbor. We manifest our sorrow and ask for pardon from the Lord. Then, through the priest, we hear Christ say to us: "Your sins are forgiven" (Mk. 2:5); "Go, and do not sin again" (Jn. 8:11). Can we not also hear Him say to us as we are filled with His saving grace: "Extend to others, seventy times seven, this same forgiveness and mercy"?

3. This is the work of the Church in every age— it is the duty of each one of us—"to profess and proclaim God's mercy in all its truth" (Dives in misericordia, no. 13), to extend to whomever we meet each day the same unlimited forgiveness that we

have received from Christ. We practice mercy, too, when we "bear with one another charitably in complete selflessness, gentleness and patience" (Eph. 4:2). And God's mercy is also shown by generous and untiring service, like that required in offering health care for the sick or in carrying out medical research with persevering dedication. On this occasion I wish to encourage all of you who are so committed to this ministry of mercy, and I thank you for your individual contributions in the field of health care. At the same time I would urge the whole community to be ever mindful of its own responsibility for this important sector of human activity.

On this day of the Lord when we celebrate the fullest expression of God's abundant mercy—the cross and resurrection of Christ—let us praise our God who is rich in mercy. And, in imitation of His great love, let us forgive anyone who may have hurt us in any way. With the Blessed Mother of God, we proclaim the mercy of God which extends from generation to generation.

In the Civil Order, Too, the Gospel Is at the Service of Harmony

On Sunday afternoon, September 16, the Holy Father offered Mass "for civil needs" in Bird's Hill Park in Winnipeg. The following is the text of his homily on that occasion.

"You shall love the Lord your God with all your heart, and with all your soul, and with all your might" (Dt. 6:5).

Dear brothers and sisters in Christ,

1. This commandment, the greatest one, was proclaimed in the Old Testament to Israel alone. It was the first and the greatest commandment of the Old Covenant that God made with the Chosen People. He gave it through Moses after the liberation from slavery in Egypt. The Covenant, which was linked to the commandments, placed on all Israelites the obligations inherent in belonging to the People of God.

The first reading of today's liturgy speaks to us in a very detailed way of how the Israelites were to know and put into practice "the commandments, the statutes and the ordinances" (Dt. 6:1) which God had taught through Moses. The Israelites were to pass them on and teach them to their children and to all the generations to come, both during the journey towards the Promised Land and when they would be living there.

"You shall bind them as a sign upon your hand, and they shall be as frontlets between your eyes. And you shall write them on the doorposts of your house and on your gates" (Dt. 6:8-9).

The Covenant with God became a fundamental source of the spiritual identity of Israel as a nation among the other peoples and nations of the earth.

2. The second reading, from St. Paul's first letter to the Thessalonians, introduces us into the dimension of the New Covenant. This Covenant is new and everlasting. It was brought about in the flesh and blood of Christ, by His death on the cross and by the resurrection, and it is universal. It is open to all the peoples and nations of the earth. For the Apostles have been sent to everyone to proclaim the Gospel: "Go therefore and make disciples of all nations, baptizing them in the name of the Father and of the Son and of the Holy Spirit" (Mt. 28:19).

St. Paul can therefore write to the Thessalonians saying: "It was God who decided that we were fit to be entrusted with the Good News, and when we are speaking, we are not trying to please men but God, who can read our inmost thoughts.... We felt so devoted and protective toward you, and had come to love you so much, that we were eager to hand over to you not only the Good News but our whole lives as well" (1 Thes. 2:4, 8).

The Gospel has become—and always continues to become—the source of spiritual culture for men and women of different nations, tongues and races. It has also become the basis of the individuality and cultural identity of many peoples and nations throughout the world.

This statement takes on singular eloquence in Canada, where, through immigration, a varied inheritance of peoples, nations and cultures becomes the common good of the whole of society.

THE GOOD OF SOCIETY

3. God's commandment to Israel expresses the good of society. Its fulfillment is the condition on which all cultural identity is consolidated, and without which there can be no lasting and effective multicultural community. God's word expressed through Moses brings with it a promise and constitutes a charter of hope for all society: "If you keep all his laws and commandments which I lay on you, you will have a long life.... Listen then, Israel, and keep and observe what will make you prosper and give you great increase" (Dt. 6:2-3).

It is in the perspective of faith that we perceive how much the Word of God—brought to fulfillment in the Gospel—contributes to the building and preservation of cultures. And we see how necessary it is to fulfill the Gospel message in order to succeed in harmonizing cultures in a pluralistic unity. In the civil order too, the Gospel is at the service of harmony. To detach culture from its link to the Gospel commandment of love would be to make impossible the multicultural interplay which is characteristic of Canada. The Church speaks to us repeatedly of the need to evangelize in depth man's culture and cultures, "always taking the person as one's starting-point and always coming back to the relationships of people among themselves and with God" (Evangelii nuntiandi, no. 20). At the same time we are alerted that "the split between the Gospel and culture is without a doubt the drama of our time" (ibid.).

The historical experience of the two founding peoples of Canada who bound themselves to live in mutual respect for the unique cultural identity of each other has providentially created that atmosphere of respect for cultural diversity which characterizes Canada today. In her own multicultural interaction, Canada not only offers to the world a creative vision of society, but she also has a splendid opportunity to show consistency between what she believes and what she does. And this is accomplished by applying Christ's commandment of love.

4. Manitoba itself truly reflects a variety of many different cultures. Besides its population of British origin and French origin—in addition to native peoples—so many other Western countries are represented here. Immigration from Western and Eastern Europe, Asia, Africa and South America contributes to making up the reality of this civil society. Latin and Ukrainian ecclesial jurisdictions compose one Catholic Church. Today I greet in a special way the Church of Winnipeg with its pastor, Archbishop Exner; the Archdiocese of Winnipeg of the Ukrainians led by Archbishop Hermaniuk; and the faithful of the Arch-

diocese of St. Boniface under the pastoral leadership of Archbishop Hacault. My greetings go to the diocesan delegations of the faithful from Saskatchewan. I greet Archbishop Halpin of Regina and the Bishops of the suffragan dioceses of Prince Albert, Saskatoon and Gravelbourg. I acknowledge with deep gratitude the presence of the high civil officials, including the former Governor-General of Canada, the Right Honorable Edward Schreyer, the Lieutenant Governor and Premier of Manitoba and the Lieutenant Governor of Saskatchewan. Yes, you come from almost "every tribe and tongue, people and nation" (Rev. 5:9). And this is expressed in our liturgical assembly today, not only through different languages but also through the different liturgical traditions of Christianity, both in the West and the East. In this Eucharist the Church in Canada celebrates her diversity and proclaims her unity in Christ and in the universal Church.

THE COMMAND TO LOVE

5. Against the broad background of history and culture, the first and most important commandment which Moses transmitted to the one Chosen People of the Old Covenant takes on a fresh eloquence in our times.

Jesus Christ says: "This is my commandment: love one another as I have loved you" (Jn. 15:12).

The commandment of love is rooted, in a new way, in love of God: "As the Father has loved me, so I have loved you. Remain in my love. If you keep my commandments, you will remain in my love, just as I have kept my Father's commandments and remain in his love" (Jn. 15:9-10).

Therefore, love of God above all things is a sharing in Christ's love—the love whereby Christ loves.

And at the same time: love of God is organically linked with love for others—with mutual love. This love makes us Christ's friends. "I shall not call you servants anymore.... I call you friends" (Jn. 15:15).

This love is a moral and existential expression of the election and calling by Christ "to go out and to bear fruit, fruit that will last; and then the Father will give you anything you ask him in my name" (Jn. 15:16).

BASED ON RESPECT

6. The pluralism of traditions, pluralism of cultures, pluralism of histories, pluralism of national identities—all of these are compatible with the unity of society.

Today we pray for the moral unity of this society—since this unity is the foundation and common denominator of all "civil needs."

From the most ancient times, Christianity has educated people—witnesses for Christ—to have a sense of responsibility for the common good of society. This is equally true when society has clearly pluralistic characteristics. The importance of the Church's teaching in this regard has been summarized by the Second Vatican Council in the penetrating words: "Let there be no false opposition between professional and social activities on the one part, and the practice of religion on the other. The Christian who neglects his temporal duties neglects his duties toward his neighbor and even God, and jeopardizes his eternal salvation" (*Gaudium et spes*, no. 43).

At the basis of this teaching is the commandment of mutual love which today's Gospel speaks about. Mutual love means, in its fundamental dimension, the relationship between human beings based on respect for the personal dignity of the other person and on real care for his or her true good.

Mutual love has particular importance for the formation of the community of marriage and the family. And then that mutual love extends to many different circles and levels of human coexistence: in different environments, communities, societies, and between societies.

In this sense this love is "social," and constitutes the essential condition for the formation of the civilization of love proclaimed by the Church, and especially by Paul VI.

MULTICULTURAL NATION

7. In this great region of Canada, mutual love between all the different communities that make up the multicultural character of this pluralistic society becomes an immense power for good. The mutual love that uplifts and unites the individual elements enables all of them, when put together, to be a particularly effective instrument of service to humanity. Love makes it possible for a vast series of talents to produce a united action. Through this united action, a multicultural society is then able to place at

the disposal of others all those blessings which it has so bountifully received.

Remember, O Canada, that the greatest richness of your multicultural character is to be able to reach out and help others—your brothers and sisters in need. This is what faith makes possible; this is what love requires. In the name of love I urge that the openness shown to so many immigrants and refugees of ethnic minorities, and the generous reception given to them, should continue to characterize and enrich Canada in the future as in the past.

PROPHETIC WORDS

In this regard it is worthwhile to recall those prophetic words of John XXIII: "The best interests of justice are served by those public authorities who do all they can to improve the human conditions of the members of ethnic minorities, especially in what concerns their language, culture, customs, and their economic activity and enterprises" (*Pacem in terris*, AAS no. 55, 1963, p. 283). This contribution of public authority must be coupled by the active efforts of all individuals and groups to continue to build a socially just Canadian society—a lasting civilization of love in which are ensured "the priority of ethics over technology, the primacy of the person over things, and the superiority of spirit over matter" (*Redemptor hominis*, no. 16)—and all this for the glory of God, who is the Father of us all.

Let us pray for this intention, especially in this Eucharistic assembly, and through this prayer let us unite ourselves with Christ. Truly, we wish to accept His invitation: "Remain in my love." Amen.

Vatican Translation

God Also Acts Through the Community of People Whom He Predestined To Be His Own

After a two-hour flight from Winnipeg to Edmonton, capital of the Province of Alberta, on Sunday evening, September 16, the Holy Father went to St. Joseph's Cathedral for an ecumenical prayer meeting. In attendance were Bishops and priests of the region, representatives of religious, and some two hundred representatives of other Christian denominations. The Pope addressed the group in English and French as follows.

Dear brothers and sisters,

My fellow Christians, and all of you who have come here this evening in order to pay honor to the mystery of God,

1. On this Sunday evening in Edmonton, the evening of the first day of the week when we Christians celebrate the resurrection of the Lord, we come together in prayer in this beautiful Cathedral of St. Joseph. We are gathered in the joy of our common Baptism, in the power of the Word of God, and in the peace and love of Christ, whom we proclaim as the Light of the world and the supreme manifestation of

God. I invite you all to reflect with me this evening on the mystery of the presence of God.

As men and women of faith, we believe that God is present in His creation, that He is the Lord of history who directs the times and the seasons, that He is near to all who call upon Him: the poor and the dejected, the sorrowing and the lonely, the weak and the oppressed. We believe that God breaks through the silence, and even the noise, of our daily lives, revealing to us His truth and His love. He wishes to dispel our fear and strengthen our hope in His saving mercy.

God personally speaks to the heart of every individual, but He also acts through the community of people whom He predestines to be His own. We see this first in the history of the Jewish people. Through Abraham, our Father in faith, through Isaac and Jacob, and in particular through Moses, God called a people to belong to Him in a special way. He entered into a covenant with them, saying: "I will be their God and they shall be my people" (Jer. 31:33). When His chosen ones sinned and went their own way, forgetting the God who saved them, God in His never-ending love intervened in their lives by means of the prophets. He called the people to repentance and promised to establish with them a new and better covenant. This New Covenant He described in this way: "Deep within them I will plant my law, writing it on their hearts.... They will all know me, the least no less than the greatest, since I will forgive their iniquity and never call their sin to mind" (Jer. 31:33-34).

And how did God establish this New Covenant? How did He write His law on the hearts of His chosen ones? With the blood of Jesus, the blood of the Lamb of God, the blood of the new and everlasting Covenant, our Savior's blood, which is the price of our Redemption and the most eloquent expression possible of the love of God for the world.

THE PRESENCE OF GOD IN JESUS OF NAZARETH

2. The presence of God is embodied in its fullness in Jesus of Nazareth, the Son of God who became the Son of Mary and who shed His blood for us on the cross. Jesus is Emmanuel, God with us, the Word made flesh, the revelation of the eternal Father. Before this great mystery of the presence of God, we stand in awe and reverence, and our hearts and voices long to break forth in songs and hymns of praise. And indeed this is most appropriate, for the first duty of a creature is to glorify the Creator, the first duty of a redeemed people is to praise their Lord and Savior. That is why I am so pleased to join you tonight in this evening service of praise. How good it is, as brothers and sisters in Christ, to join our voices in "psalms and hymns and inspired songs!" (Col. 3:16)

Psalm 103, which we are praying together this evening, shows us a person whose whole being is filled with the praise of God:

"My soul, give thanks to the Lord,
all my being, bless his holy name.

My soul, give thanks to the Lord
and never forget all his blessings" (vvs. 1-2).

"Never forget all his blessings": a heart filled
with praise never forgets the many blessings of God.
For the prayer of praise involves an act of remembering with gratitude, remembering all the ways that
God has shown His saving love. And so the psalmist
declares:

"It is he who forgives all your guilt,
who heals every one of your ills,
who redeems your life from the grave,
who crowns you with love and compassion,
who fills your life with good things,
renewing your youth like an eagle's" (vvs. 3-5).

The prayer of praise proceeds from a humble
awareness of our unworthiness and our total dependence on God, combined with a childlike trust in
God's abundant mercy. And so the psalmist continues:

"As a father has compassion on his sons,
the Lord has pity on those who fear him.
For he knows of what we are made,
he remembers that we are dust" (vv. 13-14).

To praise the Lord is also to acclaim the many
attributes of God, to extol the qualities of this great
and holy God who has established a covenant with
His people. Thus the psalmist says:

"The Lord is compassion and love,
slow to anger and rich in mercy....

His justice reaches out to children's children
when they keep his covenant in truth"
        (vvs. 8, 17-18).

3. Living in the presence of God, Christians
break forth in acclamation and praise, expressing
gratitude for the gift of faith and for all the saving
deeds of the Lord. But we must also turn to God with
prayers of petition, seeking from the Lord shelter and
safety from the forces of evil, forgiveness of our sins
and healing of our wounded lives, strength to bear
life's burdens and grace to fulfill God's will. Often the
prayer of petition must be made with a sense of
urgency and pleading. And so, the man in Psalm 141
cries out:

"I have called to you, Lord; hasten to help me!
Hear my voice when I cry to you....
To you, Lord God, my eyes are turned:
in you I take refuge, spare my soul!" (vvs. 1, 8)

The prayer of petition springs from a humble
awareness of one's great need for God's grace, and
from a deep trust in the powerful mercy of God.
Thus, it is accompanied by an attitude of adoration.
We kneel, at least in spirit, in the awesome presence
of Almighty God, and the words that we utter are like
those of the psalmist who pleads:

"Let my prayer arise before you like incense
the raising of my hands like an evening
        oblation" (Ps. 141:2).

JOINED IN PRAYER

4. Our Savior promised us: "Where two or three meet in my name, I shall be there with them" (Mt. 18:20). We know that this is true this evening as we Christians join together in common prayer. The presence of Christ fills this Cathedral as we praise His name, and as we pray for that perfect unity among Christians which He wills for His followers.

Since true prayer overflows into generous service, we are not unmindful this evening of the great needs of our brothers and sisters who suffer throughout the world. In faithful response to the Lord, whose Holy Spirit has inspired the ecumenical movement, not only do we pray together and enter into theological dialogue, but we also engage in efforts of joint collaboration to promote a more just and peaceful world. We seek to become, and help one another to be, "the salt of the earth" and "the light of the world" (cf. Mt. 5:11-16). In this way, we proclaim together the Good News of God's presence in the world in the person of Jesus Christ, who is one with His Church.

MARY, WOMAN OF FAITH AND OUR MODEL

5. The beautiful prayer known as the *Magnificat* which we pray together this evening directs our minds to God and His saving presence in human history. It also turns our attention to Mary, the Mother of our Savior. This woman of faith remains for us today a model of holiness of life. In a special way, she experienced the presence of God in her life

when she became the Mother of our Redeemer. As a woman whose heart was filled with praise, she extolled the greatness of God, proclaiming His goodness to the poor and lowly and telling of His mercy towards every generation. Together with Mary we join our voices to praise "the greatness of the Lord" (Lk. 1:46).

We do this above all in union with Jesus Christ, who remains for ever the Light of the world, and who offers us the light of life (cf. Jn. 8:12). Dearly beloved friends: let us receive this light from Him and walk in this light, for the glory of His Father, who lives and reigns with the Holy Spirit, for ever and ever. Amen.

The Poor South
Will Judge the Rich North

In Edmonton's airport in Namao, on Monday, September 17, Pope John Paul II celebrated Mass dedicated to the theme of development of peoples and solidarity. More than 150,000 faithful attended the Mass, belonging to the dioceses of the Latin and Ukrainian Rites of Edmonton and representing the ecclesial communities of the Province of Alberta and neighboring provinces, many of whom were immigrants and refugees from the Third World.

During the Liturgy of the Word the Holy Father delivered the following homily in English and French.

"I will hear what the Lord God has to say,
a voice that speaks of peace.
Mercy and faithfulness have met;
justice and peace have embraced"
(Ps. 84[85]:8, 10).

Dear brothers and sisters in Christ,

1. These are words of today's liturgy, taken from the responsorial psalm. The God of the covenant is a God of peace. Peace on earth is a good that belongs to His kingdom and to His salvation. This good is obtained in justice and faithfulness to the divine

commandments. This good, which is peace, is promised to us in different spheres: as the interior good of our conscience, as the good of our human living together, and finally as a social and international good.

This last meaning was above all what Paul VI had in mind when he wrote these memorable words: "The new name for peace is *development*." And he wrote these words in the Encyclical *Populorum progressio* (no. 87).

2. Today we come together here in Edmonton to make this theme of the development or progress of peoples the principal object of our meditations and prayers in the Eucharistic Sacrifice. In this Eucharistic community is gathered first of all the whole Church of the Archdiocese of Edmonton. And I wish indeed to greet this church with its pastor, Archbishop MacNeil, as well as the Eparchy of Edmonton of the Ukrainians, together with Bishop Savaryn and Bishop Greschuk. I also acknowledge with deep gratitude the presence of the large group of faithful from Saskatchewan, who have brought their crosses to be blessed. I likewise embrace in the love of Christ Jesus our Lord all the pilgrims and visitors. The refugees from Central America, Southeast Asia and Eastern Europe have a special place in my heart. I wish to greet all those who have come from other dioceses of Alberta—from Grouard-McLellan, Calgary and St. Paul—also from British Colombia and the Northwest Territories, as well as visitors from the United States. Likewise, I greet each ethnic and cultural group, including the German-speaking,

Ukrainian, Italian, Portuguese, Spanish; Lithuanian, Slovak, Slovene, Croatian, Hungarian and Polish; the Filipinos, Chinese, Korean and Vietnamese. To all of you who are here today: grace and peace in Jesus Christ, the Son of God and Savior of the world.

Considering our theme, I think that in a certain sense all Canada shares in this meeting at Edmonton. If the theme was proposed by the local community, it was certainly done so with a thought towards the whole society for which the cause of the development of peoples is a question of greatest importance and social and international responsibility. Especially since this "development" or "progress" is the new name for "peace."

JUDGMENT GIVEN TO THE SON

3. The liturgy leads us to consider this important theme, first of all, as it is presented in the twenty-fifth chapter of St. Matthew's Gospel.

We have listened today to the Gospel about the final judgment with the same emotion as always. This passage touches some of the most fundamental questions of our faith and morality. These two fields are strictly linked to each other. Perhaps no other passage in the Gospel speaks of their relationship in such a convincing way.

Our faith in Jesus Christ finds here a kind of final expression: "The Father judges no one, but has given all judgment to the Son" (Jn. 5:22). In today's Gospel Christ stands before us as our Judge. He has a special right to make this judgment; indeed He became one of us, our Brother. This brotherhood with the human race—and at the same time His brotherhood with every single person—has led Him to the cross and the resurrection. Thus He judges in the name of His solidarity with each person and likewise in the name of our solidarity with Him, who is our Brother and Redeemer and whom we discover in every human being: "I was hungry.... I was thirsty.... I was a stranger,...naked,...sick,...in prison..." (Mt. 25:35-36).

And those called to judgment—on His right hand and on His left—will ask: When and where? When and where have we seen You like this? When and where have we done what You said? Or: When and where have we not done it?

The answer: "Truly, I say to you, as you did it to one of the least of these my brethren, you did it to me" (Mt. 25:40). And, on the contrary: "As you did it *not* to one of the least of these, you did it *not* to me" (Mt. 25:24).

INJUSTICE AND EVIL

4. "To one of the least of these my brethren." Thus: to man, to an individual human being in need.

Yet, the Second Vatican Council, following the whole of Tradition, warns us not to stop at an "individualistic" interpretation of Christian ethics, since Christian ethics also has its social dimension. The human person lives in a community, in society. And with the community he shares hunger and thirst and sickness and malnutrition and misery and all the deficiencies that result therefrom. In his or her own person the human being is meant to experience the needs of others.

So it is that Christ the Judge speaks of "one of the least of the brethren," and at the same time He is speaking of each and of all.

Yes. He is speaking of the whole universal dimension of injustice and evil. He is speaking of what today we are accustomed to call the North-South contrast. Hence not only East-West, but also North-South: the increasingly wealthier North, and the increasingly poorer South.

Yes, the South—becoming always poorer; and the North—becoming always richer. Richer too in the resources of weapons with which the superpowers and blocs can mutually threaten each other. And they threaten each other—such an argument also exists— in order not to destroy each other.

This is a separate dimension—and according to the opinion of many it is the dimension in the forefront—of the deadly threat which hangs over the modern world, which deserves separate attention.

Nevertheless, in the light of Christ's words, this poor South will judge the rich North. And the poor people and poor nations—poor in different ways, not only lacking food, but also deprived of freedom and other human rights—will judge those people who take these goods away from them, amassing to themselves the imperialistic monopoly of economic and political supremacy at the expense of others.

THE FINAL JUDGMENT

5. The Gospel of today's liturgy is very rich in content. It is relevant to the different spheres of injustice and human evil. In the midst of each

of these situations stands Christ Himself, and as Redeemer and Judge He says: "You did it to me," "you did it not to me."

Nevertheless He wishes, in this final judgment—which is constantly in preparation and which in a certain sense is constantly present—to bear witness first of all to the good that has been done.

And here also that significant expression of the teaching of the Church takes a start, whose principal formulation became the Encyclical *Populorum progressio*. What was the inner concern of Paul VI and the universal Church became a dynamic action and a loud appeal that echoes to this day: "It is not just a matter of eliminating hunger, or even of reducing poverty. The struggle against destitution, though urgent and necessary, is not enough. It is a question, rather, of building a world where every man, no matter what his race, religion or nationality, can live a fully human life, freed from servitude imposed on him by other men or by natural forces; a world where freedom is not an empty word and where the poor man Lazarus can sit down at the same table with the rich man" (no. 47).

Yes, *development* is the new name for peace. Peace is necessary; it is an imperative of our time. And so is this development or progress: the progress of all the disadvantaged.

LINK BETWEEN JUSTICE AND PEACE

6. Today we pray in this spirit. Today's liturgy emphasizes very clearly the link between justice and peace.

In front of the Basilica of St. Anne de Beaupré, the Pope addressed a group of Amerindians and Innuits.

The interior of the Basilica of St. Anne de Beaupré.

A touching attitude of Pope John Paul with a little Indian child.

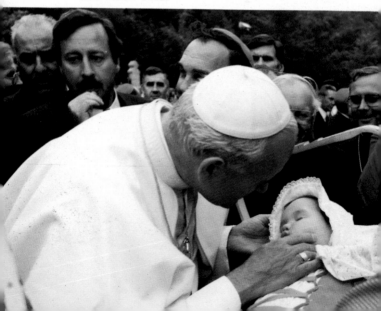

Gifts for the Pope from a little Indian girl.

Some Indian elders present a souvenir to
Pope John Paul II.

A short visit to the "Chapel of the Rosary," or the so-called Old Sanctuary. This was the first Chapel in honor of Notre-Dame-du-Cap. Today there is a spacious Sanctuary.

In Montreal, Pope John Paul is welcomed by the crowd before entering the Archbishop's residence.

The Pope's arrival at Montreal's Basilica, Mary, Queen of the World.

The Pope in prayer at the Grotto of Our Lady of Lourdes in Flatrock, Newfoundland.

After the Eucharistic Celebration in Newfoundland the Pope meets the priest-concelebrants.

The Pope deeply in touch with God during the Eucharistic Celebration at Quidi Vidi Lake, Newfoundland.

Shaking hands after the ceremony at Flatrock.

At Memorial University, St. John's,
Newfoundland, the Pope received a parka as
a gift from the young people attending the meeting.

The Pope greeted the Anglican Bishop before entering St. Paul's Anglican Church for an ecumenical prayer service.

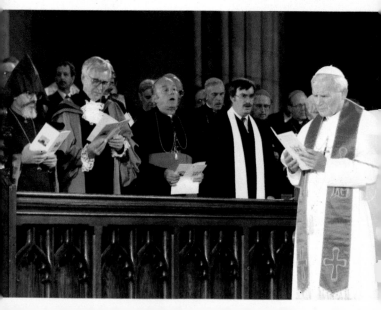

During the visit to the historical village in Huronia, Ontario, the Pope greeted Indians and gave them rosaries.

The Holy Father also greeted other persons in the village including the organizers of the tour.

In Edmonton after an ecumenical prayer service in St. Joseph's Cathedral, Pope John Paul II greeted representatives of various Christian Churches.

After the Eucharistic Celebration at Namao, Edmonton, the Pope waves goodbye to the crowd.

New Edmonton, Alberta. Woods and lakes with unlimited horizons... Through nature we come to contemplation, prayer, meditation—we come to God. What a beautiful example from our Pope.

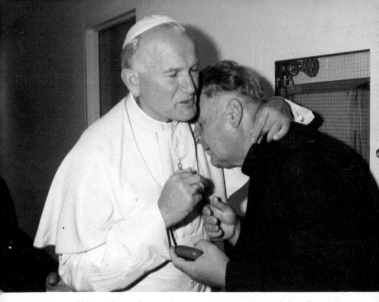

Warmth and emotion; a priest meets John Paul II.

At British Columbia Stadium, Vancouver, the Pope receives an Indian symbol which enables him to speak with authority in an assembly, according to an Indian tradition.

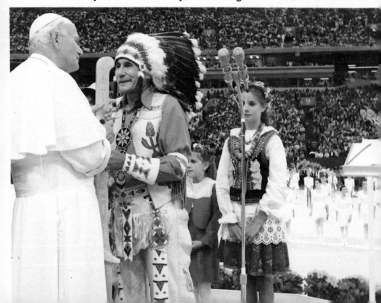

Look at the first reading from Isaiah: "There will be poured on us the spirit from above.... Integrity will bring peace, justice will give lasting security. My people will live in a peaceful home, in safe houses, in quiet dwellings" (Is. 32:15, 17-18).

This was written by the prophet centuries before Christ. How lasting and unchanging are the desires of individuals and peoples!

And later on, after Christ, the Apostle Paul writes in the letter to the Philippians: "And the peace of God, which passes all understanding, will keep your hearts and your minds in Christ Jesus" (Phil. 4:7).

Yet the condition for such peace is human behavior in every dimension of existence. Hence, St. Paul continues: "Fill your minds with everything that is true, everything that is noble, everything that is good and pure, everything that we love and honor, and everything that can be thought virtuous or worthy of praise. Keep doing all the things that you learned from me and have been taught by me and have heard or seen that I do. Then the God of peace will be with you" (Phil. 4:8-9).

PROGRESS OF PEOPLES

7. Today we are praying in Canada, in the city of Edmonton, for the progress of peoples. Hence, according to the words of Pope Paul VI we are praying for peace because we are praying for what constitutes its contemporary meaning. The words of the prophet Isaiah and of the Apostle to the Gentiles

indicate the same thing. This is what we are praying for as we celebrate this Eucharist and share in it.

May our prayer pierce the heavens! May the God of peace be with us!

May the God of peace be with us! This cry brings with it the whole drama of our age, the whole threat. The nuclear threat? Certainly!

But even more: the whole threat of injustice, the threat coming from the rigid structures of those systems which man is not able to pass through—those systems which do not open themselves so as to permit themselves to go out towards man, to go out towards the development of peoples, to go out towards justice, with all its requirements, and towards peace.

Is the global balance not perhaps ever increasing—the global balance of what we "have not done for one of the least of the brethren"? For millions of the least of the brethren? For billions?

This must also be said here, in Canada, which is as vast as a continent. And at the same time here, from this very place, it must likewise be said to all people of good will, and to all groups, communities, organizations, institutions, nations and governments, that everything we "have done" and what we will still do, what we will plan and will do with ever greater energy and determination—all of this really matters.

And the balance is increasing and must increase of what we "have done" for one person, for millions, for billions: the balance of good in human history.

The judgment spoken of in today's Gospel is constantly being prepared and is already taking place: What you did for one...for millions...for billions, "you did it to me"!

May the God of peace be with us, here in Canada and everywhere.

May justice and peace embrace (cf. Ps. 84[85]:10) once again at the end of the second millennium which prepares us for the coming of Christ, in glory. Amen.

Vatican Translation

I Proclaim Freedom
for a Just and Fair Measure
of Self-Determination
in Your Lives as People

On Tuesday, September 18, John Paul II flew to Fort Simpson to visit the native population of the Northwest Territories. Because of dense fog over Fort Simpson, the plane was unable to land there and was directed to Yellow Knife. On landing there he recorded before the TV cameras and the radio microphones the message he had intended to deliver at Fort Simpson, and it was broadcast later in the evening.

Dear brothers and sisters,

The conditions of the weather have prevented me from landing in Fort Simpson and being physically present with you.

But nothing can prevent me from being spiritually united with you. Indeed, the present circumstances have increased my desire to be in your midst, to pray with you and tell you personally of my love and affection in Christ Jesus.

I know that you all will understand the suffering that I feel at this time—the suffering of keen disappointment. With these sentiments I wish to read you the message that I have prepared for my visit:

"Grace and peace to you from God our Father and the Lord Jesus Christ" (2 Cor. 1:2).

1. From the bottom of my heart I want to tell you how happy I am to be with you, the native peoples of Canada, in this beautiful land of Denendeh. It is, indeed, an honor for me to be invited to join with you in this deeply moving spiritual celebration, in which many of you taking part are not Catholics.

In you I greet, with esteem and friendship, descendants of the first inhabitants of this land, who have lived here for centuries upon centuries. To greet you is to render respectful homage to the beginnings of human society in this vast region of North America. To greet you is to recall with reverence God's plan and Providence as they have unfolded in your history and brought you to this day. To greet you in this portion of your land is to evoke the events of human living that have taken place on the scene of God's original creation of majestic nature in these parts. At the same time my coming among you looks back to your past in order to proclaim your dignity and support your destiny.

I realize that many of you have made this pilgrimage from all parts of Canada—from the frozen Arctic and the prairie plains, from the forests and the lakehead regions, from the great mountains and coastal waters—from East and West, North and South. I am very pleased that nothing has deterred you from coming to this meeting.

I understand that the major aboriginal organizations—the Assembly of First Nations, the Native Council of Canada, the Innuit Tapirisat of Canada, the Metis National Council—collectively decided to plan this spiritual event in this northern homeland setting. This kind of cooperation, given the diversity of cultural and religious traditions that exist among you, is a sign of hope for building solidarity among the aboriginal peoples of this country.

You have chosen as your general theme for this celebration: "self-determination and the rights of aboriginal peoples." On my part I am pleased to be able to reflect with you on issues that so closely touch your lives.

2. My presence in your midst today is intended to be another expression of the deep interest and solicitude which the Church wishes to show for the native peoples of the New World. In 1537, in a document entitled *Pastorale officium,* my Predecessor Paul III proclaimed the rights of the native peoples of those times. He affirmed their dignity, defended their freedom, asserted that they could not be enslaved or deprived of their goods or ownership. At the same time my presence marks yet another phase in the long relationship that many of you have had with the Church. It is a relationship that spans four centuries and has been especially strong since the mid-nineteenth century. Missionaries from Europe, not only from the Catholic Church but from other Christian traditions, have dedicated their lives to bringing the Gospel message to the aboriginal peoples of Canada.

I know of the gratitude that you yourselves, the Indian, Metis and Innuit peoples, have towards the missionaries who have lived and died among you. What they have done for you is spoken of by the whole Church; it is known by the entire world. These missionaries endeavored to live your life, to be like you in order to serve you and to bring you the saving Gospel of Jesus Christ.

Whatever faults and imperfections they had, whatever mistakes were made, together with whatever harm involuntarily resulted, they are now at pains to repair. But next to this entry, filed in the memory of your history, is the record, with endless proofs, of their fraternal love. Jesus Himself tells us: "A man can have no greater love than to lay down his life for his friends" (Jn. 15:13).

The missionaries remain among your best friends, devoting their lives to your service, as they preach the word of God. Education and health care among you owe much to them, especially to devoted women such as the Grey Nuns of Montreal.

That marvelous rebirth of your culture and traditions which you are experiencing today owes much to the pioneering and continuing efforts of missionaries in linguistics, ethnography and anthropology. Indelibly inscribed with gratitude in your history are names like Lacombe, Grollier, Grandin, Turquetil. The list is long.

3. Today I wish to pay a special tribute to Bishop Paul Piché, who celebrates this year his twenty-fifth anniversary as pastor of this vast diocese. Bishop Piché, the Church thanks you and your confreres—as

do your people—for the communities that you have built by the Word of God and the Sacraments. Through you I thank all the heroic Oblate missionaries whom the love and grace of our Lord Jesus Christ inspired to serve the peoples of the North.

Yes, dear Indians, Innuit and Metis, the missionaries have always shared in your cultural and social life. In keeping with the teaching of the Second Vatican Council, they have striven with greater awareness to show you, as the Church earnestly desires, ever greater respect for your patrimony, your language and your customs (cf. *Ad gentes*, no. 26).

THEY BROUGHT THE WORD

4. It is in this context of esteem and love that they bring you the Gospel of our Lord Jesus Christ, along with its power to solidify your traditions by perfecting them and ennobling them even more. Their evangelization brought with it the proclamation of "the name, the teaching, the life, the promises, the kingdom and the mystery of Jesus of Nazareth, the Son of God" (*Evangelii nuntiandi*, no. 22).

It was the Church herself who sent the missionaries to you, so that you might receive the life-giving and liberating message of Jesus. This message has taken root in your hearts and become incarnate in your society, just as Christ Himself has become Indian, Metis and Innuit in you, His members. I spoke about this important topic last week, both at St. Anne de Beaupré and at Midland.

As they preach the Gospel to you, the missionaries desire to remain close to you in your struggles and problems and in your rightful striving to obtain the full recognition of your human and Christian dignity as aboriginal peoples, as children of God.

PRAISE TO MISSIONARIES

5. On this occasion, as I extol the missionary contribution that has been made over the years, I appeal to the whole Church in Canada to be ever more sensitive to the needs of the missionary North. The Spirit of God is calling the Church throughout this land to exercise the full measure of shared responsibility for the needs of God's people in the vast regions of the North. The power of Christ's Paschal Mystery that has sustained the missionaries of the past and present in total generosity will not desert the young people of today. It is the Lord Jesus Himself who is asking the whole Church in Canada to be faithful to her essential missionary character— without which she cannot exist as the Church of God.

I appeal to the youth among the native peoples to be open to accept leadership roles and respon- sibilities. I likewise appeal to the Catholic youth among you to be open to God's calling to the priesthood and religious life, and I ask all their Catholic elders, leaders and parents to look with honor upon these special vocations and to support and encourage all those who freely wish to embrace this way of life.

6. Today I have come to the beloved native peoples to proclaim anew the Gospel of Jesus Christ and to confirm its requirements. I have come in order to speak once again about your dignity and to renew

to you the Church's friendship and love—a love that is expressed in service and pastoral care. I have come to assure you, and the whole world, of the Church's respect for your ancient patrimony—for your many worthy ancestral customs.

And, yes, dear brothers and sisters, I have come to call you to Christ, to propose again, for you and all Canada, His message of forgiveness and reconciliation. It is clear from the historical record that over the centuries your peoples have been repeatedly the victims of injustice by newcomers who, in their blindness, often saw all your culture as inferior. Today, happily, this situation has been largely reversed, and people are learning to appreciate that there is great richness in your culture, and to treat you with greater respect.

As I mentioned in Midland, the hour has come to bind up wounds, to heal all divisions. It is a time for forgiveness, for reconciliation and for a commitment to building new relationships. Once again in the words of St. Paul: "Now is the favorable time; this is the day of salvation" (2 Cor. 6:2).

7. My predecessor Paul VI explained very clearly that there are close links between the preaching of the Gospel and human advancement. And human advancement includes development and liberation (cf. *Evangelii nuntiandi,* nos. 30-31). And so today, in speaking to you, I present to you the Gospel message with its commandment of fraternal love, with its demands for justice and human rights and with all its liberating power.

St. Paul wanted us all to understand the importance of Christian freedom—freedom from sin and from whatever would enslave us. It is St. Paul who continues to cry out to the world: "When Christ freed us, he meant us to remain free" (Gal. 5:1). At the same time both he and St. Peter propose to us the principle that freedom must not be an excuse for license (cf. Gal. 5:13; 1 Pt. 2:16).

Today I want to proclaim that freedom which is required for a just and equitable measure of self-determination in your own lives as native peoples. In union with the whole Church I proclaim all your rights—and their corresponding duties. And I also condemn physical, cultural and religious oppression, and all that would in any way deprive you or any group of what rightly belongs to you.

8. It is clearly the position of the Church that peoples have a right in public life to participate in decisions affecting their lives: "Participation constitutes a right which is to be applied both in the economic and in the social and political fields" (*Iustitia in mundo*, 1; cf. *Gaudium et spes*, no. 75).

This is true for everyone. It has particular applications for you as native peoples, in your strivings to take your rightful place among the peoples of the earth, with a just and equitable degree of self-governing. For you a land-base with adequate resources is also necessary for developing a viable economy for present and future generations. You need likewise to be in a position to develop your lands and your economic potential, and to educate your children and plan your future.

I know that negotiations are in progress and that much good will has been shown by all parties concerned. It is my hope and prayer that a totally satisfactory outcome will be had.

9. You yourselves are called to place all your talents at the service of others and help build, for the common good of Canada, an ever more authentic civilization of justice and love. You are called to responsible stewardship and to be a dynamic example of the proper use of nature, especially at a time when pollution and environmental damage threaten the earth. Christ's teaching of universal brotherhood and His commandment of fraternal love is now and for ever part of your heritage and your life.

10. Dear friends, dear native peoples of Canada, as you reflect on your history and work, in collaboration with all your brothers and sisters, in order to shape your own destiny and contribute to the total common good, remember always that your dependence on God is manifested by your observance of His commandments. These are written in your hearts and are summarized by St. John when he says: "His commandments are these: that we believe in the name of his Son Jesus Christ and that we love one another as he told us to. Whoever keeps his commandments lives in God and God lives in him. We know that he lives in us by the Spirit that he has given us" (1 Jn. 3:23-24). It is the Spirit that enables us to believe in Jesus and to love one another.

Your greatest possession, dear friends, is the gift of God's Spirit, whom you have received into your hearts and who leads you to Christ, and, through Christ, to the Father. With great love for all of you, my Indian, Innuit and Metis brothers and sisters, I bless you in the name of the Father and of the Son and of the Holy Spirit. Amen.

Vatican Translation

Only by Accepting and Protecting the Gift of Life Can Humanity Escape Self-Destruction

After weather conditions had forced a cancellation of the Holy Father's meeting with the native peoples of the Northwest Territories, the Pope went to Vancouver, British Columbia, on September 18, where he delivered the following address to the youth, the aging and the disabled in the local stadium.

Dear brothers and sisters,

1. This evening we have come to celebrate life in Jesus Christ. In this stadium vibrant with music and dance, as a family comprised of young and old, disabled and strong, as friends united in Christ, we praise God for the gift of life. We join our hearts and voices to glorify the Creator of heaven and earth, the Lord and Giver of life. On my part I thank you for your warm welcome and for this outpouring of love expressed in song and gesture.

In this beautiful region of British Columbia, with your towering mountains, your rushing waters, your dense green forests and mineral-rich soil, you are surrounded by an abundance of natural life, with wild animals and a plentiful supply of fish. Captivated by this grandeur and beauty, one of the first explorers of this region, Captain George Vancouver, spoke of "the innumerable pleasing landscapes and the abundant fertility that unassisted nature puts forth." How true are the words of this explorer whose name is honored by this thriving city.

We also celebrate the gift of human life, including the ethnic richness that has characterized the people of this area. There have been the Indian people, the first inhabitants of this land, who, in seeing life as the gift of a Supreme Spirit, were led to receive the Gospel of Christ when it was preached to them by the missionaries. There have been those of British extraction, too, who were the first settlers. Then came those from the Far East, those from India who came to work on the railways and in the development of resource industries. Later came immigrants from Eastern and Western Europe to push back further the frontiers of this new land. These varied immigrant peoples, together with the Indians, are represented by the performers this evening. In them we see how the many immigrant streams have contributed to the rich cultural diversity characteristic of this area. May all who have inherited these blessings truly appreciate them and thus avoid any form of discrimination against people "in law or in fact, on account of their race, origin, color, culture, sex or religion" (Octogesima adveniens, no. 16). All such discrimination is an affront to human dignity and a degradation of human life.

Above all, we celebrate tonight the gift of eternal life, which was won for us by Jesus Christ through His death on the cross. In the reading from St. John's Gospel this evening, Jesus says to us: "I have come so that they may have life and have it to the full" (Jn. 10:10). Natural life and human life are precious gifts of God. But eternal life is an even greater gift, because it is the gift of life for ever.

The grace we receive in Baptism raises the quality of our life to a level far exceeding anything we could ever imagine, for we receive the pledge of eternal or everlasting life. This everlasting life begins now; through faith in the word of God and through the sacraments of the Church, it will reach its completion in the world to come. This is the life described by St. Paul: "The things that no eye has seen and no ear has heard, things beyond the mind of man, all that God has prepared for those who love him" (1 Cor. 2:9).

I am very pleased that in the stadium tonight celebrating life with me are children and young people, senior citizens, and our brothers and sisters who suffer disabilities or handicaps of various kinds. I want to speak to each of these groups in turn.

2. Dear children and young people: my first words are for you. Do not let anyone deceive you about the real meaning of your life. It comes from God. You are here on earth because God made you. You come from Him. You belong to Him. And you will go to Him. God is the source and goal of your life. He who has given you natural life has desired that you grow up in a rich and vibrant area of God's

world. He has blessed you with many opportunities. Through Baptism, God has even given you a share in His own life. He has adopted you as His children. You are brothers and sisters of Christ.

In the Gospel reading, Jesus warns us that in the world there are thieves who come "only to steal and kill and destroy" (Jn. 10:10). You will find these thieves trying to deceive you. They will tell you that the meaning of life is to have as much pleasure as you can. They will try to convince you that this world is the only world there is, and that you must grasp everything you can for yourselves, now. You will hear some people telling you: "Look after yourselves, and do not worry about others." There will be those, moreover, who will say: "You will find your happiness in accumulating money and as many consumer goods as you can, and when you feel unhappy use the escape of alcohol or drugs."

None of this is true. And none of this brings true joy to your lives. True living is not found in one's self or in things. It is found in Someone else, in the One who created everything that is good, true, and beautiful in the world. True living is found in God, and you discover God in the person of Jesus Christ. Christ reveals God to us, and to know Christ is to know God. And in order to know yourself, your real self, you have to know Christ. That is why St. Paul can exclaim: "I believe nothing can happen that will outweigh the supreme advantage of knowing Christ Jesus my Lord" (Phil. 3:8).

I know that some of you go to Catholic schools. Why? So that you can more readily discover Christ and, in Him, the full meaning of life; so that you can live life to the full. The Church has her schools because she wants to communicate Christ to you. She wants you to come to full maturity in Him who is the perfect human being, and at the same time, the Son of God.

Dear children and young people: look to Christ.

When you wonder about the mystery of your life, look to Christ who explains to you its full meaning. When you wonder about your role in the future of Canada and the world, look to Christ. He will inspire you to fulfill your potential as Canadian citizens and as citizens of the world community. When you wonder about the life to come, look to Christ. Love Him and serve Him in your neighbor now, so that the fullness of eternal life may one day be yours.

TO SENIOR CITIZENS

3. Dear senior citizens: I now greet you, you who bear witness to the fact that the value of life lies in who you are, not in what you possess or in what you are able to do. Your life shows the continuity of the generations and gives you a horizon from which to judge new events and discoveries. You remind the world of the wisdom of earlier generations while you contribute your insights to this one.

I am happy to hear of all the initiatives happening here in British Columbia to enhance the quality of your life and, in particular, to provide you with proper housing arrangements. In its *Charter of the*

Rights of the Family, issued in 1983, the Holy See states: "The elderly have the right to find within their own family or, when this is not possible, in suitable institutions, an environment which will enable them to live their later years of life in serenity while pursuing those activities which are compatible with their age and which enable them to participate in social life" (Art. 9).

The passing of the years brings its frailties. You may be forced to give up activities that you once enjoyed. Your limbs may not seem as agile as they used to be. Your memory and your eyesight may refuse to give service. And so the world may cease to be familiar—the world of your family, the world around you, the world you once knew. Even the Church, which you have loved for so long, may seem strange to many of you as she goes forward in this period of renewal. Yet, despite changes and any weaknesses you may feel, you are of great value to all. Society needs you and so does the Church. You may not be able to do as much as before. But what counts above all is what you are. Old age is the crowning point of earthly life, a time to gather in the harvest you have sown. It is a time to give of yourselves to others as never before.

Yes, you are needed, and never let anyone tell you you are not. The Masses you have attended throughout your life, the devout Communions you have made, the prayers you have offered enable you to bestow rich gifts upon us. We need your experience and your insights. We need the faith which has sustained you and continues to be your light. We need your example of patient waiting and trust. We need to see in you that mature love which is yours, that love which is the fruit of your lives lived in both joys and sorrow. And yes, we need your wisdom for you can offer assurance in times of uncertainty. You can be an incentive to live according to the higher values of the spirit. These values link us with people of all time and they never grow old.

Be aware of your dignity, then, and once again offer your lives to our Lord Jesus Christ. Take time to know Him better than you have ever known Him before. Listen to Him in prayer as He says to you in your hour of weakness, sorrow or pain: "I am the good shepherd; I know my own and my own know me" (Jn. 10:14). He is close to you in the trials of your daily life. On your part, seek to be His faithful companions along the way of the cross. And never forget that the troubles you have to undergo are foreseen in God's plan of preparing you to live life to the full, in the company of Mary and all the saints in the kingdom of heaven.

4. Now I wish to speak to those suffering from disabilities and to those who offer them assistance. First of all, I rejoice at the sensitivity being shown to our disabled and handicapped brothers and sisters here in Vancouver and throughout Canada, through worthy agencies, associations and institutions.

Dear brothers and sisters who are disabled in some way: the value and dignity of the human person does not arise from physical or mental qualities, from efficiency, productivity or speed in one's actions. It comes rather from the fundamental fact that each individual is created by God and redeemed by the blood of His Son Jesus Christ. God calls each of you by name. He wishes you to make your individual contribution to the world and to live life to the full in the service of others. God's fatherly care embraces the healthy and the sick, the disabled, the handicapped and the strong.

Dear friends who sometimes feel so discouraged: I am filled with joy being with you today. I have come to tell you that Christ loves you and that the Church and the Pope love you, too. You are special friends of Jesus. He says to you in a very personal way: "Come to me, all who labor and are overburdened, and I will give you rest. Shoulder my yoke and learn from me, for I am gentle and humble in heart and you will find rest for your souls. Yes, my yoke is easy and my burden light" (Mt. 12:28-30). Christ is asking you to help Him to carry His cross. You fulfill in our day the role once exercised by Simon of Cyrene. You teach us, by your example, to unite our human limitations with the sufferings of Jesus, and to find joy in life.

But I have also come in order to assure you that the Church proclaims the need for you to share in the life of all society: to take your rightful part in your families, in the Church, in schools, in your places of work. The Church proclaims in a special way your right to work, as she strives to further the goal "that disabled people may be offered work according to their capabilities" (*Laborem exercens*, no. 22). She insists that to deny work to those who are not fully functional is also "a serious form of discrimination" (*ibid.*).

Dear friends whose particular vocation is service to these brothers and sisters: your work requires generosity of mind and heart, a greatness of spirit; for God calls you to love with a special intensity. I know, however, that you are the first to say that you receive much more than you give. The disabled and handicapped call forth energies from our hearts that we never suspected were there. They teach us humility, too, for they show us that human and Christian greatness does not consist in being stronger or more active than others. They show all of us the need for continual dependence upon God. In the name of Jesus Christ, the Good Shepherd, I thank you for all the care you give these important members of Christ's flock. You are the Lord's helpers in assisting these men, women and children to share life to the full.

5. Dear brothers and sisters: on this evening when we celebrate life, we are also mindful of the many threats to life which exist in our technological society. Of incalculable danger to all humanity is the rate of abortion in society today. This unspeakable crime against human life which rejects and kills life at its beginning sets the stage for despising, negating and eliminating the life of adults, and for attacking the life of society. If the weak are vulnerable from the time of conception, then they are vulnerable in old age, and they are vulnerable before the might of an aggressor and the power of nuclear weapons.

But there is a way for humanity to escape its own tyranny and avert the judgment of God: in the face of these evils which threaten life in our day, it must again proclaim in practice the sacredness of human life as a precious gift of a loving Creator—a gift to be accepted, respected and protected. "Against the pessimism and selfishness which cast a shadow over the world, the Church stands for life: in each human life she sees the splendor of that 'Yes,' that 'Amen,' who is Christ Himself" (*Familiaris consortio*, no. 30).

The Church proclaims God's plan for all human life, God's plan for the love that generates life, and God's plan for the family which, as a community of life, has the mission "to guard, reveal and communicate love" (*Familiaris consortio*, no. 17). This plan of God has been inscribed into the being of man and woman and gives a twofold dimension to their conjugal union—that conjugal union which must express intimate communion of love and life, as well as openness to procreation. Because of the inseparable connection willed by God of the unitive and procreative meaning of the conjugal act, the Church proclaims that there can be total self-giving in marriage only if these two elements are not artificially separated (*Familiaris consortio*, no. 32). In the plan of God, respect for the meaning of the body and for openness to life is a necessary condition for ensuring the full dignity of the human person, the full dignity of human life.

Life from conception onwards must be defended against all that attacks it, such as hunger and war; it must be healed of what weakens or dishonors it, such as disease and the abuse of alcohol and of drugs; it must be protected from what degrades it, such as violence, subhuman living conditions, unworthy working conditions and every such thing.

Against the thieves of our day who come "only to steal and kill and destroy" (Jn. 10:10), we are called to react with weapons of truth, justice and love. We must stand firm in our belief that Christ has already won the final victory over sin and death by His cross and resurrection, and that through faith He offers us life in His name.

In our celebration of life this evening, we look up to the Blessed Virgin Mary, the Mother of God and Mother of the Church. She who gave birth to the Savior, who is the life of the world, is with us in our celebration of life. She is close to us in all our efforts to promote life, to heal life, to improve life and to defend it against whatever would wound, weaken or destroy it. Yes, she is close to us as we strive to follow Jesus the Good Shepherd, who leads us to life everlasting.

Dear brothers and sisters: This is our destiny: to live life to the full, in communion with the Most Holy Trinity: Father, Son and Holy Spirit, to whom "be all praise, honor, glory and power, for ever and ever" (Rv. 5:13).

Vatican Translation

The Heart of Jesus Is a Call by God Addressed to Mankind, to Every Human Heart

On Tuesday afternoon, September 18, the Holy Father celebrated a Mass in honor of the Sacred Heart of Jesus at Vancouver's Abbotsford Airport in British Columbia, and delivered the following homily, mostly in English and partly in French.

"My soul, give thanks to the Lord,
all my being, bless his holy name"
(Ps. 103[102]:1).

1. With these words of today's liturgy, dear brothers and sisters, I wish to address myself, together with all of you, to the God of love. And I wish to do so through the mystery of the Heart of Christ.

I choose these words because they speak of our human heart—what the psalm refers to as "all my being." It is precisely this that we have in mind when we speak of the "heart": our whole being, all that is within each one of us. All that forms us from within, in the depths of our being. All that makes up our entire humanity, our whole person in its spiritual and physical dimension. All that expresses itself as a unique and unrepeatable person in its "inner self" and at the same time in its "transcendence."

The words of the psalm—"My soul, give thanks to the Lord; all my being, bless his holy name"—say that our human "heart" addresses God in all the unimaginable majesty of His divinity and His holiness and at the same time, in His wonderful "openness" to mankind: in His "condescension."

In this way "heart" meets "Heart"; "heart" speaks to the "Heart."

TRULY A LAND OF SPLENDOR

2. In this spirit I wish also to greet all those taking part in our Eucharistic assembly—in this Votive Mass of the Sacred Heart—as well as all those who have come to express their good will and their respectful solidarity with this praying community.

I am deeply pleased that my visit to Canada has taken me to the City of Vancouver and this gathering place of God's people. The city is indeed marvelously located between the mountains and the oceans, being the largest city of your Province, all of which is truly a land of splendor without diminishment: *Splendor sine occasu!*

The importance of your Province is certainly reflected in its forests, minerals, water, fruit and fishing, and in the beauty which attracts so many tourists. Of greater importance still are you, the people of this region. It is here that you live and work, striving to build a suitable human habitat and a just society. It is here that you struggle to solve the social problems that have become so much a part of the fabric of life in these parts. It is here that you continue your search for God and for the full meaning of human life, amid the struggle between good and evil. And to all of you today I offer the expression of my deep respect and fraternal love.

In particular I wish to greet all the Catholic faithful of the Archdiocese of Vancouver, under the leadership of Archbishop Carney. I am likewise deeply grateful for all who have made great efforts to come from other dioceses of British Columbia—Victoria, Kamploops, Nelson, Prince George, the Eparchy of New Westminster under the leadership of Bishop Chimy—and the Pacific Northwest and probably also from the United States. In the unity of the Eucharist I express my deep affection for all my brother Bishops and for all the clergy, religious and laity of the Catholic Church.

In the charity of Christ I embrace all my fellow Christians who honor me by their presence today. I recall with sincere appreciation and respect the zealous efforts made last year in this city by the World Council of Churches to proclaim Jesus Christ to the world.

With fraternal esteem I also offer my warm greetings to the members of non-Christian religions and to all the citizens of this land who have no religious affiliation. Before all of you I attest to the Catholic Church's deep interest and concern for the incomparable human dignity of every man, woman and child on this earth.

I am deeply grateful for the hospitality extended to me and for the invitation to celebrate this Eucharist. And it is in this context of public worship that I have come to you to proclaim Jesus Christ, the eternal Son of God; to proclaim the invisible God whom He reveals; and to proclaim the divine love that He communicates to the world in the mystery of His Sacred Heart.

3. When we say "Heart of Jesus Christ," we address ourselves in faith to the whole Christological mystery: the mystery of the God-Man.

This mystery is expressed in a rich and profound way by the texts of today's liturgy. These are the words of the Apostle Paul in his letter to the Colossians:

"Christ Jesus is the image of the unseen God
and the first-born of all creation,
for in him were created
all things in heaven and on earth:
everything visible and everything invisible,
Thrones, Dominations, Sovereignties, Powers"
(Col. 1:15-16).

These last words refer precisely to the "invisible" beings: the creatures that have a purely spiritual nature.

"All things were created through him and for him.
Before anything was created, he existed,
and he holds all things in unity" (Col. 1:16-17).

4. These marvelous sentences from St. Paul's letter come together with what is proclaimed to us today in the Prologue of St. John's Gospel:

"In the beginning was the Word:
the Word was with God
and the Word was God.
He was with God in the beginning.
Through him all things came to be,
not one thing had its being but through him.
And the world was made through him"
     (Jn. 1:1-3, 10).

Both in the text of John and in the text of Paul is contained the revealed doctrine on the Son—the Word of God—who is of the same divine substance as the Father. This is the faith we profess as we say the Creed—that profession of faith which comes from the two most ancient Councils of the universal Church, at Nicea and Constantinople:

We believe in one God,
the Father, the Almighty,
maker of heaven and earth,
of all that is, seen and unseen.

We believe in one Lord, Jesus Christ,
the only Son of God,
eternally begotten of the Father,
God from God, Light from Light,
true God from true God,
begotten, not made,
of one Being with the Father.
Through him all things were made."

The Son is one in substance with the Father. He is God from God.

At the same time, everything that is created has its divine beginning in Him, as the Eternal Word. In Him all things were made and in Him they have their existence.

5. This is our faith. This is the teaching of the Church about the divinity of the Son. This Eternal Son, true God, the Word of the Father, became man. These are the words of the Gospel: "The Word was made flesh, he lived among us" (Jn. 1:14).

In the Creed we profess: "For us men and for our salvation he came down from heaven: by the power of the Holy Spirit he became incarnate from the Virgin Mary, and was made man."

Here we more directly touch upon the reality of the Heart of Jesus. For the heart is a human organ, belonging to the body, belonging to the whole structure, to the spiritual and physical makeup of man: "And the Word was made flesh."

In this makeup the heart has its place as an organ. At the same time it has a meaning as the symbolic center of the inner self, and this inner self is, by nature, spiritual.

The Heart of Jesus was conceived beneath the Heart of the Virgin Mother, and its earthly life ceased at the moment Jesus died on the cross. This is testified to by the Roman soldier who pierced the side of Jesus with a lance.

During the whole of Jesus' earthly life, this Heart was the center in which was manifested, in a human way, the love of God: the love of God the Son, and, through the Son, the love of God the Father.

What constitutes the greatest fruit of this love in creation?

We read it in the Gospel: "He came to his own domain and his own people did not accept him. But to all who did accept him he gave power to become children of God..." (Jn. 1:11-12).

Here is the most magnificent, the most profound gift of the Heart of Jesus that we find in creation: man born of God, man adopted as a son in the Eternal Son, humanity given the power to become children of God.

6. And therefore our human heart "transformed" in this way can say and does say to the divine Heart what we hear in today's liturgy:

"My soul, give thanks to the Lord,
and never forget all his blessings.
It is he who forgives all your guilt,
who heals every one of your ills,
who redeems your life from the grave,
who crowns you with love and compassion.
The Lord is compassion and love,
slow to anger and rich in mercy"
(Ps. 103[102]:2-4, 8).

These are the words of the psalm in which the Old Testament speaks of the mystery of God's love. How much more do the Gospels tell us of the divine Heart of the Son—and indirectly of the Heart of the Father:

Heart of Jesus, abode of justice and love!
Heart of Jesus, patient and most merciful!
Heart of Jesus, fountain of life and holiness!

Finally we can repeat with Isaiah that those who hope in the divine Heart "renew their strength, they put out wings like eagles. They run and do not grow weary, walk and never tire" (Is. 40:31).

7. The Heart of Jesus Christ is a great and unceasing call from God, addressed to humanity, to each human heart! Let us listen once more to the words of St. Paul in today's liturgy:

"Now the Church is his body,
he is its head.
As he is the Beginning,
he was the first to be born from the dead,
so that he should be first in every way;
because God wanted all perfection
to be found in him
and all things to be reconciled through him and
    for him,
everything in heaven and everything on earth,
when he made peace by his death on the cross"
    (Col. 1:18-20).

This is the definitive perspective that is opened up before us by our faith in the Heart of Jesus Christ. He is the Beginning and the End of everything created in God Himself. He is the Fullness.

Towards this fullness in Him goes all visible and invisible creation. Towards this fullness in Him goes all humanity, reconciled with God by the blood of Jesus shed on the cross.

Lord Jesus Christ,
Eternal Son of the Eternal Father,
Born of the Virgin Mary:

We ask You to continue to reveal to us the mystery of God: so that we may recognize in You "the image of the invisible God"; that we may find Him in You, in Your divine Person, in the warmth of Your humanity, in the love of Your Heart.

Heart of Jesus, in whom dwells the fullness of divinity!

Heart of Jesus, of whose fullness we have all received!

Heart of Jesus, King and center of all hearts, for ever and ever. Amen!

Vatican Translation

The World Needs Witnesses of God's Gratuitous Love

After a flight from Vancouver to Ottawa on Wednesday, September 19, the Holy Father visited the monastery of the Servants of Jesus and Mary in Hull, a city of the province of Quebec, separated from the federal capital by the Ottawa River. Pope John Paul II celebrated Mass for more than two hundred contemplative nuns and delivered the following homily, mostly in French.

My dear sisters,

1. "The Spirit and the Bride say, 'Come....' Come, Lord Jesus" (Rv. 22:17, 20). The Church, inspired by the Spirit present in it, continues to address this call to the Lord Jesus. She awaits His return. The Church awaits Him, as a bride yearning after her beloved Husband who is at the right hand of the Father. She has already "washed her robes" in His redeeming blood. She hopes "to feed on the tree of life." She knows that she already shares in His life in a mysterious and partial way, through faith, the sacraments, prayer and charity. It is with Him that she works to renew this world according to His Spirit.

But she is impatient for a complete renewal, for the full vision of her Spouse. For the moment, her life is hidden in God.

The whole Church must live in this expectancy and bear witness to it. But consecrated souls have made "a charismatic choice of Christ as the exclusive Spouse." This choice already enables one "to be anxious about the affairs of the Lord" but also—when it is made "for the kingdom of heaven"—it brings this eschatological reign of God closer to the life of all people. Consecrated persons bring into the midst of this passing world news of the resurrection to come and of eternal life (cf. my letter, *Redemptionis donum*, no. 11).

SPECIAL CHARISM

2. All religious men and women have this charism at the heart of the Church. But it is even more obvious in the case of cloistered sisters who give up all activity in the world in order to be present to the Lord alone. And in this place it is first of all to you that I speak, dear contemplative sisters. The Church considers your place in the Mystical Body of Christ essential to the life of the Church, to its full development, and this, even in the young churches whose energy is monopolized by the tasks of evangelization (cf. *Perfectae caritatis*, no. 47, and *Ad gentes*, no. 40). In fact, the prayer of contemplatives has played a considerable role in the deepening of faith in Canada. That was certainly the insight of Father Mangin and Sister Marie-Zita de Jésus when they founded here, almost a hundred years ago, the Servants of Jesus and Mary. These religious women honor in a special way the Sacred Heart of Jesus in the Eucharist,

the supreme gift of His love, before which they keep a continuous vigil. Your spiritual apostolate, dear sisters, is it not to support the ministry of priests and to collaborate in the eternal plan of the covenant for all believers: "that they might be one"? I think also of all the men and women who have established the contemplative life in Canada according to complementary spiritualities. So, in addition to all the religious here today, I greet with affection and I encourage all those who lead a monastic life in Canada!

BE ON WATCH

3. "The kingdom of heaven will be like this: ten bridesmaids took their lamps and went to meet the bridegroom. Five of them were foolish and five were wise." My sisters, wait for the groom as these wise virgins did. Always be ready. Always be open. In your waiting for the Lord, be on watch.

Your convent life is organized in such a way as to encourage the experience of God. Your withdrawal from the world, with its solitude; your silence, which is a listening silence, a silence of love; asceticism, penance, the tasks which lead you to share in the redemptive work; fraternal communion which is always being renewed; the daily Eucharistic Celebration that unites your offering to that of Christ.

May the weariness, routine and monotony involved in your convent life not make you lose your vigilance, may the occasional impression that God is absent or temptations or even the normal trials of growing in mystical union with Christ not discourage you! May the lamp of your prayer, of your love, never stop burning! Keep it well supplied with oil, day and night.

TRINITARIAN LIFE

4. For, even within a community, your path is still a personal one. Just as the wise virgins were incapable of making up for the carelessness of the foolish virgins, no one else can take your place in welcoming the Trinitarian life into the depths of yourself, there where the love received responds in adoration, praise and gratitude to love. It is then that you make your own the prayer of the psalmist we were reading a moment ago: "God, you are my God, I am seeking you, my soul is thirsting for you, my flesh is longing for you, like a land parched, weary and waterless; I long to gaze on you in the sanctuary and to see your power and glory. Your love is better than life itself.... All my life I will bless you.... I meditate on you all night long.... I sing for joy in the shadow of your wings. My soul clings close to you, your right hand supports me" (Ps. 63[62]:2-5, 7-9).

This ineffable meeting with the personal and living God can take place only in the darkness of faith. The groom stands behind the door while you are still outside in the night. It is always in the light of faith that God gives Himself. But the signs of God are so discreet in the ordinariness of your everyday life that you must be vigilant if you are to persevere and grow in faith in imitation of Mary. The "treasure" that awaits you in heaven will only be the eschatological fulfillment of what is hidden in the inner "treasure" of the heart (cf. *Redemptionis donum*, no. 5).

HIDDEN BUT FRUITFUL

5. Your lives have a hidden but assured fruitfulness. "Whoever remains in me...bears fruit in plenty" (Jn. 15:5). In the solidarity that unites all the members of Christ, you are like the heart, as St. Theresa of the Child Jesus put it. Without your love, charity would grow cold. In the Church that prays, suffers and evangelizes, your part is the link with God. Your offering makes you like Christ so that He can use your whole being for the work of redemption according to the pleasure of His love. And God hears the prayer of praise and intercession that rises up from your hearts and pours out His grace, without which there would be neither conversion to the Gospel, growth in faith nor vocations of apostolic workers in the Church (cf. *Ad gentes*, no. 40).

THIRST FOR THE ABSOLUTE

6. The Christian community in Hull seems to have clearly understood your vocation, as has the neighboring community of the city of Ottawa. People are attached to your monastery and support it. They do not hesitate to entrust you with their sorrows and their joys, their plans and their prayer intentions.

More and more people—and among them, many young people—are seeking places of grace, of prayer, of contemplation. They are thirsting for the Absolute. Some come to your monasteries in search of spiritual values. To all these seekers after God, show by the truth and the transparency of your persons that belonging to Christ makes you free and that experience of God fulfills you. Without shirking the requirements of contemplative life, find ways of expressing for the culture of our time your radical option for God. To those who say: "We do not know how to pray," say again and again by your existence that dialogue with God is possible for "the Spirit too comes to help us in our weakness" (Rom. 8:26). To those who want to do something great with their life, testify that the path to holiness is the most beautiful of adventures. It is not just the work of our efforts, but that of the infinite tenderness of God in the vastness of human misery. May your monasteries allow passers-by to approach the sources of living water: "Then let all who are thirsty come: all who want it may have the water of life and have it free!" (Rv. 22:17)

NUMEROUS RELIGIOUS

7. My meditation seemed to be focused on cloistered nuns. But all along I have had in mind all the women who have devoted themselves to God in religious life in Canada. There are almost forty thousand of them! What I said about the spirit of consecrated life is also valid for all the sisters dedicated to an active or apostolic life. Circumstances have not permitted a special meeting with them as a group, and I regret that. I have seen many of them at every stage of my visit, with the People of God. But I was waiting for this opportunity and now, this evening, I am happy to greet them all from this place of contemplation and to address to them this message.

Dear sisters, in the Church, you carry out services that are precious to Christian communities and to the world: among other things, you are involved in teaching catechism, in education, in hospital care, in supporting the elderly and in parish activities.... Happy are the villages and the cities where sisters are still present! You exercise a certain professional activity, with preference for activity which allows you to express charity and to give witness to faith, and that, in a community way.

ROOTED IN BAPTISM

8. But that is not the original mystery of your life. You freely consecrated yourself to the Lord who was the first to choose you. Your religious vows are intimately rooted in the consecration of Baptism, but express it with greater fullness (cf. *Perfectae caritatis*, no. 5). You share in a special and permanent way in the Redeemer's death on the cross and in His resurrection. The paschal nature of your life is evident in each of the "evangelical counsels" which you have committed yourselves to practice in a radical way. At the same time you become truly free in order better to serve. You stake your all, not on "having," but on the quality of being, the quality of the person renewed in Jesus Christ.

More than ever before, our world needs to discover in your communities and in your lifestyle the value of a simple and poor life in the service of the poor, the value of a life freely committed in celibacy in order to consecrate itself to Christ and, with Him, to love especially those deprived of love, the value of a life where obedience and community life silently protest the excesses of an independence that is sometimes irresponsible and barren.

Above all, the world needs witnesses to the free gift of the love of God. To those who doubt about God or who have the impression that He is absent, you show that the Lord is worth seeking and loving for Himself, that the kingdom of God, despite its apparent foolishness, is worth devoting one's life to. Thus, your lives are a sign of the indestructible faith of the Church. The free giving of your life to Christ and to others is perhaps the protest that most urgently needs to be made to a society where profit-making efficiency has become an idol. Your choice amazes, questions, interests or irritates the world, but it never leaves it indifferent. In any case, the Gospel is always the sign of contradiction. You will not be understood by all. But never be afraid to manifest your consecration to the Lord. It is your honor! It is an honor to the Church! You have a special place in the Body of Christ where everyone has his or her role to assume, his or her own charism.

If, with the Holy Spirit, you seek the holiness which corresponds to your state of life, do not be afraid. He will not abandon you. Vocations will come to you, and you, you will keep the youthfulness of your soul, which has nothing to do with age. Yes, my dear sisters, live in hope. Keep your eyes on Christ and walk firmly in His steps in joy and in peace.

9. I cannot develop any further now this message to all the Canadian nuns. On March 25 of this year, I wrote a special letter to you and to all religious men and women, entitled *Redemptionis donum.*

This evening, at the end of my long apostolic journey across Canada, I am very happy to be, together with Bishop Adolphe Proulx of this diocese, the guest of the sisters. As Jesus loved to withdraw to Bethany to the home of Mary and Martha—the one more contemplative, the other more active—I have come to your home in order to pray with you. As Peter and the other Apostles withdrew to the Cenacle, together with Mary the Mother of Jesus, I come to invoke the Holy Spirit. May He pour out His light and His power upon all the inhabitants of this dear country, so that the Church here might grow in holiness! Pray with me for all religious, for all those who are consecrated, for the men and women who are members of Secular Institutes. Let us pray for the priests, who are the ministers of the Eucharist and the guides of consciences. Let us pray for those who educate people in the faith. Let us pray for those who undergo persecution for their faith.

Here, close to Ottawa where I shall meet this evening with political authorities and where tomorrow I shall celebrate the Mass for Peace, let us pray for all those who must contribute to establishing more justice, more peace and more fraternity, in Canada and in the less privileged countries.

Lord Jesus, may Your kingdom come! Amen.

From the English edition of L'Osservatore Romano

True Peace Will Come Only When Hearts and Minds Are Converted to Compassion, Justice, Love

On Wednesday, September 19, Pope John Paul II met with the Governor General of Canada, Madame Jeanne Sauvé, and with the members of the two branches of the Canadian Parliament and representatives of the Diplomatic Corps accredited to Canada. The meeting was held in Ottawa's Rideau Hall, the official residence of the Governor General.

The Holy Father delivered the following message in French and English.

Your Excellency, the Governor-General,

Mr. Prime Minister of Canada,

Honorable Members of Government,

Honorable Members of the Legislative and Judiciary
      Institutions,

Your Excellencies, Members of the Diplomatic Corps,

Ladies and Gentlemen,

    1. I have looked forward to this encounter with so many distinguished personalities in this capital city of Canada since the beginning of my apostolic

visit and all through the different stages of my journey in this unique country of Canada. I am very pleased to have been able to meet already this evening with the Governor-General, and to speak with her about matters that concern Canada and the world. I am deeply touched by the presence of all of you here, and I wish to thank you most cordially for the honor you thus show me as Bishop of Rome and chief pastor of the Catholic Church. It is not possible for me at this moment even to try to analyze or summarize the deep and lasting impressions which the many unforgettable events of my visit with the people of Canada have made on me. Let me say only that I give thanks to Almighty God for the moments of grace which He has bestowed on me in the many encounters of prayer, sharing and dialogue with so many people in this country.

2. In meeting today with you who represent not only the people of Canada but also the peoples of many nations, my thoughts go once again to the whole world and to the links that bind together all of humanity: North and South, East and West, men, women and children, old and young. My thoughts and concerns, as those of the whole Church, go out to the industrialized nations that are faced with new problems which impel them to re-examine their old and trusted presumptions; and to the nations that struggle to achieve their own development, reinforce their sovereignty and assume their rightful place in the family of nations. We all know that no nation can live and pursue the good of its citizens in isolation from other nations. Today, more than ever before, we have become aware—or shall I say, we have been

forced to become aware—that all nations are bound together in mutual dependence and solidarity.

Any solution devised by one nation or region to solve its problems has a necessary repercussion on the lives and pursuits of other nations as a consequence of economic, monetary, financial and political mechanisms. But at the same time, all peoples are accepting more clearly and with greater commitment a common responsibility for the universal common good. The growing sense of solidarity and shared responsibility among nations is one of the hopeful signs of our times that must inspire all peoples to ever greater availability for collaboration. Legitimate national interests cannot be achieved through sterile confrontation, but only through open, continuing and trustful dialogue and cooperation. All individuals and peoples must know that they are the stewards of a common heritage and the servants of a common destiny.

3. The particular setting and circumstance of today's encounter, in this capital city of Canada, at the end of my pilgrimage *"a mari usque ad mare,"* allows me to offer a word of praise to the Canadian people and their leaders for the many achievements which they have realized by giving tangible expression to their sense of world solidarity. Richer by reason of its own experience of collaboration between many different groups in the common pursuit of the well-being of all Canadians, this country has also, in the field of international collaboration and responsibility, endeavored to follow the path of an effective commitment to world peace

and of selfless contributions to the development of the less advanced nations.

4. We owe it to the many people and nations that, in the decades since the Second World War, have sincerely and honestly been striving to create a world of peaceful relations and international justice, not to let our perception of the world situation be obscured by pessimism or defeatism. Real progress has indeed been made in many areas and has to be acknowledged with praise.

At the same time, we cannot close our eyes to the persistence of many unsolved problems and to the many situations of conflict and injustice which still remain as a dark mark on the international scene and as an unavoidable challenge to the international community. We cannot close our eyes, nor should we harden our hearts, in the face of the untold suffering and needs that afflict millions of our fellow human beings. Today, society is not lacking in information and statistics about the ills of the world. It is, however, lacking in sensitivity when it does not allow certain facts to influence its action: the absence of agreements to reduce and eventually to halt the arms race; the investment of scientific talent and funds in weapons of mass destruction; limited wars that continue to kill people in countries not one's own; disregard for the value and dignity of unborn life; experimentation on human embryos; the starving or undernourished children in countries affected by chronic drought or underdevelopment; the lack of basic health care; the massive flight to urban concentrations that cannot offer employment, education or food; the loss of liberty, including the freedom to practice one's religion. In all of this there is the absence of sufficient concern for the ethical dimensions that underlie and are connected with the problems of society.

PUBLIC RESPONSIBILITY

5. I appeal to you today, ladies and gentlemen, and through you to all the people whom you represent in different ways, to be the bearers of a new vision of humanity: a vision that does not see society's problems in terms of economic, technical or political equations alone, but in terms of living people, of human beings created in the image and likeness of God and called to an eternal destiny; a vision that is built upon and therefore promotes true human values; a vision that inspires action and overcomes complacency, insensitivity and selfishness.

Is it not, in a particular way, the mission of all those entrusted with public responsibility—on both the national and international levels—to promote this vision of humanity that is capable of marshaling the good will that lives in the heart of every citizen? Is it not their responsibility to produce the political will that brings about the changes that are necessary so that all the human and technical potential at the disposal of society can be utilized? None of us can remain passive in the face of today's challenges; we know that the modern world possesses an immense amount of technical knowledge and means that can be employed to help solve the problems of humanity. It is my conviction that in your executive, legislative and judiciary roles within Canada, and in your international service to your respective countries, you are in a unique position to promote, in all your initiatives, the new vision of humanity, which affects every area of human endeavor and which is at the basis of all legislation, civil activity and social exchange. Be assured of my own support and encouragement.

NEW VISION OF PEACE

6. Nobody will deny that today's world is truly in need of a new vision of peace. People are being killed in war-torn countries. People live in fear of the ever present possibility that tensions and conflicts will be settled by the might of weapons and not by the force of reason. People feel threatened by the very existence of powerful arsenals of destruction and by the absence of meaningful progress in disarmament negotiations. People suffer from hunger, malnutrition and disease. Many lack education and the possibility of living meaningful lives, while at the same time they see immense funds being engulfed in the arms race. It is important to state again and again that war is made in the hearts and the minds of the men and women of our times, and that true peace will come about only when the hearts and minds of all are converted to compassion, to justice and to love.

ALL ARE INVOLVED

In the new vision of peace there is no place for self-centeredness and antagonism. We are all involved; we all carry the responsibility for our own conversion to thoughts and actions of peace. One person alone cannot change the world, but all of us together, strong in the conviction and determination that peace begins in our own hearts, will be able to create a peaceful and peace-loving society. On my part I have decided to devote my annual message for the forthcoming celebration of the World Day of Peace to the theme: "Peace and youth go forward together." Today's world population is made up, in large measure, of young people. Their commitment to peace will make a meaningful difference for the future of the world, and the contributions of everyone—when put together—will change the world.

DIGNITY
OF THE PERSON

7. The relationships between individuals and between peoples are at the core of the problems of society. These relationships must be based on a vision of the human person that proposes and extols the dignity and sacredness of every human being. The dignity of the human person is the basis of all human rights. We cannot but rejoice at the growing awareness that exists of the importance and centrality of respect for human rights for the building up of society in peace and in justice. It remains necessary, however, in the promotion of respect for human

rights, to refer back to their ultimate foundation: the human person and his or her dignity viewed in all their dimensions. Every human being lives at the same time in the world of material values and needs and in that of spiritual aspirations and achievements. The needs and the hopes, the freedoms and relationships of the human person never concern one sphere of values to the exclusion of the other. It is in this light that human rights and liberties, and the corresponding duties and responsibilities have to be viewed.

Today I wish to draw your attention in a particular way to what I consider to be extremely fundamental in the whole question of all human rights: the right to religious freedom. Religious liberty is a right that directly concerns what is essential in the human person and what fully manifests his or her dignity: the relationship to God, the Creator and the ultimate destiny of every human being. It is all the more reprehensible that various forms of denial of religious freedom and of discrimination against believers and the whole community of the Church still take place, notwithstanding the existence of constitutional legislation and international instruments which guarantee the right to religious liberty.

I wish at this time, in union with all men and women of good will, to proclaim again the right to life, and to make a renewed plea that the right to life of the unborn be respected. We must abhor the fact that in not a few societies abortion has become socially acceptable and is made readily available. Abortion is being presented as the ready answer to many problems: the problems of unwanted pregnancy; the problems of the unmarried pregnant woman, the problems of a fast growing population, the problems of the poor. Not only does society permit the destruction of unborn human beings, it often tries to justify that destruction. When respect for human life is systematically denied or refused, the dignity of every human being and the sacredness of all human life is being attacked.

PROBLEM OF REFUGEES

8. In inviting you, ladies and gentlemen, to be the bearers of a new vision of peace and justice, I must speak of a phenomenon of increasing urgency today—one in which, I know, you have a great interest: I am referring to refugees and those who migrate. There are many factors to account for this reality and situations vary greatly from place to place. There are political refugees, and refugees forced from their homes by human or natural forces. There are those seeking to flee from injustice, oppression and persecution. There are immigrants seeking an opportunity for work, so that they can take care of the needs of their families, and those who migrate in order to find better and more promising opportunities. Whatever the reasons, the refugee and the immigrant must be understood in a basic twofold relationship: a relationship to the homeland or country of origin, and to the new land that is theirs by choice or necessity.

This new situation, which has taken on wide dimensions in many parts of the world, entails losses and raises challenges both to the individuals and to the nations concerned, and to all humanity as well. It

is important today that we all share a greater understanding of refugees and immigrants, whatever the
causes of their present circumstances or whatever the
possibilities they might have before them. And from
this understanding may there develop a greater
sensitivity to their needs and to their human dignity.
Above all, the world needs to understand the detach-
ment and pain entailed in every sort of migration.

ENTITLED TO RESPECT

Every one of these persons carries into new
environments those traditions and values belonging
to a culture which is a precious heritage. At times
these new environments can be inhospitable to the
refugee or immigrant, or hostile to his or her background. The sons and daughters of a culture and a
nation—of any culture or any nation—have a right to
maintain their just traditions, to take pride in them
and to have them respected by others. While it would
not be right for them to seek to impose their inherited
cultures on others, it is quite proper for them to
expect that the respect and honor their cultures
deserve will be accorded to them as a rightful
inheritance. They are entitled to expect that this
respect will be a first step to a complementarity of
traditions that will enrich the citizens of the host
country as a whole, as well as sustain and support the
refugees and immigrants themselves.

Here in Canada, as I mentioned in Winnipeg, so
much has been done over the years to honor and help
the refugees, all those who have immigrated to this
land, all those who have known the problems of
migration. Besides official assistance, the whole pri-

vate sector, including families and many religious groups, has generously endeavored to serve these brothers and sisters. The results in this field have also been a great credit to the government policy of this country and to all its people. Today I would encourage Canada and all the nations represented here to pursue these splendid efforts, and to resist any temptation to grow tired in performing this good work. Be assured that the Holy See supports this cause and stands by all of you in order to proclaim before the world the importance of your activities and their effectiveness in helping to build true peace.

AN UPLIFTING VISION

9. Ladies and gentlemen: I present to you these elements of an uplifting vision of humanity for your reflection and encouragement as you discharge the lofty responsibilities that are yours. Be always the bearers of this vision here in Canada and throughout the world. Let it become an incentive and a moving force towards actions and commitments that will make the world a world where peace and justice reign. This, dear friends, is the world which God in His goodness has entrusted to our care.

I Pray
That God Will Bless You
and Your Families

On his last day in Canada, September 20, the Holy Father's first engagement was a visit to Ottawa Cathedral where he thanked all those responsible for the organization of his visit. The following is the text of his address.

Praised be Jesus Christ!

In this final stage of my long pastoral visit to Canada, I give thanks to God for all that He has permitted me to see and hear, from east to west, in very diverse assemblies.

Here we are in this magnificent city of Ottawa, the capital of Canada, where this afternoon we will be celebrating the Mass for Peace. Yesterday evening, I met officials from the government, the parliament and the diplomatic corps. Their role is an important one for the Canadian people and for the world community. I also greeted the local civic authorities.

In a little while I shall be meeting with my brother Bishops, who are entrusted with the care of the Catholic Church in Canada. I wish to thank Archbishop Joseph-Aurèle Plourde for welcoming me so warmly to the cathedral of his Archdiocese.

This is an opportunity for me to express my heartfelt gratitude to all those who, for months now, have been involved in the preparation and then in the carrying out of this visit. In Rome I received many reports of this intense work of preparation. In the past twelve days I have seen for myself the fruits of this work.

Dear friends, with your Bishops and the General Secretariat of the Conference, you have carried out a large number of initiatives. You have chosen the places and occasions that seemed to you the most fitting. You have prepared the people by informing them about the Church in Canada, about Rome and the Pope, and about the meaning of my pastoral visit. Thanks to you, many of your compatriots have prepared themselves spiritually for this visit. In my view, this was the most important thing.

I wish to thank the various groups represented here, who have made all the technical arrangements in such diverse areas as transportation, communications, the printing and transmittal of documents, and the coordination of policing, protocol and security services.

I wish to mention by name:
—the staff of the Secretariat of the Canadian Conference of Catholic Bishops;
—the staff of the Papal Visit Secretariat;

—the representatives of the dioceses of Ottawa and Gatineau-Hull, who were responsible for the part of the visit that concerned them;

—the Canadian Government Task Force;

—the guests of Archbishop Plourde, who have made their own contribution, especially through their meaningful commemoration of this visit.

I am particularly appreciative of the collaboration which was established for this undertaking between the Provincial and Federal Authorities and the various ecclesiastical groups. And through you I thank the thousands of people who have had a hand in all the services, at the various stops throughout the country, in a selfless and discreet manner, without always being able themselves to assist at the ceremonies, while they contributed to their success.

In addressing myself more especially to the faithful who have had responsible roles, I dare add that this fine work is not yet finished. It will be necessary to draw the maximum profit from this experience, to point out its value for the Canadian people, and permit them to meditate on it. I am sure that many of you are already part of those dedicated groups who have the habit of supporting similar services in your ecclesial communities. I congratulate you and I encourage you. The Church needs structures for the fulfillment of her mission in so many spheres. She needs competent and generous people. Indeed, she needs an impetus, a spiritual inspiration which she finds in prayer, in her liturgical life, in her commitment to charity, and I do not doubt that you have met these spiritual requirements in your work of organization.

We are here in the cathedral, and I cannot visit such churches without reflecting on the sense of the sacred which they help to develop in order to facilitate an encounter with the living God, and without evoking the image of the Christian assemblies for which they exist. It is of capital importance that these signs of God arise in the hearts of our cities, and above all that our faithful diligently strive to visit these spiritual places for personal prayer or for the celebration of the sacraments. In this way they can set out again on the roads of this world with the light and the strength of the Lord! This morning, our prayer consists above all in rendering thanks to God and recommending to Him your intentions, in union with the Virgin Mary.

To all of you, ladies and gentlemen, dear brothers and sisters, I repeat my deepest thanks. I offer my fervent prayers for all the responsibilities which you exercise in society and in the Church. I pray that God will bless you and your families.

From the English edition of L'Osservatore Romano

The Meaning
of Our
Episcopal Ministry

On September 20, the Holy Father met the Conference of Catholic Bishops of Canada in the Convent of the Sisters of Charity in Ottawa, and he addressed them as follows.

Dear brothers in the Episcopate,

1. Here we are, almost at the end of my pastoral visit. You desired this visit and have actively organized it; you have prepared your Christian people for it well. In the various stops of the journey, I found not only the local Bishop but many others who wished to join us since I could not go to their dioceses. For all of this I am deeply grateful.

And now we are gathered together to reflect, in the sight of God and with the light of the Holy Spirit whom we have invoked, on the grace and role which He has entrusted to us, as successors of the Apostles. These were magnificently re-expressed in the texts of the Second Vatican Council, above all in the Constitution *Lumen gentium* and the Decree *Christus Dominus*. These are the texts which will guide our reflection, for they permit us to stir up within ourselves an awareness of our apostolic mission.

In *Lumen gentium* we read: "In the person of the bishops, then, to whom the priests render assistance, the Lord Jesus Christ, supreme high priest, is present in the midst of the faithful.... Indeed, it is through their unique service that he preaches the word of God to all peoples and constantly administers to the faithful the sacraments of faith.... Through their wisdom and prudence he directs and guides the people of the New Testament on their journey towards eternal beatitude. Chosen to shepherd the Lord's flock, these pastors are servants of Christ and stewards of the mysteries of God...to whom is entrusted the duty of affirming the Gospel of the grace of God...and of gloriously promulgating the Spirit and proclaiming justification..." (no. 21).

This is the meaning of our episcopal ministry which includes especially the tasks of teaching, sanctifying and governing. These tasks are exercised in hierarchical communion with the Head of the College of Bishops and its members. In other words, to take up again the words of the Council: "The bishops, in a resplendent and visible manner, take the place of Christ himself, teacher, shepherd and priest, and act in his person" *(ibid.)*.

2. This mission is sublime and formidable. It supposes that, as Peter did, we repeat to Christ the fullness of our faith (cf. Mt. 16:16) and our love (cf. Jn. 21:15-17). To accomplish this mission as the Apostles

did, we have received by episcopal consecration a special outpouring of the Holy Spirit (cf. *ibid.*, no. 21), who remains with us, and at whose disposition we must constantly place ourselves in prayer to do His work and not our own.

In all cases, it is a question of service (cf. *ibid.*, no. 27), of the service of the Good Shepherd who gives His life for His sheep. This humble and generous service necessarily requires courage and authority: "The bishops, as vicars and legates of Christ, govern the particular churches assigned to them by their counsels, exhortations and example, but over and above that, also by the authority and sacred power which indeed they exercise exclusively for the spiritual development of their flock in truth and holiness..." *(ibid.).* And you know well that, as the Council said further, the power of each Bishop—which remains integral in the midst of the Episcopal Conference—is "defended, upheld and strengthened" by the supreme and universal power of the Successor of Peter *(ibid.).*

PREACHING THE GOSPEL — FIRST TASK

3. Placing the preaching of the Gospel as the first task of the bishops, the Council specified that they are "heralds of the faith...they are authentic teachers, that is, teachers endowed with the authority of Christ, who preach the faith to the people assigned to them, the faith which is destined to inform their thinking and direct their conduct; and under the light of the Holy Spirit they make the faith shine forth.... With watchfulness they ward off whatever errors threaten their flock" *(ibid.,* no. 25).

All the ethical reflections and the questions which we can and must raise as pastors before the human, social and cultural problems of our times— about which I shall now speak—are subordinated to the proclamation of salvation in Jesus Christ.

In this sense, dear brothers, lead your Christian people to drink from the living water itself. It is necessary to speak to them from a theocentric and theological perspective. Only the Word of God holds the key to our existence and enlightens our paths. This is why, in my homilies, I tried to place the faithful face to face with this Revelation from on high, to lead them to contemplate the glory of God, who wishes for man the fullness of life, but in a way which transcends man's experiences and desires. The redemption places us before the "justice" of God, before the sin of man and the love of God which ransomed him. Man has need of his Redeemer to be fully man.

Humanism—which we want to promote in collaboration with our brothers and sisters of other religions and with non-believers of good will—depends, for us Christians, on God the Creator and Redeemer. *Nisi Dominus aedificaverit donum....* Secularization, taken in the sense of wanting to realize in practical life a humanism without reference to God, would be a negation of the Christian faith. That is why we must proclaim the Good News of God in season and out of season, in all its power and originality; we must proclaim the whole Faith which the Church expresses, beginning from the early kerygma. And as I said to one of your groups during the *ad limina* visit (September 23, 1983), it is necessary to encourage and call the faithful to conversion. If the world no longer dares to speak about God, it expects from the Church, and especially from the bishop, and from the priests, a word which witnesses to God with strength and conviction, in a persuasive and adapted language, without ever reducing the greatness of the message to the expectation of the listeners. I have noted that this was one of the concerns of your Theological Commission. Here, in actual fact, come together all the problems of the initiation to the Faith, or of its deepening, for adults, youth and children, about which we spoke at the time of the *ad limina* visits.

RESPONDING IN FAITH
TO NEW QUESTIONS

4. As heralds of the faith, we are necessarily guides of consciences, like Moses who led his people to encounter the God of the Covenant and to receive the Commandments connected with the Covenant. The Council says it well: faith must direct one's thought and one's conduct.

I know the care which you have taken to help your contemporaries become sensitive to certain moral attitudes inspired by the Christian spirit. You have published a number of documents in this vein. The values of honesty, justice, the dignity of man and woman, work, aid, charity, social love and solidarity with the poor and the disinherited in the face of the new economic and cultural situations claim your attention in particular. At the same time, you seek to respond in faith to the new questions posed by the sciences, technology, and the sometimes disturbing developments of human biology. I understand and I approve this preoccupation. You wish to avoid a break between Christian teaching and life, between the Gospel and culture, between faith and justice. Indeed, what kind of faith is it which would not seek to incarnate itself in daily conduct? And would it have credibility in a world which at times doubts the existence of God? The letters of St. Paul, after explaining the Christian mystery, proceed to concrete exhortations which flow from it.

I am thinking here of two other Gospel demands. First, the dignity of family life. "Happy the pure of heart" (Mt. 5:8). You observe the breakdown of the family and the crisis in marriage. How many children and parents suffer from broken homes, separations, divorces! You yourselves moreover have sought to improve the legislation on this point. You also see the many "free unions" which refuse or delay a total and exclusive commitment of the two partners in the Sacrament of Marriage. You know that abortion is very widespread. And many have recourse to contraceptive means instead of respecting, in self-control and a mutually agreed effort, the double finality of the conjugal act: love and openness to life. Among the causes of these evils, there is a generalized tendency to hedonism; there is a forgetting of God; there is without a doubt an ignorance of the theology of the body, of the magnificent plan of God for conjugal union, of the necessity of an asceticism in order to deepen a love which is truly worthy of man and woman, and to correspond to the life of the

Spirit present in the couple. Sex education, the preparation of young people for marriage and support for family life should be top priorities here. Despite frequently passionate opinions to the contrary, it is expected that the Church would help to save human love and respect for life.

On the other hand, the consumer society, the seduction of artificial needs, the situation of over-abundant riches, and a general striving for profit render more difficult the important application of the beatitude: "How happy are the poor in spirit" (Mt. 5:3). How is it possible to educate, despite everything, to poverty and simplicity of life, in order to keep the heart free, open to the kingdom of God and to one's neighbor? Is it not necessary, among other things, to open people's eyes to the immense regions of the world where many live in complete destitution?

In this domain, as in many others, we must unceasingly remember the appeal of St. Paul: You who have been sanctified, who have become children of God, called to holiness and inhabited by the Spirit of God: "Do not model yourselves on the behavior of the world around you" (Rom. 12:2). Let us always remember the pastoral courage of St. John Chrysostom, whom we honored at Moncton.

A SENSE OF PRAYER

5. Our people have to struggle to keep the faith and Christian morality, partially because they have not discovered a sense of prayer, or because they no

longer attempt to pray. I wish to speak of that prayer which seeks, in dialogue with God or preferably listening to God, the contemplation of His love and conformity with His will. The graces of renewal and conversion will only be given to a Church that prays. Jesus begged His Apostles to watch and pray (cf. Mt. 26:41). With our priests, with our religious and many of the laity who have rediscovered prayer, in the joy of the Holy Spirit, let us be teachers of prayer.

Prayer is inseparable from the sacraments. In this regard the Council said the following about the role of the Bishops: "Through the sacraments, the regular and fruitful distribution of which they direct by their authority, they sanctify the faithful" (Lumen gentium, no. 26). I will mention only two extremely important domains. First the Sunday Eucharistic assembly. How can a people which wishes to be Christian neglect it? The causes are many, but at any rate, we pastors must do all we can to restore a sense of the Lord's Day and of the Eucharist, and to see that our liturgies are carefully prepared and characterized by the active participation of the faithful and the dignity of prayer.

SACRAMENT OF PENANCE

You easily understand why I underline another main point of pastoral sacramental practice: that of the Sacrament of Penance or Reconciliation. The frequent reception of this sacrament bears witness to the fact that we believe in the Church as a communion of holiness, and in Christ's action to build up this communion. The entire renewal of the Church depends on the personal conversion which is sealed in a personal encounter with Christ. To foster this is to contribute effectively to the whole renewal willed by the Second Vatican Council and promoted by the postconciliar reforms; otherwise, the whole of our pastoral practice suffers a serious lack, and the effectiveness of all the activity of the Church is affected. Our communion with the universal Church requires that the discipline of the whole Church be respected just as it has been defined by the Congregation for the Doctrine of the Faith, which has stressed its link with a divine precept (June 16, 1972). The last Synod, in which many of you participated, gave special emphasis to the absolute necessity of Penance: the spirit of penance, a sense of sin, and the request for pardon in the Sacrament of Penance with a personal accusation of one's sins to a priest.

You are aware that in the last few years, this centuries-old practice of the Church has been neglected. There have truly been commendable efforts to point out the communal aspects of Penance, to make all of the faithful conscious of the need for conversion, and to lead them to celebrate together the mercy of God and the grace of reconciliation. But this communal renewal must never lead to abandoning the personal act of the penitent; and one can even say that it is the right of Christ, with regard to each person whom He has redeemed, to be able to say through His minister: "Your sins are forgiven" (cf. *Redemptor hominis*, no. 20).

Dear brothers in the episcopate: help your priests to give priority to this ministry, after the Eucharist, but before many other activities which are less important. Let us help them to be convinced that in this way they cooperate marvelously in the work of the Redeemer, as dispensers of His grace. If this conviction is ensured, the practical problem will be able to find solutions, even with fewer priests. If our faithful would ever lose a sense of sin and of this personal pardon, if they would no longer find a sufficient number of priests available for this essential ministry, a principal dimension would be lacking in the authenticity of their Christian lives. And even the approach to the Eucharist, which seems to have remained frequent, would leave the conscience perplexed about the demands that communion involves for the members of the Body of Christ, communion with Him who is the Head: the "Christ who invites to the Eucharistic banquet is the same Christ who calls to penance, who repeats: 'Repent'" (cf. *ibid.*).

I have insisted at length on this point, but I know that many of you, quite in keeping with the benefit of a communal preparation, have already sought in the course of this year how to react to this crisis of the personal request for pardon.

6. I have mentioned the ministry of priests. I know how close you are to them, like fathers, and I know that you offer them encouragement in these difficult times, when some of them feel displaced, because fewer of their faithful are practicing the faith and their own place in society seems less clearly defined, and because a new style of needed collaboration between them and the laity is not always easy to find. During this period of cultural change and

postconciliar adaptation, your priests, as is the case in many countries, are particularly in need of being strengthened by means of a well-balanced theology and very clear pastoral directives, in conformity with the new Code of Canon Law.

Then, naturally, we all think about replacements. This is a concern I fully share with you. On September 23, 1983, I spoke at length with many of you about vocations. Signs of hope are appearing in the seminaries of many of your dioceses. But we need to continue resolutely to call and to provide a solid spiritual and theological formation. It is especially vocations to the religious life that have become scarce. The pastoral care of vocations requires us to work closely with Christian families and with youth. It always presupposes explicit prayer for this intention. Yes, let us have many prayers offered for vocations to the priesthood and to the religious life.

7. Through us the People of God are gathered together in unity. This is the mission of bishops, and, with them, of their priests. The Council specifies: "In any community existing around an altar, under the sacred ministry of the bishop, there is manifested a symbol of that charity and unity of the Mystical Body, without which there can be no salvation" (Lumen gentium, no. 26). Through us, the various groups of believers, and of Christian apostles at work in their own environment and according to their own charism, gather around the same Lord. And like the Good Shepherd, we must assure, as far as possible, that all the members of the flock walk together, without allowing some to feel abandoned or mis-

understood because they have greater difficulty in accepting the pace of reforms. We are guardians of unity, promoters of fraternal openness, educators in tolerance between contrasting opinions, always giving example of mercy in regard to our brothers and sisters who may be more sensitive to scandal, sometimes not without reason (cf. 1 Cor. 8:12).

The Church in Canada has made a marvelous effort to help the laity to assume their full responsibility as baptized and confirmed members of the community. Yes, as Bishops and priests, let us not be afraid to give them our trust. It is their task, with the proper preparation, to bear witness in the midst of the world, a witness that, without them, would be lacking in the Church. They are even capable of helping priests to renew their priestly zeal. During this visit I have spoken often of the ministries that the laity, men and women, can increasingly fulfill within their communities, with respect, naturally, for what belongs exclusively to the ordained ministry. And I have spoken too of the apostolate that is their very own, within the family, in the world of work, in education, in public affairs. The laity and their associations are charged with carrying into the fabric of society the principles of social doctrine which your documents emphasize.

8. I am well aware of other areas in which you are pastorally committed; for example, in the important field of ecumenism, about which we have spoken in the course of this visit.

On another level, the Church of which you are the pastors can make a valued contribution to building up a sense of fraternal solidarity in your country. Canada—I have become more aware of this—is extraordinarily rich, not only in material goods, but in cultural and linguistic traditions. The francophone and anglophone elements are foremost, without mentioning the Amerindians and the Innuit. As well as this, every part of Canada has welcomed numerous groups of immigrants who have adopted this country as their home. In such conditions, I am convinced that the Church has the task of promoting mutual acceptance, esteem and recognition, of promoting the fuller participation of everyone in the life of society, in helping all to overcome all forms of chauvinism or exaggerated nationalistic sentiment. These must not be confused with legitimate pride in one's origin and cultural heritage, or with the beneficial complementarity of variety.

9. But your responsibility as Bishops extends beyond your own country. The Council has insisted on this point when it traces the consequences of the doctrine of collegiality: "Each bishop, as a member of the episcopal college and a legitimate successor of the Apostles, is obliged by Christ's decree and command to be solicitous for the whole Church. This solicitude, though it is not exercised by an act of jurisdiction, contributes immensely to the welfare of the universal Church" (*Lumen gentium*, no. 23).

Naturally, the concern and assistance of one particular Church for another must always be provided with this collegial and fraternal spirit, fully respecting the responsibilities of the Bishops of other countries and their Episcopal Conference, trusting the perception that they have of the spiritual needs of their people and the directions to be taken in their concrete situation. In every case it is a question of strengthening the bonds of peace, love and solidarity, always with the greatest openness to the universal Church.

To exercise this solidarity is to "promote and to safeguard the unity of faith and the discipline common to the whole Church" (ibid.). A particular Church will not be in a position to resolve its problems, except in this perspective.

But it is also necessary "to instruct the faithful in love for the whole Mystical Body of Christ, especially for its poor and sorrowing members and for those who are suffering for the sake of justice" (ibid.).

This meets one of your concerns: to contribute unceasingly to the opening of the eyes, hearts and hands of your Christian people—in the total picture of being so very favored by nature and technical progress—to a concern for less favored countries, telling especially of the concerns of peoples who lack the minimum necessities of bread, health care and liberty. Many forms of aid are possible, which are respectful of these partners of the Third World, or of the "South," who for their part help us, in return, to re-establish a hierarchy of values. You also prepare your fellow citizens to participate in an international plan for the solution of the problems of peace, security, ecology, development.

10. The spiritual needs of our brothers and sisters of the other churches should hold a primary place in your universal charity. "The task of proclaiming the Gospel everywhere on earth devolves on

the body of pastors.... With all their energy, therefore, they must supply to the missions both workers for the harvest and also spiritual and material aid...." And in a particular way, "in a universal fellowship of charity, bishops should gladly extend their fraternal aid to other Churches, especially to neighboring and more needy ones" (ibid., no. 23). Everyone knows how admirable has been the missionary commitment of many Canadians: priests, men and women religious, and laity, in Latin America, Africa, Asia and also in the Great Canadian North. Let us not allow the source of missionary vocations to dry up! Let us not let the conviction about the urgency of the universal mission wither, even if this mission requires other forms of solidarity.

11. Finally, this is an area where the solidarity and common witness of Bishops and their churches should manifest themselves ever more clearly. We are sensitive to injustice, to the unequal distribution of material goods. Are we sufficiently sensitive to the damages done to the human spirit, to the conscience, to religious convictions? This fundamental freedom of the practice of one's faith is abused every day in vast regions; it is a most grave violation which dishonors humanity and which affects us believers very deeply. At Lourdes last year I decried the distressing situation of our persecuted brothers and sisters, but there is on this point a kind of conspiracy of silence which must be broken. I ask you, my brother pastors, to make this appeal with me. I ask you to sensitize your faithful to it, see that prayers are offered for these brothers and sisters. Their courage in the faith aids in a mysterious way the whole Church. It awakens Christians who are half asleep in an easy life,

enjoying all freedom, and at times too worried about problems which are quite relative in comparison with these essentials.

12. In a more general vein, dear brothers in the episcopate, I thank you for all you have done, and will do, to participate, by affective and effective collegiality, in the mission of the universal Church, in communion with the Successor of Peter—*cum Petro et sub Petro* (cf. *Ad gentes*, no. 38)—and in collaboration with the departments of the Holy See.

Yes, before the Lord, you bear the charge of your particular churches, but in each one the universal Church is present, for "Christ is present, and by virtue of Him the one, holy, catholic, and apostolic Church gathers together" (*Lumen gentium*, no. 26).

May Christ, the Good Shepherd, grant to each of you the pastoral courage necessary for your sublime mission! May the Holy Spirit give you light and strength to lead the Canadian people on the paths of the living God, so that they might be sanctified for the sanctification of the world! May God the Father keep you in hope and peace!

I shall continue to keep all your pastoral intentions in my prayers, even as you pray for me. Let us entrust them to the maternal heart of Mary. And may the all-powerful God bless you, the Father, the Son and the Holy Spirit!

The Moral Conscience of Humanity Must Not Yield to Violence

On September 20, John Paul II preached his last homily in Canada during the Mass for justice and peace celebrated on Le Breton esplanade in Ottawa. The following is the text.

1. "Happy are those who hunger and thirst for justice..." (Mt. 5:6).

"Happy are the peacemakers" (Mt. 5:9).

At the end of my pilgrimage on Canadian soil, in your capital city, Ottawa, in this Mass, we pray for justice and peace.

We pray for justice and peace in the contemporary world and we base our prayer on the beatitudes of Christ according to the Gospel of St. Matthew. We pray for peace, and the way to peace is through justice. That is why those who truly hunger and thirst for justice are at the same time peacemakers.

I would like the theme that focuses our prayer today in the context of the Eucharistic sacrifice, to unite all those who participate in it, all those who are gathered by the thousands here at the foot of the splendid Gatineau Hills, by the banks of the river of the Ottawans, around His Grace Joseph Aurèle Plourde, Archbishop of your city, to whom I express fraternal greetings; and also to Madame Governor General and the other civil authorities, to the inhabitants of the capital, to all Canadians, and to all those who join us from afar. This river was in the past the gateway to the heart of your continent, when European cultures initially came into contact with those of its first inhabitants. Today, I am among you as a pilgrim of peace and, in my last homily on Canadian soil, I would like to expand on everything I have said during my pastoral mission here. I would like to make a final synthesis based on the eight beatitudes of Christ.

THE DIVINE MASTER

2. In the beatitudes, we encounter, first of all, a person: the Divine Master. It is of Him that Isaiah speaks when he announces that a great light has shone on those who dwell in the land of deep shadow (cf. 9:1).

Those same words ring out on the night of Christmas: "For there is a child born for us, a son given to us and dominion is laid on his shoulder" (9:5).

The power laid on the shoulder of the Child born in the night of Bethlehem is confirmed by the majesty of the cross. The crucified One truly carries in Himself the whole power of the redemption of the world.

And it is He, Christ crucified, whom Isaiah calls: "Wonder-Counselor, Mighty-God, Eternal-Father, Prince of Peace" (9:5).

God forever confirmed the power of the crucified Christ when He raised Him up. The Redeemer, risen from among the dead, says to the Apostles as He leaves them: "All power in heaven and on earth has been given to me. Go, therefore, make disciples of all nations..." (Mt. 28:18-19).

Thus, Christ always remains in the midst of humanity as this "great light" of Isaiah which shines "on those who dwell in the land of darkness."

He remains the "Prince of Peace" and the "Wonder-Counselor." The way to justice and peace begins with the redemption of the world which Christ accomplished by the power of His cross and resurrection.

VIOLENCE THREATENS

3. This is critical to remember at a time when human beings, when nations and all of humanity are desperately seeking the way to peace. *Genus humanum arte et ratione vivit:* Human beings live by wisdom, by culture and by morality. Violence is in complete contradiction to such a life. Violence creates the justifiable need for defense. And at the same time, violence threatens to destroy the sources of human life. Not only does it threaten to kill human beings, millions of men and women, but it threatens to destroy all that is human.

In the midst of this threatened human family, Christ continues to stand as the Prince of Peace, as the defender of all that is human.

The Gospel of the eight beatitudes is nothing other than a defense of what is most profoundly human, of what is most beautiful in human beings, of what is holy in them:

"Happy are the poor in spirit....

"Happy the gentle....

"Happy those who mourn....

"Happy the merciful....

"Happy the pure in heart....

"Happy are those who are persecuted in the cause of right....

"Happy are you when people abuse you and persecute you and speak all kinds of calumny against you on my account.... This is how they persecuted the prophets before you" (cf. Mt. 5:3-12).

4. The Gospel of the eight beatitudes is a constant reaffirmation of what is most profoundly human, of what is heroic in human beings. The Gospel of the eight beatitudes is firmly linked to the cross and the resurrection of Christ. It is only in the light of the cross and the resurrection that what is human and heroic in human beings will recover its strength and its power. No form of historic materialism can give it either a foundation or a warrant. Materialism can only question, diminish, trample underfoot, destroy, shatter that which is most profoundly human.

The Gospel of the eight beatitudes is, at its very roots, tied to the mystery, to the reality of the redemption of the world.

Indeed the reality of the redemption of the world is the sole basis for the beatitudes, and more particularly of those two which are so very important amidst the dangers of our time:

"Happy those who hunger and thirst for justice...."

"Happy the peacemakers...."

Awareness of redemption touches in its depth the heart of those who are tormented by the threats now facing the world.

If we can accept the Gospel of the beatitudes of Christ we shall not be afraid to face up to these threats.

AN EXISTING BOND

5. The moral conscience of humanity is discovering, by various means, the bond that exists between justice and peace. We should do everything necessary so that this consciousness, recovered at the price of immense sacrifice since World War II, will not be submerged anew by the spread of violence.

Contemporary men and women, nations, humanity, seek untiringly the ways which lead to justice and peace. Unceasingly the Church participates in this great task. Particular churches and episcopates share in this effort, as does the Holy See. It is a human, Christian and apostolic duty.

PLEA OF THE CHURCH

6. Pope John XXIII addressed a remarkable appeal to the world in his Encyclical *Pacem in terris*. There he analyzed at length the conditions for peace,

and he invited us to become artisans of peace and justice in all the spheres in which the human community acts.

In its turn, the Second Vatican Council, when it considers the place of the Church in the context of the modern world, again takes up this reflection; it asks us to safeguard peace and to build up the community of nations (*Gaudium et spes*, II, V).

Pope Paul VI did not cease to act in that sense. To the General Assembly of the United Nations he issued this prophetic cry: "War never again!" He emphasized the links between peace and the development of peoples, of which I have spoken a few days ago in Edmonton. Paul VI also instituted the World Day of Peace on January 1. From that time on, at the beginning of each year, all are called to prayer and action for peace; it is the occasion for the Pope to renew his appeals to all people, so that they may opt for peace and take the necessary steps to overcome tensions and to dispel growing dangers.

Shortly after my election, I was able to answer the invitation of the United Nations and to assure the international community not only that the Apostolic See supports their efforts but that "the Catholic Church in every place on earth proclaims a message of peace, prays for peace, educates for peace" (Discourse to the 34th General Assembly of the United Nations Organization, October 2, 1979, no. 10).

Today, I renew my appeal. For we know that after the World War, tensions and confrontations have not ceased, that they provoke wars which, while localized, are no less murderous. And we know that the sources of the conflicts are found wherever injustice kills, or wherever the dignity of people is scoffed at. To build peace we must establish justice.

What moral conscience could resign itself, without reacting, when there exist "frightful disparities between excessively rich individuals and groups on the one hand, and on the other hand the majority made up of the poor or indeed of the destitute..." (ibid., no. 18)?

What moral conscience could resign itself to superficial arrangements which cover over injustice, as long as somewhere on the planet man is wounded "in his most personal belief, in his view of the world, in his religious faith, and in the sphere of what are known as civil liberties" (ibid., no. 19)?

Will we be peacemakers hungering for justice if we consent without reacting to "the breathtaking spiral of armaments" presented as being "at the service of world peace" (ibid, no. 22), while the arms race is a real threat of death and while its economic cost deprives so many countries of the effective means for their development?

Our duty remains urgent at this time. We shall be peacemakers if our conscience makes us aware of the dangers, energetic to winning acceptance for dialogue and sharing, attentive to respecting the point of view of others at the same moment that we defend our own rights, faithful to love for humanity, and receptive to the gift of God!

We shall be disciples of Christ and true brothers and sisters among ourselves if together we take our part in the thrust of civilization which for centuries has been in one direction: that of guaranteeing "the objective rights of the spirit, of human conscience and of human creativity, including man's relationship with God" *(ibid.,* no. 19). We shall be peacemakers if all our action is based on respect for the One who calls us to live according to the law of His kingdom, and from whom all power comes (cf. Jn. 19:11).

7. In this way, therefore, one cannot permit the moral conscience of humanity to give in to violence. It is necessary to maintain that close link which unites peace and justice, peace and the defense of the inviolable rights of individuals and of nations!

It is necessary to protect people from death—millions of people—from nuclear death and death from starvation. It is necessary to protect from death all that is human!

With this intention, today our prayer for justice and peace rests upon the Gospel of the eight beatitudes.

In a word, what does this Gospel proclaim? Let us read it one more time:

"How happy are the poor in spirit: theirs is the kingdom of heaven.

"Happy are the gentle: they shall have the earth for their heritage.

"Happy those who mourn: they shall be comforted.

"Happy those who hunger and thirst for what is right: they shall be satisfied.

"Happy the merciful: they shall have mercy shown them.

"Happy the pure in heart: they shall see God.

"Happy the peacemakers: they shall be called children of God.

"Happy those who are persecuted in the cause of right: theirs is the kingdom of heaven.

"Happy are you when people abuse you and persecute you and speak all kinds of calumny against you on my account. Rejoice and be glad, for your reward will be great in heaven!" (Mt. 5:3-12)

Let us allow ourselves to be seized by the Spirit of Christ. May He fill us with the truth of these words, with the power of the love that inspires them! May our prayer enable us not only to seek peace, but to bring our will into harmony with the will of God as it is revealed to us by Christ. For peace among people will always be precarious if we are not at peace with God, if we do not conform ourselves in our most inner being to the plan of God for the history of the world. May our justice be the reflection of His justice! Recognizing our sinfulness, let us allow God to reconcile us with Himself, the Author of life, and, at the same time, with our brothers and sisters. This reconciliation, which we cannot fully realize by ourselves, we shall attain by grace if we faithfully unite ourselves to the immense supplication of those who pray.

8. In a word, then, what does the Gospel of the eight beatitudes proclaim?

It says that the poor in spirit, the gentle, the merciful, those who hunger and thirst for justice, the peacemakers—all these are invincible! It says that the final victory belongs to them! To them belongs the Kingdom of Truth, of Justice, of Love and of Peace! May their weakness, their difficulty in surmounting what divides and opposes, not deject them. Human forces are not enough to apply the Gospel, but the strength of Christ permits the purification and the conversion of hearts, for He gave Himself so that humanity might possess His peace!

And it is this perspective which Christ by this Gospel and Redemption has truly opened up to those who practice His beatitudes.

Hear me, you who in various parts of the world suffer persecution in the cause of Christ; you, the poor suffering from oppression and injustice as if you were daily being ground into dust by those systems which crush humanity! You all who are truly people of good will!

We say that Christ is Wonder-Counselor.

We say that Christ is Prince of Peace.

We say that Christ is the crucified and risen One.

"Dominion is laid on his shoulder."

"Wide is his dominion...for his royal power which he establishes and makes secure in justice and integrity" (Is. 9:6).

"Your kingdom come!"

From the English edition of L'Osservatore Romano

Be Faithful to the Inspiration of Your Saints

At the farewell ceremony at Uplands Military Airport, Ottawa, the Holy Father gave the following address in the presence of the Bishops of Ottawa, the Governor General, Madame Jeanne Sauvé, and the new Prime Minister, Mr. Brian Mulroney, with his wife.

Ladies and Gentlemen,
Dear brothers and sisters:

1. The time has come for me to leave Canada and to say good-bye to you. I do so not without regret, having had the opportunity to visit so many men and women and so many varied and interesting places in your vast country. Nevertheless, I am filled with joy, for I feel that we lived together moments of grace.

Among you I greet in friendship my brother Bishops, who invited me, who prepared this pilgrimage with great care, who welcomed me on behalf of you all and who accompanied me; I reiterate to them all my deep gratitude. Through you here, who represent the whole Canadian community, I wish to thank the priests, the religious and the laity for their kind and sincere welcome, for the witness of their faith and for their spirit of service in the Church. I would like to greet in particular the other Christian communities, with whom I am happy to have been able to make a number of contacts, and of whose zeal in promoting the cause of unity I have gained a better appreciation.

I would also like to thank the civic officials, who have played such a major part in organizing my journey and who have shown such a deep appreciation of the pastoral meaning of my visit. I thank them for being so kind as to come even here to bid me farewell. I have vivid memories of our meetings, especially upon my arrival in Quebec City, and quite recently in Ottawa itself. I wish to express my gratitude to the Governor General, to the Prime Minister, to the Honorable Members of the Judiciary, to the Speakers and Members of the Senate and the House of Commons, to the provincial premiers and to the members of the diplomatic corps, who have joined here with Canadian civic dignitaries and officials. With these civic authorities, I wish to thank all those who, for many months, working in numerous groups, have given them their effective, courteous and often discreet cooperation, participating in the many organizational, security and transportation arrangements required for this long trip.

GENEROUS PEOPLE

2. The visit that I have just completed has given me a better appreciation of the beauty and diversity of your country, and of the generosity of your people.

I have enjoyed our meetings, thanks to your characteristic openness and enthusiasm. I cannot speak now of all that I will keep in my heart; that goes beyond what can be expressed in a few words.

Permit me to say only that throughout my trip I have been struck by the richness and continued vitality of all that has been passed on to you by your predecessors: the Amerindians and Innuit and the half-castes, the French and English, the immigrants from many other countries of Europe, of the West and East, without forgetting all those who have come from the numerous regions of Latin America, of Africa and of Asia.

The happy combination of all these elements of your heritage in a free and enterprising people makes Canadians particularly well suited to remaining open to all the calls of the world, to promoting peace and to living actively in generous solidarity with those of our brothers and sisters who are most in need and with those who have heavy burdens to bear.

3. At this moment of my departure, I wish for the Canadian people a happy future, the development of all their qualities, a life lived in harmony and in respect for their cultural and spiritual differences. This is facilitated, I am aware, by the institutions of this country. You have before you many challenging tasks, both in order to face the internal difficulties which remain, notably the economic crisis, and in order to develop your positive contribution to international life. May the awareness of these duties lead you to fulfill them with the courage, the nobility and the unselfishness of those who find their joy in the service of their brothers and sisters!

4. To you, the members of the People of God in this country, I entrust one of my best remembrances of the different stages of this pilgrimage: together we have been able to live a striking experience of the Faith that unites us. I am well aware that the sympathy that you have manifested in my regard expresses, beyond my person, your real bonds with the universal Church, with the Church rooted in the faith of the Apostles ever since the resurrection of the Lord and the beginning of the missionary era of Pentecost.

In my coming to your communities, I have discovered with joy that you are continuing what the great founders whom you so greatly honor began. They brought the Gospel here, sometimes at the price of their lives; they built an edifice which continues to be full of life despite the difficulties and changes of our times. Be faithful to the inspiration of the known and unknown saints who have sown in this land the seed that was destined to bear fruit.

We have celebrated together, we have prayed to the Lord, we have been in communion with Him, we have listened to His Word. Your fervor is the sign that the message of the Successor of Peter, who has come to bear witness to Jesus Christ, has found men and women ready to work for a new world. It is the sign that the Christians of this country have the Holy Spirit living within them—the Holy Spirit who infuses into our hearts the love of God, who strengthens us in hope and gives fullness to our faith.

May my pilgrimage to the shrines of God's People mark a positive step for all of you on the long road that leads humanity to renewal through the gift of God, and to the fullness of fraternal solidarity on the road of holiness!

I reiterate at this time my keen disappointment at not being able to visit the Indians, Innuit and Metis people at Fort Simpson. From the very beginning of the preparations of my pastoral visit to Canada, I attributed great importance to this encounter, and I now renew to all of them the expression of fraternal love and esteem that I communicated through my message to them. I truly hope that God's Providence will give me another occasion to meet with them. (And excuse me...for thus inviting myself a second time to Canada.)

I shall continue to pray for you and with you. Today I ask the Father of all love, the Son who dwells among us, and the Spirit of power and light, to fill you with every blessing.

With joy I assure you all once again of my gratitude and I renew from the bottom of my heart my good wishes for all the people of Canada.

From the English edition of L'Osservatore Romano

INDEX

abortion 295, 323, 336
Abraham
Father in faith 263
Acadians 146f.
adoration 266
alcohol 164, 290, 296
America
modernity of 21
Amerindians 4, 6, 19, 38ff., 46, 146, 343, 359
André Bessette, 65f.
Anne, St. 39, 44
annunciation 49
anthropology 281
apostles 360
apostolate 173f.
exercise of the Christian 171
lay 167
of the Church 168
primary aim of Church's 172
armament 353
arms race 319, 353
asceticism 309
Assembly of First Nations 280
atheism 70
Augustinian Hospital Sisters of the Mercy of Jesus 13

Baptism 34, 97, 105, 117, 148, 156, 168, 190, 239ff., 244, 289f., 313
Basilian Fathers 248
beatitudes 34, 70, 76, 202, 347f., 351, 354, 356
believer(s) 1, 7, 9, 20
Benedict, St. 232
Bishop(s) 67, 72ff., 79, 149, 161, 194, 332f., 341, 343
Bishop of Rome 13, 16, 23, 82, 96, 147
see also *Successor of Peter; Pope*
Bourgeoys, St. Marguerite 63, 80f.
Byzantine Rite 234, 236f., 245, 249
clergy of 248

Cartier, Jacques 3, 18
catechesis 72, 76, 158, 244
catechetics 149
catechism 40
catechists 171
Catherine de Saint-Augustine 19
Catherine of Siena, St. 86
Catholics
Ukrainian Byzantine 246
celibacy 12, 14, 78, 186, 193, 313
Chabanel, St. Noel 219
charism 92, 149, 161, 308
charity 14, 148, 168, 170, 202, 307, 313
children 108, 171, 177, 207, 224, 289, 291, 319, 336
Chiwatenwa, Joseph 220
Chosen People 254
Christianity 259
and the Indian peoples 221
Eastern 249
Church 23, 43f., 72, 97, 106, 173, 209, 221, 240ff., 283, 307, 329, 338ff., 344
and civil matters 42
and ecumenism 201
and the Paschal Mystery 56
apostolate of 168
communion of persons 164
founded on Apostles 168
in Canada 258
in Poland 205
liturgical life of 242
members of 168
missionary efforts of 220
Mystical Body of Christ 344
social doctrine of 112
Ukrainian Catholic 245f.
universal 150, 206
Code of Canon Law 341
collegiality 346
colonists 13, 19
commandment(s) 254, 256, 260, 270, 286

Daughters of St. Paul

MASSACHUSETTS
50 St. Paul's Ave., Jamaica Plain, Boston, MA 02130; **617-522-8911.**
172 Tremont Street, Boston, MA 02111; **617-426-5464; 617-426-4230.**

NEW YORK
78 Fort Place, Staten Island, NY 10301; **718-447-5071; 718-447-5086.**
59 East 43rd Street, New York, NY 10017; **212-986-7580.**
625 East 187th Street, Bronx, NY 10458; **212-584-0440.**
525 Main Street, Buffalo, NY 14203; **716-847-6044.**

NEW JERSEY
Hudson Mall—Route 440 and Communipaw Ave.,
Jersey City, NJ 07304; **201-433-7740.**

CONNECTICUT
202 Fairfield Ave., Bridgeport, CT 06604; **203-335-9913.**

OHIO
2105 Ontario Street (at Prospect Ave.), Cleveland, OH 44115;
216-621-9427.
616 Walnut Street, Cincinnati, OH 45202; **513-421-5733; 513-721-5059.**

PENNSYLVANIA
1719 Chestnut Street, Philadelphia, PA 19103; **215-568-2638.**

VIRGINIA
1025 King Street, Alexandria, VA 22314; **703-683-1741; 703-549-3806.**

SOUTH CAROLINA
243 King Street, Charleston, SC 29401; **803-577-0175.**

FLORIDA
2700 Biscayne Blvd., Miami, FL 33137; **305-573-1618; 305-573-1624.**

LOUISIANA
4403 Veterans Memorial Blvd., Metairie, LA 70006; **504-887-7631;
504-887-0113.**
423 Main Street, Baton Rouge, LA 70802; **504-343-4057; 504-381-9485.**

MISSOURI
1001 Pine Street (at North 10th), St. Louis, MO 63101; **314-621-0346;
314-231-1034.**

ILLINOIS
172 North Michigan Ave., Chicago, IL 60601; **312-346-4228; 312-346-3240.**

TEXAS
114 Main Plaza, San Antonio, TX 78205; **512-224-8101; 512-224-0938.**

CALIFORNIA
1570 Fifth Ave., San Diego, CA 92101; **619-232-1442.**
46 Geary Street, San Francisco, CA 94108; **415-781-5180.**

WASHINGTON
2301 Second Ave., Seattle, WA 98121; **206-441-3300; 206-441-3210.**

HAWAII
1143 Bishop Street, Honolulu, HI 96813; **808-521-2731.**

ALASKA
750 West 5th Ave., Anchorage, AK 99501; **907-272-8183.**

CANADA
3022 Dufferin Street, Toronto 395, Ontario, Canada.